Introduction to Nigerian Literature

Introduction to
Nigerian Literature

edited by Bruce King

Africana Publishing Corporation   University of Lagos

Published in the United States of America 1972
by Africana Publishing Corporation
101 Fifth Avenue
New York, N.Y. 10003

University of Lagos
Lagos, Nigeria

Library of Congress Catalog Card No. 73-180669

ISBN   0-8419-0111-2

Printed in Great Britain by
T. and A. Constable Ltd., Hopetoun Street, Edinburgh

Contents

Acknowledgements

The publishers wish to thank the following for permission to quote copyright material:

André Deutsch and the Macmillan Company, New York, for extracts from **The Interpreters** by Wole Soyinka;
Faber and Faber Limited and Grove Press, Inc., New York, for an extract from **The Palm-Wine Drinkard** by Amos Tutuola;
David Higham Associates, Ltd for extracts from **People of the City** by Cyprian Ekwensi, published by William Heinemann Ltd;
Hutchinson Publishing Group Ltd and David Higham Associates, Ltd for extracts from **Jagua Nana** by Cyprian Ekwensi;
Methuen & Co. Ltd for an extract from **Idanre and O her Poems** by Wole Soyinka;
Oxford University Press for extracts from **The Swamp Dwellers, The Lion and the Jewel, A Dance of the Forests, The Trials of Brother Jero** and **The Road** by Wole Soyinka.

Introduction

by Bruce King

We are now used to Nigerian writers winning international literary prizes; we expect their plays to be performed in London and Dakar as well as Lagos and Ibadan; we are not surprised when their poems are analyzed in serious critical journals. This was not always so. It is easy to forget that Nigerian literature in English is a recent phenomenon. While there is a long and still undocumented tradition of Nigerian writers in English, it was only in the early 1950s that authors emerged who are worthy of serious literary attention.

Amos Tutuola's *The Palm-Wine Drinkard* (1952) was one of the first novels written in English by a Nigerian. It quickly gained an international reputation and in a sense put Nigeria on the map of world literature. Among the reasons why it is liked abroad are its imaginative use of tribal myths, its fresh use of English, its free mixture of the spiritual and the human worlds. Unfortunately many Nigerians have been embarrassed by Tutuola's supposedly bad English and his seeming lack of sophistication. It would be a pity if the appreciation of Tutuola in Europe and North America should lead to his being undervalued at home, for he is a genuine writer of considerable, if uneven, talents. It is probable that if he were not well known abroad he would have become a local literary cult with critics exclaiming against those who failed to see his originality.

As Professor Dathorne's essay shows, Tutuola uses the manner of a folk artist for serious purposes. Unlike some writers who seem to approach Nigerian culture as anthropologists attempting to reconstruct the tribal past or as sociologists attempting to record the texture and tempo of urban life, Tutuola creates moral fables from the imaginative use of tribal mythologies and legends. His exact relationship to previous Yoruba writers and his degree of originality in inventing his stories, though topics for debate, are not of prime literary interest, for Tutuola has an instinctive sense of literary form. Like many natural writers Tutuola can be read at any age since his themes grow out of adventure stories. The opening paragraphs of his novels are among the best in modern literature. He takes us directly into the setting and theme of his books. Despite the use of repetition he is very good at exposition.

His writing is fresh, and his comparisons make lively use of Nigerian English. His supposedly bad English can be seen as functional, an aspect of the content of his stories. It would be pointless to write of adventures in the Nigerian spirit world in the style of Hemingway or T. S. Eliot. Tutuola's bad English is appropriate both to the character of his narrators and for creating the necessary frame of mind for the kind of stories told. No doubt Tutuola stumbled on his style accidentally at first by translating Yoruba expressions into English; but it has become a conscious technique in his later novels.

Ajaiyi and His Inherited Poverty (1968) is a good example of the recent direction of Tutuola's work. The book has a clear and obvious moral purpose; although there are several digressions in the action, the plot is related to the themes. *Ajaiyi* is meant, I think, to show the superiority of the modern world to the tribal past. In the book the past is character-ized by cruelty, tyranny, blood sacrifice and evil. Traditional gods are shown as cruel and demanding. By way of contrast the All-Mighty Creator, the Christian God, is shown as merciful. The life in the Town of the Creator offers a standard of happiness by which the rest of the action in the book should be judged. Tutuola uses his seeming simplicity and naïveté for a sophisticated artistic purpose. The am-biguous time scheme allows the narrator's adventures to cover approximately two hundred years and enables Tutuola to trace a development of moral awareness from the past to the present. In terms of themes this development is a movement from tribal religion to Christianity, from tribal values to individualized conscience, from concern with material values to a more profound spiritual awareness. Tutuola's achievement, however, is more in his imaginative recreation of African culture than in his moral didacticism. If the Town of the Creator is alive and vital, it is because heaven has been translated into an African festival of drumming, feasting, dancing and praise-singing. Even the sayings which his stories illustrate are typically African ways of teaching and owe nothing to European culture.

If Nigerian literature in English can be said to have begun with *The Palm-Wine Drinkard*, the second event of major significance was the publication in 1954 of Cyprian Ekwensi's *People of the City*. At first it may seem that no two writers could be more dissimilar than Tutuola and Ekwensi. Tutuola's books are romances and allegories, which utilize traditional Yoruba myths and recognize no barrier between the living and the dead. Ekwensi works within recognized conventions of the English novel and belongs to a tradition of realistic writers who find their subject-matter in the flux of modern urban life. His writings are concerned solely with the living, and he sees traditional customs and rituals as an anthropologist might, carefully noticing the exotic and the sensational. Although he has sympathetically portrayed the

Fulani of Northern Nigeria, he is most at home among those who inhabit the fringes of urban society, when he portrays the temptations, corruptions and the expediencies to which people are forced if they are to survive. Tutuola and Ekwensi are alike, however, in having to create literary structures in which to give expression to the Nigerian experience. It is significant that both writers are often accused of being unable to create solid literary structures in which form, event, action and theme are harmonious and unified. Ekwensi and Tutuola are also alike in having to forge a literary language of their own. Neither is a master of traditional English and neither is a model for good writing as taught in the schools or as used by the educated. However, just as Tutuola's style is appropriate for his uneducated narrators, so Ekwensi's use of pidgin English is appropriate to his characters, the semi-literate, semi-educated who make up the greater part of metropolitan life. Both Tutuola and Ekwensi can be seen as wrestling with the problem of what is uniquely Nigerian in Nigerian literature. They both have approached the problem at first unconsciously and later with dedication, from dissimilar angles and using different subject-matter. They are both popular novelists in the sense that their writing grows out of the common life of the community, whether in its tribal legends or in recent urban experience, rather than from a superior intellectual or educational vantage point.

While I would not make large claims for Ekwensi, he is of historical importance. He was, I believe, the first West African novelist, whether writing in English or French, to record the tempo and texture of city life. He was the first West African writer to treat of the various moral and ethical conflicts inherent within modern African society. Such later fiction as *The Interpreters* and *A Man of the People* can be seen as more aesthetically satisfying extensions of the subject-matter and themes of Ekwensi's novels. It is ironic that Ekwensi should be looked upon as in some way an immoral writer. As Douglas Killam points out, Ekwensi is actually a moralist, intent upon showing how the pressures of modern society force people into illegal and immoral conduct. His view of Nigerian society may be limited, but no one can deny that what he portrays exists. Ekwensi's faults are as an artist rather than as a moralist.

It could be argued that the real tradition of Nigerian literature in English begins with Chinua Achebe's *Things Fall Apart* (1958). It begins a tradition not only because its influence can be detected on subsequent Nigerian novelists, such as T. M. Aluko, but also because it was the first solid achievement upon which others could build. Achebe was the first Nigerian writer to successfully transmute the conventions of the novel, a European art form, into African literature. His craftsmanship can be seen in the way he creates a totally Nigerian texture for his fiction: Ibo idioms translated into English are used freely; European character study is subordinated to the portrayal of communal life; European economy of form is replaced by an aesthetic appropriate to the rhythms of traditional tribal life. Achebe's themes reflect the cultural traits of the Ibos, the impact of European civilization upon traditional African society, and the role of tribal values in modern urban life.

Although his writing lacks the infectious spontaneity of Tutuola's and the intellectual sophistication which is Soyinka's trademark, Achebe is, in my opinion, the most competent literary craftsman in Nigeria today. Each of his novels is a success and shows a control in the handling of his material of a kind which often escapes Tutuola and Soyinka. Other writers may be more promising, or show signs of genius, but in the case of Achebe there is a solid body of accomplished work which is fully achieved in its own terms and which can be evaluated, judged or criticized as literature, without reference to some of the controversies which so often erupt over the evaluation of African literature.

Achebe has a sense of irony and is especially good at social satire. It is remarkable how often his evocation of society, whether the tribal past or the present, is tinged with the sharp eye of the detached observer. His first four novels trace the progressive deterioration of a traditional culture until it has become corrupt and inefficient. Many of the problems of modern Nigerian society are seen as having their roots within tribal customs and values. The tragic forces which cause the ruin of Okonkwo in *Things Fall Apart* are implicit within the tribal culture depicted and are not merely the result of European colonization. In this sense Okonkwo is destroyed, and brings ruin on others, because he is excessive in his adherence to the values of his society; those who can compromise, change with the times and adjust are seen as more sensible. This does not make Okonkwo any less tragic or heroic. Despite Achebe's objective manner of narration, his characters are portrayed with sympathy and achieve noble stature in the course of the novels; the principles they uphold are also seen as noble and engage our sympathies. But such principles are often flawed and inherently unsound in the face of social change. Achebe is like such nineteenth-century English novelists as George Eliot and Thomas Hardy in presenting a tragic universe in which exceptional individuals are crushed by larger cultural forces. One is tempted to describe it as a deterministic universe, since the causes of the tragedy are inherent within the culture itself and its relationship to larger realities.

Although *Things Fall Apart* is one of the best known books of African literature, it is not necessarily Achebe's best novel. *Arrow of God* (1964) and *A Man of the People* (1966) are in my opinion better. In *A Man of the People*, he allows a thoroughly corrupt politician to have an immense warmth and vitality. His zest for life is given full credit and he comes alive on the pages of the novel. The seeming hero of the book, however, is not very likeable; it is implied that his disapproval of corruption comes as much from pride, failure and jealousy as from absolute moral standards. Only an excellent craftsman would have dared to reverse our normal expectations of the sympathetic hero and the unsympathetic villain. It could be argued of course that Achebe has always cast a wary eye on his heroes, or it could be argued that *A Man of the People* attempts to satirize all of Nigerian society, whether the corrupt politician, the intellectual, or the masses who see no wrong in corruption. In either case Achebe's ability to step back from total involvement with his main characters is an example of his artistry, a sign of his concern with literature as an art, and sets his work off from those who mistake literature for journalism, sociology and anthropology.

With Wole Soyinka Nigerian literature in English entered another new phase. Soyinka's writing often has a sophistication, a brilliance, a self-confidence lacking in the work of his predecessors. This does not mean that Soyinka is necessarily a better writer. The quality of his work is often uneven; but if Soyinka is uneven he has, I feel, reached greater artistic heights than any Nigerian writer so far. *The Lion and the Jewel* (1963) seems to me the best literary work to come out of Africa, and *The Interpreters* (1965) the most brilliant, but not the most successful, novel. Even when Soyinka fails, as I feel he does in *Kongi's Harvest* (1967) and his long poem *Idanre* (1967), his failures are of interest for the artistic and intellectual complexity of what he attempts.

The sophistication of Soyinka's work is the reflection of a lively mind, sceptical, witty, alert, ironic, articulate and at home in the realm of ideas. Soyinka is obviously so at home among the classics of world literature that he brings to his work an intuitive sense of form, of literary convention, and of the situations which have worked for other writers. This has several advantages. He knows the kinds of situations which will produce laughter, the kinds of dramatic rhythms which are aesthetically satisfying. He seems unhampered by problems of form. Consequently his writing is fluid, relaxed, and capable of subtleties. If this facility in handling of words and form can lead to the brilliant and charming dance-like movements of *The Lion and the Jewel*, it can also lead to the undisciplined incoherence of plotting found in *Kongi's Harvest*, where the dramatic rhythms are perfect but the actual events are vague and unclear.

Soyinka is also a witty writer. He is often comic even when his subject-matter is serious and profound. He has an urbanity of spirit and a sense of the humorous even when treating of what he disapproves. Oba Danola in *Kongi's Harvest* is a marvellously engaging character, even though immoral and primarily concerned with his own comforts. The satire on Kongi, although sharper and more bitter, is lightened by a consciousness of Kongi's absurdities. Soyinka has shown that disapproval need not consist of invective and scorn.

As Professor Jones points out, Soyinka's writing, although firmly set in Africa, is universal in its themes. The question of the relative value of progress versus the past, although set in a Nigerian context in *The Lion and the Jewel*, is in fact the old debate found in the plays of George Bernard Shaw over what is the life force. Evolution towards the future may come from the corrupted past rather than from ineffectual representatives of the present world. Energy, cunning and the ability to survive may be of more importance than book learning. Soyinka is often profound. In *Kongi's Harvest* the seeming conflict between tradition and a form of African socialism is subsumed by a larger philosophical theme. Daodu, imitating Christ at the beginning of the presentation of the yam to Kongi, offers a philosophy of pleasure, love and life in contrast to Kongi's death-bringing social and political ideas.

While there is a strong pessimistic streak in Soyinka's view of life, it is not the facile pessimism which arises from an easy cynicism. Rather it is very much connected with Ogun, the Yoruba deity whom Soyinka has turned to, as European artists have turned to various muses, for inspiration and vision. Ogun, god of iron, war, harvest and the creative essence, is the subject of Soyinka's long poem *Idanre*. The spirit of harvest, the spirit of creation, the promise of the future are seen as essentially tragic. New life can only be born at the cost of pain to the old. Destruction is necessary if there is to be renewal. The poem is a vision of an essential cosmic process. The gods of various African, European and Oriental religions are treated as equivalent to each other. The poem is also meant to be applicable to present-day Nigeria and Africa. It is an amazing attempt at writing an African *Paradise Lost*, explaining the ways of the gods to men. While I do not feel the poem fully succeeds, it is typical of Soyinka to have attempted it.

Despite its many accomplishments to date, Nigerian literature in English is still in its infancy and has not undergone the test of time. Reputations will undoubtedly rise and fall, masterpieces will be written, some of what is significant today will be seen as only of historical interest. Canons of taste will be established and challenged, and critical standards will develop from constant comparison of an increasing body of authors and works. With one exception all the Nigerian writers mentioned in this book are still living. They might write better books which will enhance their stature; or they may never pass their present achievement, in which case they are likely to be surpassed by others. Gabriel Okara is an example of someone who has published one promising novel, *The Voice* (1964), and some excellent poems, and who, when he has a greater body of work behind him, may well be an important writer. Unfortunately he has not yet published enough to be given the kind of critical attention called for by Soyinka or Achebe. The one exception to this warning is Christopher Okigbo, who died in 1967 at the age of thirty-seven. Okigbo left a small body of poems which already have a considerable reputation. With the exception of manuscripts which may still turn up, his poetry must be judged on the basis of what we have, as there will be no more.

Okigbo's poetry is immediately attractive but difficult to interpret. It is perhaps best to approach him as a poet's poet, someone whose verse gives immediate pleasure in its sound and imagery before the reader can interpret its meaning. Paul Theroux, himself a writer, approaches Okigbo's work in this fashion. Okigbo was influenced by Ezra Pound and T. S. Eliot; from them he learned to use striking images which create significance by contrast and pattern rather than, as in traditional English poetry, by developing statements into arguments. From them he learned how to write poetry which, though based on personal experience, has a broader cultural significance. At any moment Okigbo could be writing about a love affair, his own spiritual condition, Nigeria, Africa or mankind. While the origins of the emotions behind his poetry will no doubt be traced by later criticism, his achievement is to have transformed such feelings into images capable of wider resonances. Okigbo is an example of a traditional romantic paradox: intense, vital, visionary, he seeks limits, form and order. His poetry is filled with oblique, angular statements which are saved from pretentiousness by self-mockery, parody and irony. In the later poems the turning back upon himself creates pathos in contrast to the more generalized symbolism and saves the verse from becoming excessively rhetorical.

If Okigbo was influenced by Pound and Eliot, his poetry is African in its themes, imagery and form. It is not necessary to point to images of drums, clappers and elephants to prove this. The forms he has chosen with their oblique allusions, choral-like responses and open-endedness utilize the conventions of tribal songs and praise-singing within the more economical boundaries of European verse. I remember once asking him how long his 'Lament of the Masks for W. B. Yeats' was going to be. He told me that as it was based on a traditional praise-song it could go on for ever, and so it was just a question of slicing off as much as was wanted. It is typical of Okigbo's sense of humour that I still don't know how much this was true and how much was exaggeration. Perhaps the best advice that one can give the reader of Okigbo's poetry is the same advice that one gives to students beginning to study T. S. Eliot. Don't worry about the meaning at first. Let the poetry

7

work on you, especially the sound. On a second reading the form will emerge, on a third the themes and symbols will begin to have a coherence.

Among the second generation of well-known Nigerian writers, J. P. Clark is perhaps the best example of an all-round man of letters. Poet, dramatist, critic and translator, he is also editor of the influential magazine *Black Orpheus*. While Clark is best known for his plays, *The Song of a Goat* (1961) and *Ozidi* (1966), it is probable that his most lasting achievement will be in poetry. Generally speaking, one can say that the plays show a lack of knowledge about rudiments of production and stagecraft. In *Ozidi* the attempt to transform Ijaw legend into drama results in a number of scenes which seem impossible to produce; there are also seemingly extraneous events, such as the ending, which, while no doubt having a place in Clark's source material, do not seem related to the main themes of the play. Clark's poetry shows more awareness of form and of the need to find proper vehicles for his themes. The rhythms and rhyme scenes of his poems provide a discipline that his temperament seems to need. The well-known poem on Ibadan will have a place in anthologies of African poetry for some time to come. Among Nigerian writers Clark is the only one so far who is also a literary critic. While Soyinka sometimes writes criticism it usually has to do with intellectual issues rather than specific literary works. Clark's criticism is essentially that of a poet rather than a teacher. If the essays are not well argued or developed, they are full of insights and suggestions. Probably because his *America, Their America* (1964) was flashy and journalistic, Clark's reputation has suffered and his poetry has not received the attention that it might deserve.

Form and style in Nigerian literature in English are often perceptibly different from those found in European literature. How much of the difference is the result of new literary conventions developing out of African culture and how much of the difference is simply the result of inexperience in handling European literary forms? Dr Adetugbo's essay wisely leaves such questions unanswered as they can be seen in their proper light only when there is a longer tradition of Nigerian literature in English from which to judge. Such questions, however, demand our attention even if no answer can be given. Nigerian writers, for example, seem more interested in communal rather than personal problems. Consequently, characterization in their novels and plays is often lacking in depth. Does this result from a new approach towards literature in which individual psychology is less important than public themes? Or is it simply the result of being unable to imagine characters with any fullness? Do the unwieldy plots of Tutuola, Soyinka and Ekwensi show an inability to handle form or are they closer to some as yet ununderstood Nigerian aesthetic norm? That there are cultural differences which are reflected in literary form or subject-matter is obvious. Nature in Nigerian literature may contain spiritual presences or it may just be there as a neutral scene; but it never seems to offer the comfort often found in English and American descriptions of the natural world.

The main question, however, is to what extent Nigerian literature should conform to European artistic genres. One might say that Nigerian literature should not in any way conform to European literary categories; but this would be too simple an answer. There may be traditional Nigerian dramatic forms such as the masquerade or various ceremonies, but outside infusion is obviously needed if local forms are to be developed and given artistic permanence. The very act of writing a script and performing it before a large audience in a limited amount of time requires an awareness of artistic problems for which European literature can serve as a model. The question, therefore, is not whether European drama is relevant to Nigeria, but rather how it can be used. Soyinka's introduction of mime, masquerading and dances into his plays while retaining the highly formalized plot structure of European drama is an example of the kind of fusion possible and it has enabled him to reach an international audience. The difficulties in staging Clark's *Ozidi* show the problems which result from a less thoughtful attempt to adapt traditional material to the stage.

It may be assumed that because Nigeria has a long tradition of oral verse the problems faced by poets of adapting to English would be fewer than those of dramatists and novelists. But this is not so. The problems may in fact even be greater because there is a living, vital tradition with different tendencies. The difference between oral public verse and printed personal poetry is much greater than is sometimes realized. Uncertainty as to what audience one is writing for can affect rhythm, phraseology, imagery and the whole tone of a poem. There is also the difficulty of expressing nuances of feeling in what is often a second language, where words do not have exactly the same meaning as in your first language. Then there is the question of verse form. If one's aesthetic expectations have been formed by oral tradition, can one so readily adopt the sonnet or the heroic couplet as a means of expression? Yet what happens if you try to write a traditional praise-song using the English language which lacks the rhetorical devices that create artistic purpose in some Nigerian languages? How do you find equivalent effects?

Similar problems also come to mind when one thinks of rhythm and metre. Can Nigerian poets handle traditional English iambic rhythms or free verse patterns based upon such rhythms with any security? Should they need to? But if not, what is to replace them? Can you translate rhythms inherent to various Nigerian languages directly into

English? And even if you could, would they be expressive and meaningful to Nigerians from various parts of the country and from different tribal backgrounds? Metre in English poetry is itself a compromise between various possible rhythmic systems and has changed over the centuries. It will take time before any commonly accepted compromise becomes the natural mode for Nigerian poetry written in English. Until then each poet is faced by a problem and an opportunity. Any metre or rhythm can be attempted and is perhaps as valid as any other system. While we can expect brilliant experiments in this direction, each experiment risks the possibility of utter failure and of some day seeming quaint or naïve. But it is necessary to experiment because the rhythms of poetry must reflect the rhythms of the spoken language. Metre may underlie cadence in English verse, but the movement is still created by the spoken voice. When poets such as Clark or Soyinka have attempted to follow rigidly traditional English metric forms, their poetry often seems stilted and the metre a straitjacket from which they cannot burst free into song. If such problems exist, so does the possibility of something new and exciting, some fusion in which traditional Nigerian poetic devices will be found to enrich English poetry and provide undreamt-of opportunities for Nigerian poets.

It was once felt that Nigerian literature grew out of the study of English literature. But, as the writings of Tutuola, Ekwensi and Clark show, modern Nigerian literature has many roots, including tribal poetry and legend, traditional drama, and even that unclassifiable body of pamphlets and short stories printed in Onitsha and other urban centres. While literature in Nigerian languages can only be touched upon in a book of this length, it is hoped that the essays included here may create a more balanced view of the variety of literary expression in Nigeria. The growing body of modern printed literature in Nigerian languages is especially impressive in both scope and achievement. The novels of D. O. Fagunwa are regarded as classics among the Yoruba, and the plays of Duro Ladipo, in Ulli Beier's translations, seem to me to be of high artistic value. As Professor Babalọlá shows, Hausa, Yoruba and Efik are among the Nigerian languages which have a history of published literature. Nor does art need to be printed. It is certain that centuries of tribal life have created literary riches, the extent of which is only now being explored. There is a need to record traditional oral poetry and dramatic festivals before they are lost for ever; there is also a need to subject them to literary analysis and evaluation, rather than merely regarding them as forms of folklore. Attention will also need to be given to the influence of translations from English into Nigerian languages. I am thinking in particular of the probable influence of the Yoruba translation of *The*

Pilgrim's Progress and the Bible on Tutuola and, perhaps, Fagunwa. Until more research has been done and more texts made available, it will be impossible to write a real history of Nigerian literature.

There was once a time when African literature was written in New York and Paris by black men attempting to justify their cultural heritage. Although such literature contributed to the political and cultural awakening of Africa, its values were shaped by the expectation of its American and European audience. In making passion and emotion the prime characteristics of African culture, the writers of this period were accepting European views of other people as more primitive, more spontaneous and less rational. As literature actually written in Africa developed, the focus changed. Ibadan, Abidjan and Johannesburg replaced Paris and New York as centres of African writing. Critics began asking whether the work of American Negroes and West Indians is part of African literature. Now that there is a considerable body of African literature we can see, as Clive Wake points out, that it differs from country to country and that there are national characteristics. Tutuola and Achebe have more in common in their treatment of the English language than either has with Senghor's or Dadier's use of French. It is only necessary to compare *Things Fall Apart* with Camara Laye's *L'Enfant Noir* to see two radically different approaches to the portrayal of tribal life. Where Achebe is objective and stands at a distance from his material, Camara Laye is subjective and works from within the consciousness of the narrator. Where Achebe creates a new form and texture for novels written in English, Camara Laye writes in the French tradition of novels which trace the journey from adolescence to maturity. Examples of such differences can be multiplied. It is only to be expected that the literature of each African country will share some features of a continental heritage while being unique to itself. The influence of different political and social histories, the influence of different tribal cultures, even the influence of different tribal languages, are bound to show. Just as each European nation has its own literature so each nation in Africa can be expected to produce its own literary tradition.

Oral Poetry

A good deal of the oral literature of many Nigerian cultures is preserved in poetic form. The field of oral poetry is therefore a very important one from a literary, linguistic and anthropological viewpoint.

Despite the intensive work now being done on the oral poetry of the major Nigerian language groups, our knowledge of this interesting field still remains fragmentary. More work needs to be done by way of collection, transcription and analysis. Perhaps the greatest need is the collection of oral poetry by tape recorders so that at least we are sure that something is preserved for posterity. This is a very urgent task in view of the violent changes now ravaging many established aspects of several Nigerian cultures.

In the following pages we have attempted an analysis of some of the forms of oral poetry among the Yoruba, the Hausa and the Edo. Space does not permit us to touch on all forms of oral poetry in these cultures, but we have chosen a few examples to show the nature of the oral poetry of each of the three cultures. It is hoped that this approach will be a useful introduction to Nigerian oral poetry.

1 Yoruba
by Wándé Abímbọ́lá

The field of Yoruba oral literature is a vast one. It includes the folktales [Àló], the myths and legends [Ìtàn], and chants [Àròfọ̀] of various kinds. Yoruba oral literature is rendered both in prose and poetry forms. The folktales [Àló], for example, are rendered mainly in prose form with a few lines of poetry coming in the midst of a long passage. The myths and legends [Ìtàn] are also primarily rendered in prose form. The chants [Àròfọ̀] are, however, rendered mainly in poetic form, and it is this aspect of Yoruba oral literature that this paper intends to discuss.

There are various forms of Yoruba oral poetry. The most important forms include Ifá, Ìjálá, Oríkì, Iwì, Ọfọ̀, Rárà, Ìgbálá, Ègè and Àrọ̀.

The most important of all the forms of Yoruba oral poetry is Ifá (chants associated with the profound system of Yoruba divination corpus). The corpus consists of two hundred and fifty-six branches known as Odù. Each Odù consists of an unspecified number of poems known as Ẹsẹ.

Another important form of Yoruba oral poetry is Ìjálá (hunters' poetic chants), rendered mainly for entertainment. Related to Ìjálá both in form and content is Iwì (chants associated with Egungun, the Yoruba ancestor god). Closely related to Ìjálá and Iwì is Oríkì (praise poems) which is chanted as a salute to Yoruba lineages and personalities. Oríkì can also take the form of salute to animals and even to inanimate objects. Nearly all forms of Yoruba oral poetry make use of Oríkì in one form or the other.

In the following pages I will draw examples from Ifá and Ìjálá— two of the best-known forms of Yoruba oral poetry—to illustrate the usual form and content of Yoruba oral poetry.

The form of Ẹsẹ Ifá

Each one of the various forms of Yoruba oral poetry mentioned above has its own structure. The structure of Ẹsẹ Ifá is analyzed below.

Ifá verse has a distinct structure of its own. The poems can be presented either in chanted or recited form. Whether chanted or recited, the poem begins with the mention of a list of names of Ifá priests who are believed to have been involved in a previous divination. In actual fact, these names could be names of animate and inanimate objects personified as Ifá priests. After mentioning the names of the Ifá priests involved in a past divination, the words 'A díá fún' [Ifá divination was performed for . . .] are mentioned. These three words are very important as one way of determining whether a piece of Yoruba oral poetry belongs to Ifá verse or to another form of Yoruba oral poetry.

After 'A díá fún' the name of the person for whom the past divination was performed is also mentioned. The reason for the past divination is mentioned next. It is not unusual, however, to omit altogether the reason for the divination. The pronouncement of the Ifá priests [who performed the divination] to their clients is then mentioned. This usually includes a portion asking the client to perform certain sacrifices. The next step mentions what happens to the client after he performed or refused to perform the prescribed sacrifices. The next step contains the reaction of the client to the result of the divination. This usually takes the form of jubilation or regret depending on whether the client was obedient or disobedient. The last step contains a song which usually draws a fitting moral out of the whole story.

13

The example below shows the eight divisions of a typical Ifá poem.

Part i   Àdánáà yá òkété;
Àfàkálẹ̀ẹ gbòrọ̀;
Bí tẹ̀tẹ̀ ẹ̀gún bá so lódò,
A tiiri gógọ́ọ́gọ́ sínú omi.

Part ii   A díá féèkán aláwọ̀ọ mìnìnjò.

Part iii   Òún le níyì báyìí?
Ni èèkán dáfá sí.

Part iv   Wọ́n ní pípọ̀ ni iyìi rẹ̀,
Ṣùgbọ́n kó rúbọ.

Part v   Ó sì rú u.
Ó rú abẹ mẹ́wàá
Àti aṣọ mìnìnjò kan.

Part vi   Abẹ mẹ́wàá tí ó rú náà
Ni àwọn awoo rẹ̀ẹ́ kàn mọ́ ọn lẹ́sẹ̀,
Tó fi ńṣọkọ fún gbogbo ẹranko.
Aṣọ mìnìnjò tó rú náà
Ni wọ́n dà bò ó lára,
Tó sọ ọ́ di arẹwà ẹranko.

Part vii   Ijó ní ńjó,
Ayọ̀ ní ńyọ̀;
Ó ńyin àwọn awoo rẹ̀,
Àwọn awoo rẹ̀ ńyin Ifá
Ó ya ẹnu kótó,
Orin awo ní ńkọ.
Ẹsẹ̀ tí ó nà,
Ijó fà á.

Part viii   Ó ní:
Àdágbiyì ẹranko ò,
Àdágbiyì ẹrkano.
Òòṣà ló fiyì féèkán,
Àdágbiyì ẹranko.[1]

Part i   The giant rat makes fire but does not warm himself by
                it;
            Gbòrọ̀[2] creeps all over the ground;
            When a thorny stem of tẹ̀tẹ̀[3] grows seed by the river-
                side,
            It bends its trunk heavily towards water.

Part ii   Ifá divination was performed for Tiger,
               The one with lovely and shining skin.

Part iii   Could he possibly have honour?
               That was the reason why Tiger performed Ifá divina-
                   tion.

Part iv   He was told that much was the prospect of honour for
                   him,
               But he should perform sacrifice.

Part v   And he performed it.
               He performed sacrifice with ten knives
               And one lovely and shining cloth.

Part vi   The ten knives which he used for sacrifice
               Were fixed to his fingers by his Ifá priests,
               And with it he does havoc to all other animals.
               The lovely and shining cloth which he also
                   used for sacrifice
               Was used to cover his body
               And it made him a beautiful animal.

Part vii   He was dancing,
               He was rejoicing;
               He was praising his Ifá priests
               And his Ifá priests praised Ifá.
               He opened his mouth,
               And the song of Ifá entered therein.
               As he stretched his feet,
               Dance caught them.

Part viii   He said: O! Animal created to have honour.
               Animal created to have honour.
               It is Òòṣà[4] who gave honour to Tiger,
               Animal created to have honour.

In its form, Ifá verse makes use of several poetic devices, e.g. suspense, play upon words, parallelism, simile, metaphor and repetition. Below, I will discuss one of these poetic devices in detail.

The following example plays upon the syllable 'ká'. This syllable is used either as a prefix, suffix or infix to denote a noun or a verb. Examples of nouns where 'ká' has been used as suffix are: Ìká, Lákaá and Àká. Examples of nouns where 'ká' has been used as an infix are: Oníkàá-mògún, Akáwùú, Akáagbòn and Akáagun. Examples of verbs where 'ká' is used as prefix are: Káwó, Kásè and Káyé.

1 Àró Ìká kìí jajá;
2 Òdòfin Ìká kìí jàgbò;
3 Ẹjẹmu Ìká kìí jòrúkọ;
4 Olórí Íká ò gbọdọ̀ jorí ajá.
5 Káwọ́ fún mi,
6 Kí nkásẹ̀ fún ọ.
7 Akáwùú níí pààrọ̀ ọrun, èèkàn.
8 Kálẹ̀-káákààkáá.
9 Ìyá lakáagbọ̀n;
10 Baba lakáagun;
11 Àbúròo wọn lakààkààgbasà;
12 Ẹ̀gbọ́ọn wọn lakáàkaàkáwọ́.
13 Nígbà èkíní,
14 Mo wọlé Oníkàámògún,
15 Èmi ò bá Oníkàámògún ńlé. . . .
16 Ó wáá kù dẹ̀dẹ̀ kí n wọ káà kẹrìndínlógún,
17 Mo wáá bá Oníkàámògún.
18 Ó káwọ́ Ifá,
19 Ó fi lérí,
20 Ó faṣọ àká bora.
21 Pààká mẹ́ta ló jókòó ti Oníkàámògún.
22 Oníkàámògún mọ àká mẹ́ta
23 Sáàrin ìta.
24 Ó so ibaaka mẹ́ta
25 Mọ́ ìdí àká.
26 Ó pe Lákaá
27 Pé kó yanko fún ìbaaka
28 Ní ìdí àká.
29 Ìbaaká ta Lákaá léjìká.
30 Lákaá-lá,
31 Akààkààgbasà
32 Àti Sásíoró
33 Ló dífá fún Sáàbámọ̀
34 Níjó tí wọn ńlọ lèé bèèrè ọ̀rọ̀ wò lọ́wọ́ Oníkàámògún.
35 Wọ́n ní èé ti jẹ́ tẹ́ ẹ fi ńjóóko káakàa wọ̀nyí?
36 Tí ìyá fi ńjẹ́ Akáagbọ̀n;
37 Tí babá fí ńjẹ́ Akáagun;
38 Tí àbúrò fí ńjẹ́ Akàakààgbasà;
39 Tí ẹ̀gbọ́n fí ńjẹ́ Akáàkaàkáwọ́?
40 Wọ́n ní nítorí pé o,
41 Apá àwọn ò káyé ni.
42 Ọ̀rúnmìlà, afèdèfẹ̀yọ̀,
43 Ẹ̀là Ìsòdè,
44 Ifá, jápá akápò ó káyée rẹ.[5]

16

1 The Àró[6] of the city of Ìká does not eat dogs;
2 The Òdòfin[7] of the city of Ìká does not eat rams;
3 The Ẹjẹmu[8] of the city of Ìká does not eat he-goats;
4 The head-man of Ìká does not eat the head of dogs.
5 Lift away your hand for me,
6 So that I may lift away my leg for you.
7 It is the spindler of cotton who changes spindles and knots.
8 The person whose name is Kálẹ̀-káákààkáá.
9 Mother's name is Akáagbọ̀n;
10 Father's name is Akáagun;
11 Their younger brother's name is Akàakàagbasà;
12 Their elder brother's name is Akáakaàkáwọ́.
13 On the first occasion,
14 I entered the palace of Oníkàámògún[9],
15 I did not find Oníkàámògún at home. . . .
16 As I was about to enter the sixteenth palace building,
17 I found Oníkàámògún.
18 He put his hands, full of Ifá divination instruments,
19 On his own head,
20 He covered himself with àká[10] cloth.
21 Three small masqueraders [pààká] sat by Oníkàámògún.
22 Oníkàámògún built three storage barns [àká]
23 In the middle of the open space in his compound.
24 He tied three mules
25 To the supporting poles of his storage barns.
26 He called upon Lákaá
27 To give food to the mules
28 At the foot of the storage barns.
29 The mules kicked Lákaá on the shoulders.
30 Lákaá whose other praise-names are Lá,
31 And Akàakàagbasà
32 Together with another person named Sásíoró
33 Were the people who performed Ifá divination for Sáàbámọ̀
34 On the day they were going to ask for the solution to a problem
     from Oníkàámògún.
35 They asked why all of them were bearing names sounding káakàa?
36 Why mother is named Akáagbọ̀n;
37 And father is named Akáagun;
38 And their younger brother is named Akàakàagbasà;
39 And their elder brother is named Akáakaàkáwọ́?
40 They answered that that was because
41 Their hands could not support the world.
42 Òrúmìlà, speaker of all languages,

43 Èlà of Ìsòdè[11],
44 Make the hands of Ifá priest able to support his own life.

The form of Ìjálá

Ìjálá, like Ifá, has its own distinct form which distinguishes it from other forms of Yoruba oral poetry. It also has its own typical poetic devices. In the following pages I will discuss parallelism as one characteristic poetic device in Ìjálá poetry.

The use of parallels is perhaps the most typical poetic device in Ìjálá poetry. 'The use of parallels renders the language of Ìjálá poetically figurative.'[12] Two examples of such parallels are given below:

i Àkò ló sìkejì àpó,
Olóòdẹ ló sìkejì ọba.[13]
[The scabbard is the close companion of the shed post
The chief hunter is the first counsellor of the king.]

In the above example, a parallel is drawn between the importance of the King in the city and the importance of the role of the Chief Hunter who guards the city.

ii Ó ló dijọ́ Ifá
Tó bá padà lẹ́yìn babaláwo;
Ó dijọ́ òpèlé bá padà lẹ́yìn ìṣègùn;
Ó dijọ́ Aláwùràbí bá padà lẹ́yìn 'Mọle;
Lòun ó ò tóó padà lẹ́yìn ìwọ erin.[14]
[He said
On the day when Ifá would desert an Ifá priest;
Only on the day when the divining chain would desert a healer;
Only on the day when Allah would desert a Muslim;
Would he also stop pursuing the elephant praise-named Láayé.]

In example [ii] above, parallels are drawn between the perseverance and courage of a hunter in pursuing the elephant and the constant watch of Ifá over the priest of Ifá; the constant use of the divining chain by healers; the constant care and protection of Allah over the Muslim.

The content of Ẹsẹ Ifá

The content of Ẹsẹ Ifá represents the whole range of the Yoruba world-view.

> Ẹsẹ Ifá deals with all subjects. It deals with history, geography, religion, music and philosophy. . . . There is certainly no limit to the subject matter which Ẹsẹ Ifá may deal with. Ẹsẹ Ifá is, therefore, a story or a group of stories taken from the rich experiences of our forefathers. These stories are lists of what have happened before in history. They are lists of precedents carefully laid down for us. The underlying philosophy of the whole system is that history repeats itself.[15]

Below are two examples of the subject-matter of Ẹsẹ Ifá. The first example tells of the practice of fortifying cities in traditional Yoruba society and how in times of peace fortification was neglected.

i   1 Pòngbá pòngbá là á bódi;
     2 A díá fÓdi,
     3 A bù fún Yàrà
     4 Ìgbà tì ńrayéè láì níí kú
     5 Ìwà Odí mò mò ḿbàjẹ́ o,
     6 Gbogbo òtò kùlú,
     7 Ẹ kọ́kọ́,
     8 Ẹ kádàá,
     9 Ẹ lọ túnwà Odi ṣe.
    10 Pòngbá pòngbá là á bÓdi,
    11 Odí mò dOdi ìgbàlèrò[16].

    1 Town-wall is always found in an impregnable state;
    2 Ifá divination was performed for Town-wall,
    3 Ifá divination was performed also for Moat.
    4 When they were going to earth never to die again
    5 The well-being of Town-wall is getting bad.
    6 All wise men of the city,
    7 Take hoes,
    8 Take cutlasses,
    9 And improve the well-being of Town-wall.
   10 Town-wall is always found in an impregnable state,
   11 Town-wall is now a wall of peace time.

    The second example below tells about the advantages of a good home to any person.

ii   1 Òsánṣọ gbá yìgí;
     2 Òwẹ̀wù gbá yìgí;

    3 Agírírí òkúta;
    4 A díá fún Iléere
    5 Tíí ṣaya Ọ́rúnmìlà.
    6 Iléere èé kú.
    7 Iléere èé wó.
    8 Iléere èé rọ̀run.
    9 Ààṣẹ̀ Iléere àṣígbà ni.
10 Ẹ̀rìgì, ọkọọ rẹ̀, èé rọ̀run àrèèbọ̀.[17]

    1 He who ties cloth on the loins and moves gracefully;
    2 He who wears a garment and moves gracefully;
    3 The very hard stone;
    4 Ifá divination was performed for Good-home
    5 Who was the wife of Ọ̀rúnmìlà.
    6 Good-home does not die.
    7 Good-home does not fall down.
    8 Good-home does not go to heaven.
    9 The door of Good-home is always opened by many.
10 Ẹ̀rìgì [Ifá], her husband does not go to heaven without coming back.

The content of Ìjálá

Ìjálá makes extensive use of praise-poems or salutes to various lineages, gods, individuals, birds and animals. These salutes, known as Oríkì, form an important part of Yoruba literature as a distinct form of oral poetry. When Oríkì is employed in Ìjálá, it takes the form of the latter and its content is also slightly modified. The following are examples of praise-poems in the content of Ìjálá. The first example is a salute to Ṣàngó, the Yoruba god of thunder, while the second example is a salute to the Baboon.

i Salute to Ṣàngó.

    1 Olúfínràn, ọbaa Kòso;
    2 Ọba asángiri;
    3 Ọba alàgiri;
    4 Ọ̀làgiri kàkàKà kọ́mọkùnrìn kò.
    5 Ṣàngó, ekuru gbágbá lọ́dàá;
    6 Ilẹ̀ gbogbo àkùrọ̀ lojò.
    7 Ènìyàn tí a bú léyìn tó sì mọ̀;
    8 Ènìyàn tí a bú léyìn tó sì gbọ́.
    9 Ogunlabí, etí lu kára bí ajere
10 Mọ́ bu u;
11 Mọ́ ṣa a;
12 Mọ́ sọ̀rọ̀ọ rẹ̀ léyìn.

13 Baba Bánkọ́lé.
14 N ó lọ lọ́nà ibẹ̀ un.
15 Ṣàngó ò!
16 A ru òwú rÒwu;
17 Ò rù 'fẹ̀ẹ̀fẹ̀ refẹ̀.
18 Ò ru gùdùgbú tà n'Gúgùgbú;
19 Láì ṣọmọ ẹranko kelebe.
20 Ṣàngó o!
21 Dégòkè,
22 Àrẹ̀mú.[18]

1 Ṣàngó whose other name is Olúfínràn, King of Kòso;
2 The king who cracks walls;
3 The king who splits walls;
4 He who splits walls with force and curls up young men.
5 Ṣàngó, plenty of dust in the dry season;
6 All land is marsh-land in the rainy season.
7 A man who was abused in his absence and he knew all;
8 A man who was abused in his absence and he heard all.
9 Ogunlabí, with ears all over the body like a colander.
10 Don't abuse him;
11 Don't strike him;
12 Don't talk of him in his absence.
13 Father of Bánkọ́lé.
14 I will continue to travel on that road.
15 Ṣàngó, I call you!
16 He who carried raw cotton to the city of Òwu;
17 He who carried new yam flour to the city of Ifẹ̀;
18 He who carried gùdùgbú yam tubes to sell at Gúgùgbú town;
19 Whereas he was not a small animal.
20 Ṣàngó, I call you again!
21 You, whose nick-name is 'Dégòkè,
22 Whose praise-name is Àrẹ̀mú.

ii Salute to Akítì [Baboon]

1 Láaré
2 Òpómù, a kájá lódẹ.
3 Ajá mọde tán,
4 Ajá wáá fÒpómù jẹ o.
5 Òbọ ǹlé o,
6 Apàtàkì
7 Abìlagbà lọ́wọ́.
8 Ọdẹ a fún bí alámọ̀ léyìin wọn.
9 Ọmọ OníṢànpọ̀nnáa mọ́ ṣàdan kù.

10 Òdéfìlà mójú gún,
11 Onílù ẹgàn.
12 Arápòólà ṣagbèjí ẹnu.
13 Ẹran tá à fẹ́mọ lọ́wọọ rẹ̀
14 Tí ńgbàna lọ́wọ́ ẹni
15 Mo rí i ńlẹ̀
16 Mo ba rẹ̀kẹ̀rẹ̀kẹ̀.
17 Kò sí ńlé,
18 A pín pàkọ́ dè é.
19 Ó délé.
20 Ó sunkún ẹnu.
21 Ò toko bọ̀ gbẹ́nu rọ̀ bí àpò Ìdọ̀ọ̀mì.
22 Olójú arédè tíí róbìnrin ará oko.
23 Kànkà kanka lórí ìgbá,
24 Baba Ìjímèrè.
25 Bọ̀ọ̀kìní orí òkè.
26 Ẹni tẹ́wà ńpa bí ọtí.
27 Ládoógí, a bẹnu bọọbọọ bí oobọ.
28 Abìpọn lẹ́nu.
29 Abìtìkùn láyà.
30 Ó ṣojú hòròhóró jẹko ànaa rẹ̀.[19]

1 Baboon, whose other name is Láaré.
2 You are also known as Òpómù who teaches dog how to hunt successfully.
3 Dog masters hunting,
4 Dog eats up Òpómù.
5 Monkey, I greet you,
6 The very important one.
7 He who has a whip on the hands.
8 Whom the hunter pursues and in the process besmears his smock with earth.
9 Animal speckled all over the body like a patient cured of severe small-pox.
10 He who wears a fitting cap for his face,
11 Drummer of the forest.
12 He who covers his mouth with slab-like jaws.
13 Animal from whom one has not received a wife
14 But who receives prostration homage from one.
15 I saw him on the ground,
16 I hid myself carefully.
17 While he was not at home,
18 An extra share of occiput was reserved for him.
19 He returned home,

20 Weeping for an extra share of mouth.
21 He returns from the farm and hangs his heavy mouth downward like Dahomean's bag.
22 He whose beautiful eyes see farmers' wives.
23 Bulky thing on locust-bean tree,
24 Father of Red Patas Monkey.
25 Gentleman on hill top.
26 Whose beauty intoxicates him like liquor.
27 Ládoógí, whose mouth protrudes like a ginning rod.
28 He who has a wooden spoon for a mouth
29 And a heavy door-bolt on the chest.
30 He who takes his deep and sunken eyes to raid the farm of his father-in-law.

Problems of Collection

The collection of Yoruba oral poetry raises some problems for researchers. Some of the forms of Yoruba oral poetry, for example Ifá and Iwì Egungun, belong to secret societies who guard these forms of literature jealously against any outside influence. Unless a man is therefore initiated into the secret societies that possess these forms of literature, it may be difficult or even impossible for him to collect anything.

Recently, however, the attitude of cult members to the collection of the literature in their possession has changed. They have been made to realize the importance of committing these forms of literature into writing. This change of attitude has helped towards the collection of Yoruba oral poetry. It does not, however, remove the urgent need for collecting more of these forms of poetry as our knowledge of this field still remains fragmentary.

2 Hausa

by D. Muhammad

Perhaps the most delicate problem in the appreciation of Hausa oral poetry is to draw a distinction between what is poetry and what is merely song. As has been recognized by Don Scharfe and Yahaya Aliyu, 'there are certain kinds of rhythmic utterance which one would hesitate to classify as poetry, yet which are clearly related to it, and which illustrate the linguistic and social bases of the oral tradition'.[20] The fact that linguistically there is no distinction[21]—wàƙà applies both to poetry and to song—further complicates the issue. One may from this be tempted to regard every song as poetry, but this no Hausa would accept. And to say that what Hausa knows and has is song and not poetry is as unhelpful as it is erroneous. Another complicating factor is that every poem can be, and often is in practice, set to music, whether this musical accompaniment be in the form of the talking drum, *Kàlàngú*, the stringed instrument, or simply clapping with the hands. Yet most Hausas would regard the songs of, say, Narambaɗa, which are set to *Kòtsó* music, as belonging to a distinct category from those of, say, Audu Yaron Goge who practises *gògé* music, not so much because the music differs as that in the one the words claim prior attention, while in the other the music is at least equally important.

As pointed out earlier, oral Hausa poems are sung and chanted rather than said. This quality also belongs to many a literary poem, but whereas the literary poem observes regularity of rhyme, the oral one is freer. And although it makes abundant use of silent stresses and modulation, oral poetry has a fairly regular prosody. It is usually in the last line of a verse, which is often shorter or longer than the preceding, that the punctuating heavy beat shifts its place.

One of the characteristic features of Hausa folktales is to include a poem in the middle or end of the narrative. The case of a girl called Lado is an example. Lado, having been abandoned by her fleeing parents during wartime, is adopted by a sympathetic couple. When she comes of age, they intend to marry her to a man who, unknown to them, is her real brother. By some singular instinct, Lado asks to be given millet to pound and sings the following song to the rhythm of the pounding:

> Ìn dákà gɛ́rɔ́ ní Ládɔ̀
> In daka gero tín-kwá-tìn
> In daka gero ni Lado
> In daka gero gídán míjì
> Úwǎtá dà tá hàifɛ́ nì
> Gǎ shí nǎ zámá sùrúkǎ nátà
> Ùbáná da ya haife ni
> Ga shi na zama suruka násà
> Ìn dáka gɛ́rɔ́ ni Lado
> In daka gero tin-kwa-tin.

> Let me pound millet, I Lado
> Let me pound millet, tin-kwa-tin
> Let me pound millet, I Lado
> Let me pound millet in my husband's house
> My mother who bore me
> I thus become her in-law
> My father who bore me

I thus become his in-law
Let me pound millet, I Lado
Let me pound millet, tin-kwa-tin.

As the last example illustrates, repetition is often a characteristic of folk poetry. Another feature of the oral poetry is the abundant use oi metaphor and idiom, as for instance in the poem sung by bridesmaids to the bride advising her not to succumb too easily to the bridegroom. Each line can be repeated two or more times and the girls clap to the major beats indicated. (Where a drum is available it supplements the clapping.)

Kánwằ/tắ
    Kár / kì bắ / dà bádò
Ín kín / jế
    Kar / ki ba / da bado
Dàddàu / rế
    Kar / ki ba / da bado
Àbù nằ / rúwá
    Shìn / káfá / dà bádò.

My Sister,
    don't give the lily
If you go
    don't give the lily
Try hard
    Not to give the lily
The water thing:
    Rice and lily.

Another poem in this category illustrates regularity of rhythm in the first three lines, the last word of each line, which is disyllablic, being outside the main beat span:

Gắ yákù, yế, gắ yákù mún káwố
Gắ yáku, màsú gídắ ga yaku mun kawo
Tắ ƙi ci tắ ƙi shá sái đán kàrén kứká
Kứká kàmán gwánkí
Ján ídò kàmán gáutắ.

Here's your daughter, ye, here your daughter we brought
Here's your daughter, members of the household, here you
    daughter we brought
She would not eat, would not drink but weep and weep
Her cry like the roan antelope's
Her eyes [red] as the bitter tomato.

25

There is in Hausaland a large number of professional singers, some of whom may be termed poet-singers. Without exception these set their poems to music. Mamman Shata, who practises *Kalangú* music, sings practically for all classes, while Narambaɗa and Danƙwairo, who both practise *Kòtsó* music, and Jankidi, who is a prominent *Táushí* singer, attached themselves to palaces of great emirs who patronize them as poet-laureates. Understandably, the major content of this court poetry centres on praise of the patron, his ancestors and other relatives; but sometimes it transcends these and in more recent times, has included an appraisal of the political situation in Hausaland and in Nigeria as a whole. Jankidi added to his fame by composing a long poem on the occasion of Nigerian Independence, a poem which illustrates the concern for grandeur and pageantry characteristic of this poet. Jankidi is the retainer of the Emir of Katsina of whom he has sung most flatteringly, just as Danƙwairo has found in the late Sardauna a subject worthy of his great verses; and Narambaɗa, whatever or whomever he may sing about, places his poems in the great mainstream of his poetry—the praise of Sarkin Gobir Na-Isa.

Praising his patron, Narambaɗa at one point says that he never dealt in coins but in currencies:

> Fáifằ nis sánì
> Zằmànìn Bằbán Rábí
> Bàn sán súlàllá bá.

> It's paper-money I knew—
> During the reign of Baban Rabi
> I knew no shillings.

Narambaɗa characteristically punctuates his poetry with philosophical statements:

> Mùtúm kà hánằ má àbínái
> Állàh ín yái núfìn bằkà
> Bá kà yá kài bá yá jìn shằwáràr kówá.

> It's man that refuses to offer you his.
> Allah—when He intends blessing you—
> Bestows on you without heeding anybody's advice.

But praise is by no means the sole preoccupation of these professional poets: satire also occupies an important place, for antagonists of a patron or a rival poet are understandably acidly satirized. Referring to a prince who is an enemy of his patron, Narambaɗa sings:

> Ɗán Sárkí dúkà áb bằ kówắ
> Ɗan sarki duka ab ba kómí

Sànnán yáts tsìrí yắwòn bánzá
Sái fá yà kwán nàn gòbé, yà kwán càn jíbí . . .

A prince who is a nobody
A prince who is nothing
Further takes to wandering
Only passing the night here tomorrow, sleeping there the day
after . . .

Mamman Shata is one of the more modern and more versatile of these professionals, whose poetry directs itself to a variety of subjects ranging from a small girl, through an Emir, to the praise of the Federal troops in the Nigerian Civil War. One of the most interesting pieces is that composed on his first pilgrimage to Mecca and the overawing sensation he felt on seeing the Red Sea. His versatility is not only in the variety of his interests but also in the spontaneity of his singing tunes. It is because of this double versatility that he has come to be the most popular of the professional poets.

But this is not to say that the court poets are all limited in their interests. In one of his poems, for instance, Narambaɗa describes the excellencies of a racehorse:

Íkòn Állàh 'Dánfílíngé
Dőkìn ískà 'Danfilinge
Kő bísà tùrkẽ nái na kwắná
Yáná nán tắré dà mártábőbí . . .

    .   .   .

Dáwắkí nà súkwà sún kwán hàníníyà
Bàrí gòbé tà zám tá bánzá
Mài tsế̃rẽ̀ músù níg gá yắ zố . . .

God's work, 'Danfilinge
The aerial steed
Even while passing the night on his tether-post
He still has his honours . . .

    .   .   .

[Other] race-horses have passed the night neighing
Let the morrow be fruitless:
It's their winner that I see come.

3 Ɛdo

by E. Ogieiriaixi

Ɛdo oral poetry is generally associated with some social purpose, so it is not often that one finds the poet as an individual engrossed in his own personal emotions. This is particularly so because of the highly centralized nature of the society; even events which have no direct connection with court festivals must revolve round a social unit such as the family or round the rites of groups. It is to be expected, therefore, that the oral poems that have been analyzed so far fall mainly into the categories of praise-songs and hymns, dirge, narrative, satire and ballad.

The major genres of Ɛdo oral poetry are classed as follows:

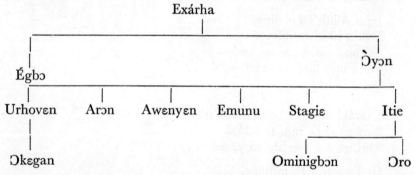

Perhaps the best way to have an insight into the nature of the poetry is to examine in some detail two poems—a narrative satire, *Iyayi*, and a lyric, *Eri¹ agbɔn ye*.

Iyayi[22]

Iyayi ʋɛn,
Iyayi ʋɛn, n¹ oʋiɔkpobɔzigho!
ɛi ghi le n¹ ɔdɔ, ɛi ghi tɔn n¹ egbaxian,
ɛdɛ ghaghi gbe, ɔ ¹gha zɔiku xian;
ɔ ghi zɔiku, ɔ mueʈɔ fĩobɔ.
A ghi nɔ ɔɛn, ɔ y¹ɔxuɛ, sɛhi;
A ghi nɔ ¹ɔxuɛ, ɔxuɛ z¹ Olukumi.

Mɛi ma hˡẽdo fo, amawˡ Olukumi.
ɛvɔnguɔvandia, ɛi ghi ma vˡ egbe;
ɛvɔnguɔvandia!

Iyayi dear,
Iyayi mine, daughter of the 'rich',
She cooked neither for a husband, nor for an acquaintance.
At break of day, from grubbing she made her meal;
When at it, with a knife she cut her hands.
And when queried, she summoned Parrot to witness her 'defence';
Parrot spoke Olukumi[23].

Am not full competent in ɛdo, much more Olukumi.
The problems caused by a maid are trying ones;
The problems caused by a maid!

Eriˡ agbɔn ye

A mugbo—ɔka, ɔi ma ma,
Axa nˡowinna, ɛi rhiˡ ebe giˡɔvan.

A na rhiˡ oxuo, nˡɔi ma guobɔvan,
Olɔxuɛnxuɛn, ɔɽˡ a fiee
A na biɔmɔ nˡɔi ma xˡɔvan,
Afianma, ɛi giˡ a viɛ.

Ogbewɛnkɔn owˡ iɽɛn riˡ ɛdo,
Nˡiɽɛn ya riɔba:
ɔ ghi sˡ ɛdo, Ominigbɔn, ˡghiˡ guɔnvɛn!

Imaʒɛhiagan, ɔgbˡ Ayaɽu okan,
ɔ na wɛ: 'Dˡ ɛdɛ nˡu gha biɛ?'
Ayaɽu ghi xian xa, ɔ na wɛ:
'Dˡɛdɛ nˡu gha dˡ imɔto?'

ɛi ɽˡɛvɔnvan, ɔgbuloko, nˡɔ rˡAzama,
ɔ na sˡigbina vˡ Élasolobi.
Ai ma guan, ɛvɛn fo vˡunu.

Nˡɔ xian muigbina, ɔ ɽˡɔ ghi ka muɛzɔ
ɛzɔ gha re, igbinai giˡa mu.
ɔxuɛ, nˡɔvɛnkɛ, ɔxuɛ, nˡɔvɛnɽo:
ɔ zowˡ eva, ɔ zɛe ghˡaɽo;
ɔ zowˡ eva, ɔ zɛe ghˡiyeke.

A na wɛ, nˡa gualˡ ɔe:
A gualˡ ɔe yo; a gualˡ ɔe re,
Ai ma ɽɛn eke nˡɔ laghe.

29

oxuo, nˡɔʋɛnkɛ; oxuo, nˡɔʋɛnɽɔ;
ɔ wɛ ɔdɔ gha wu nɛ,
Iɽɛn lɛlˡɛe riˡ owa:
ɔdɔ ghi wu, ukpɔn ɔ ghi silo.

Ugɛgɛ, ɔ ɽˡ oxuo zɛ:
ɔdɔe na gbˡ ukpɔbian;
ɔ na ba tie: 'ɔʋoxanʋɛn,
Ghˡeʋin nˡerhaʋɛn mu re,
Nˡima gba ɽe'.

ɔ na guakpaegbe, gbˡ ɔdɔ ginegbe:
'Lahɔ, ghɛi giˡ ɛe fian ʋˡobɔ ɽe.'

ɔba uku, ɔkɔlɔkpɔlɔ;
Ogie nˡɔ gbɔʋan,
ʋˡɛdɛ nˡuwui xˡɔ̃ʋan:
ɔba ghaa gbˡ ɔʋinzeghudu,
ɔ ghigha hi;
ɔ ghaa gbˡ ɔʋanʋiɛɽɛ,
ɔ ghigha begbe.

Iyayi, nˡoʋiudo,
A wˡɛe zɔse ɔkpa,
ɔ wɛ, ʋˡ iɽɛn ya ɽu?
ɛdɛ ghi riˡ ɛdɛ,
Eveɔmɔ ˡghi viɛ.

Ekita, ɔwe nˡa fi ema fua,
Nˡa gha ghi iɽɛn ghˡ ɛɽinʋin,
Nˡɔ gha ka rhiˡ ɛe ɽe:
Ɛseɔʋan ɔ gbɔʋan;
Oghiɔnʋan ɔ sinʋiɔnʋan.

Ɛwei diguɛ tu ɔʋan,
ɔ bolˡ iguɛ:
ɔ kpa tuɔʋan,
ɔ gha bolˡ uhun.

That's the World

If one makes a corn farm, and it fructifies not,
The sparrow sues one not for same.

If one compacts marriage with an incompatible woman,
One furrows for self a fiery way.

If a child treads not the path of his parents,
Sad are the latters' days.

Ogbewɛnkɔn set for ɛdo to seize the seat of King;
He arrived all right,
But took to divination!

Imaʒɛhiagan, of Ayaʈu in jest she asked:
'When will you bear a child?'
Fair is fair, and Ayaʈu asked:
'When will you buy a car?'

ɔgbuloko of Azama caused a quarrel like Élasolobi[24].
It was no one's fault he did; there was a fight,
And a moderator was the worse for it:
When a fight ensues, moderation is a farce.

Parrot, the clown; parrot the jester:
Two steps to the fore he took; two steps to the rear he took.
'Look for the parrot,' it was said:
To and fro the search was sought,
And none could claim the parrot's way.

Woman the clown; woman the jester; says she:
'For sure will I follow him, my husband,
If in time he's claimed by the hands of death.'
When husband in time did die,
She wore the latest in dress.

Woman is a naughty child:
Ukpɔbian fell a prey to a preying husband,
And husband in jest to the wife did say:
'Here's a gift from my dad for us to eat.'
The wife jumped, clasped the husband:
'Please, don't let the animal bite.'

ɔba, uku, ɔkpɔlɔkpɔlɔ,
Ruler that kills one the day one most hates to die:
When he's about recalcitrants,
He prays he deals not with the like again;
When he's about the weakling,
He fears, lest he ends with a fractured hand.

Iyayi, daughter of Udo town,
Was asked to choose a friend,
And she scoffed at the idea.
Years later, Iyayi wept
'Cause she had no child.

The dog did request to be thrown away a morsel
To put to test he and the spirits
Who shall be first to eat the food:
One's kindness often turns persecutor;
Our enemies often turn out our saviours.

The goat kneels not to greet anyone,
Yet its knees are sore:
If it were to do so,
Sore would be its head.

The rhythm is stress-timed[25] and the metre or ideal pattern is basically iambic. That is, the metric line consists of feet each having two syllables in which the first syllable is unstressed and is followed by a stressed one, thus: ˘ ˈ. Characteristically, the tone-bearing unit in the stressed syllables—usually a vowel—is relatively higher pitched than the tone-bearing unit (i.e. the vowel) in the unstressed syllable. Also, the duration of the former is longer.

The initial two verses of each of the poems are scanned below:

Ǐyá | yǐ ʋέn,| Ǐyá | yǐ ʋέn, ‖ nˈǒʋíɔ | kpǒbɔ́ | zǐghó,
ɛǐ ghí | lĕ nˈɔ́ | dɔ̆, ‖ ɛ́i | ghǐ tɔ́n | nˈĕgbá | xǐán. ˘ ˈ

Ǎ mú | gbˈɔ̆ká, ‖ ɔǐ má | mǎ, ˈ ˘ ˈ
Ǎxá | nˈǒwín | nǎ, ɛí ‖ rhiˈ ˘ebé | giˈɔ̆ʋán.

Notice that a silent stress could occur at the end of a verse, and that a natural pause or caesura is also a regular feature midway in the line.

The lines are not rhymed, but the second of every two lines tends to be end-stopped thereby producing closed couplets. In a few cases, closed couplets alternate with open couplets. In any case, the effect is epigrammatic or oracular.

The parrot features in each of the two poems. A question that could readily come to mind about this bird is 'What role does it play in Ɛdo oral poetry?' Like the tortoise of Ɛdo folktales, it appears to be an animal representative of a particular human quality, in this case, craftiness. This is sufficiently clear in the poems. Thus, when the narrator in the poem *Iyayi* complains of the parrot speaking 'Olukumi', he was in other words, complaining of the craftiness of Iyayi, the maid, who, probably, is from a place called Olukumi. Similarly, the parrot personifies woman's craftiness as a wife in the second poem.

Iyayi, also occurring in the two poems, is representative of the recalcitrant spinster, while the dog and goat, which are respectively the subjects of the last two stanzas of *Eriˈ agbɔn ye*, are merely *ad hoc* personifications of some types of men—a fitting closing gambit generalizing in the true epigrammatic mood of the poem.

The second poem exhibits an interesting structure. It opens with traditional folk wisdom put in the form of wise saws and a two-part structure reflected in the opening and closing couplets of each stanza, both reminiscent of the eighteenth-century couplet in England. The first three stanzas serve as an introduction which has the function of enlisting the interest of the listener. The poem proper [*Eri¹ agbɔn ye*] begins in the fourth stanza which is 'fuller' in content, having more lines as the narrative progresses.

The poem constantly moves from the particular incident being narrated to general truths. Again, as in *Iyayi*, the syllables are so equally weighted that they cannot be pronounced rapidly in sequence. When the fact of the regular occurrence of a caesura in the middle of the line is added, one finds that the emotional tone of the poem is stately, and meant to point at a universal truth in a deliberate philosophical mood. Every man's experience is of relevance for all, and the particular incident is made an exemplum. Even the title of the poem, *That's the World*, is quite indicative.

But in this approach to knowledge and truth, stereotyping is encouraged, as is borne out by the conclusion drawn about woman:

> 'Woman is a naughty child.'

The reference to 'car' in the second poem gives an idea about the possible date of composition of the poem, and that, at the earliest, would be the close of the last century, as that was about the earliest time motor vehicles were introduced to Benin City by the British.

The 'ɔgbuloko of Azama' who 'caused a quarrel like Élasolobi' is not a historical figure. But the effect of introducing him beside an important social figure, Élasolobi, into the incident being narrated is that it gives importance to a fight, a commonplace affair, which is being used as an exemplum. The audience may not have intimate knowledge of the quarrel in which ɔgbuloko was involved, but, their interest having been enlisted by reference to him in comparison with a great historical figure, the narrator can then go on to say what to him is the important thing—to warn against engaging in disputes.

In the poems, imagined dramatic situations are vivid, and it is easy to see in the fully stated stories the narrative element—Who is speaking? To whom? Under what circumstances? What is the speaker's attitude toward the subject of his discourse? toward the audience? etc. In this respect, for example, the poet's quoting the words of his characters renders the poem more explicit in its dramatic situation.

Nor are the poems wanting in diction that produces in the mind stimulating effects. Visual and auditory images (onomatopoeia) are effectively used, particularly in the opening stanzas of the poem or in the opening couplets of a stanza. In this line from the poem *Iyayi*: 'Iyayi ʋɛn,/Iyayi ʋɛn, n¹ oviɔkpobɔzigho!', 'n¹ oviɔkpobɔzigho' communicates, in the rising and falling pitches of its syllables, the picture of a very leisurely class with a magic wand for making money. But the audience realizes that such people do not exist in the world of experience, and that anyone who is human, like Iyayi, and who is said to belong to that caste, must be living in a dream world. So, with the careful use of such an apt word by the poet, the curiosity of the audience is aroused, and the desire to hear the particulars of the activities of the one who does things out of the ordinary is keen.

Towards this end, we find the poet also uses metaphor and personification, rhetorical devices such as anticlimax and hyperbole (as in the example given in the preceding paragraph) and, while there is no conscious rhyming of the lines, the use of assonance in opening couplets imparts great intensity to the lines, and makes for effective versification:

> . . . ɔgbuloko, nˡɔ rˡAzama,
> ɔ na sˡigbina ʋˡ Élasolobi . . .

By and large, Ɛdo oral poems are chanted. The instrumental accompaniment could be a harp, drum, hand claps or maracas, depending on the occasion. But the fact that the poems are often sung makes it difficult to distinguish between songs as songs, and poems. To the Ɛdos, both appear to be one, and while they may be 'the interpretative dramatization of experience in metrical language', the experience is not individual but collective, and the poems turn out to constitute one of the traditional ways or media our ancestors found for effectively conserving their experiences, their philosophies, their ethos and their history, in the absence of formal writing.

Notes

1 Wándé Abímbọ́lá, *Ìjìnlẹ̀ Ohùn Ẹnu Ifá, Apá K̀ìní*, Collins, Glasgow, 1968, p. 65.

2 Gbọ̀rọ̀: a type of vegetable creeping stem.

3 Tẹ̀tẹ̀: another vegetable herb.

4 Òòṣà—Òòṣàálá: the Yoruba god of creation.

5 Abímbọ́lá, Vol. I, pp. 121-4, (*Ìká Méjì*, chapter 5).

6 Àró: an Ògbóni title.

7 Ọ̀dọ̀fin: another Ògbóni title.

8 Ẹjẹmu: an Egúngún title.

9 Oníkàámògún: king of the city of Ìká.

10 Àká: a type of cloth used in ancient times.

11 Ẹ̀là of Ìsòdè: Ẹ̀là is another name for Ọrúnmìlà and Ìsòdè is the name of a place.

12 S. A. Babalǫlá, *The Content and Form of Yoruba Ìjálá*, O.U.P., 1966, p. 68 (I have slightly modified Babalǫlá's orthography and translation in some cases).

13 Ibid., p. 68.

14 Ibid., pp. 68-9.

15 Abímbǫlá, *African Notes*, Vol. 2, No. 3, April 1964, p. 14.

16 Abímbǫlá, *Ìjìnlẹ̀ Ohùn Ẹnu Ifá, Apá Kìíní*, Vol. I, p. 124, (*Ìká Méjì*, chapter 6).

17 Ibid., Vol. I, p. 124 (*Ìká Méjì*, chapter 7).

18 Babalǫlá, op. cit., p. 223.

19 Ibid., p. 97.

20 *Black Orpheus*, 21, April 1967, p. 31.

21 More recently, especially among those versed in Arabic literature, the Arabic loan word for poet— *shā'ìr*—is increasingly gaining currency to distinguish it from the Hausa word for ordinary singer, *máwàkí*.

22 Iyayi is the name of a girl (an incompetent housemaid) about whom the poem is composed.

23 Olukumi is spoken in Midwestern Nigeria. To Ɛdos, Olukumi is Greek.

24 Élasolobi is said to have been a great Ɛdo warrior, a contemporary of ɔba Ɔʒɔlua. He loved to fight aided by very few men. His end came as a result of trusting too much to his single might. The uloko tree, unsurrounded by other trees of significance, is likened in its fall when a strong wind blew, to the fall of Élasolobi in similar circumstances. The reference is historical and understood by the audience. The poet plays on this.

25 Stress in Ɛdo should not be equated with the English stress; stress in Ɛdo is syllable prominence.

Traditional Nigerian Drama

by Ola Rotimi

Ritual drama, traditional drama, folk opera and Nigerian drama in English: these are the four major forms of Nigerian drama. Of these, the second, traditional drama, is perhaps the most difficult to define. The reason for this is that traditional elements can be found in all these forms in varying degrees. For instance, such plays as J. P. Clark's *Ozidi* and Wole Soyinka's *A Dance of the Forests* belong to Nigerian drama in English; their medium of expression is English, and in the structure of the plays we can see the writers' awareness of the demands of modern theatre. On the other hand, the dependence of these plays on such ritual sources as the Egungun,[1] in the case of *A Dance of the Forests*, and on legend, as with J. P. Clark's play, coupled with an all-pervading atmosphere of fantasy, makes a good case for their being regarded as basically traditional Nigerian drama. Even the sheer size of their casts is reminiscent of a typical community pageant. Wole Soyinka significantly describes the occasion for his play's setting as 'the Gathering of the Tribes'; and J. P. Clark's play opens on 'spectators . . . settling down all around . . .' Both plays have a cast of at least forty.

Like Nigerian drama in English, the term 'ritual drama' explains itself: drama that has to do with ritual ceremonies or ceremonies of worship. One might only want to add that mime is the essential index of drama here. Folk opera, a term coined by Ulli Beier,[2] covers that type of presentation that thrives on music, song, dance, extended story-line, a message of a moral nature which is sometimes made obvious in the title of the play,[3] broad acting gestures, and the vernacular of the people which may range from an isolated local dialect[4] to commonly understood pidgin English.[5]

Traditional Nigerian drama is the immediate offspring of ritual drama, which is the earliest form of the Nigerian dramatic heritage. Folk opera and Nigerian drama in English both developed individually, and not in direct response to an already existing native form or to one another. The parallel here is the mediaeval theatre of Europe which came into being in ways divorced from Graeco-Roman antecedents.

To establish a detailed identity for traditional drama, one needs not only to trace its development from its parent body, ritual drama, but also, more important perhaps, to appraise this development in terms of the world-view of early Nigerians who themselves determined that development.

The idea of 'homeopathic and contagious' magic, as explained in George Frazer's *Golden Bough* and brought even closer home by the renowned Nigerian scholar in psychiatry, Professor T. A. Lambo, offers an explanation of this world-view. It was a common belief among Nigerians in the past, as it still is among some today, that:

> if a man finds the hair or nail belonging to, or even a piece of material which has been worn by, an enemy . . . he has only to 'use' them in order to bring about his enemy's death or to injure him.[6]

What this belief demonstrates, in essence, is a haunting feeling of anxiety which sees life itself as a potential enemy. Compelled by the need for survival in a brute milieu, and impelled by the instinct to understand, if not to master, the mysteries that haunted their nights and the fears that stalked their days, our forbears, as generations after them do today,[7] believed in the power of certain rituals or magical acts to bring about a wish. 'The beasts of the field',[8] being man's closest co-tenant on earth, must have been the most immediate target for these magical projections in which mimetic actions were a highlight, further enlivened by 'cries, grunts and growls'[9] intended to lure the reality of the animal desired.

Such dramatic action, or mimesis, has survived in the Nigerian dramatic heritage as ritual drama. A good example of it can be witnessed in the ancestor-worship ceremony of the Yoruba Egungun, the Ibo Mmuo and the Ijo Owu. In each case, the reality of the dead whose memory is being honoured is invoked not only through chanting and drumming but more importantly through a series of eerie vocal sounds imitating the 'weird nasal voice'[10] assumed to belong to the world of the dead. In time, as with the Hindu theatre, these 'gestures, sounds and movements were abstracted from this naturalistic representation and developed into symbols and patterns which signified the *dance*'.[11] This is significant since the dance was later to become a major concern of traditional Nigerian drama. In the meantime, however, the need to maintain constancy of good wish-fulfilment evoked from our forbears an intense trust in the efficacy of this ritual act. To further ensure constancy in good results, some formalization of procedure along lines prescribed by credos, taboos, incantations and spells was necessary. The upshot of this, then, was religion or cult worship.

Ironically, while the ceremonials of worship caught on, developed and became further elaborated with the ritual of sacrifice,[12] the dramatic element of mimesis remained static—stunted, as it were, by that which it had nurtured: religion. However, on occasion, mimesis was activated by dialogue which usually took the form of invocation and response between god (priest) and man (initiate). Examples of this abound in the ancestor worship ceremonies of the Kalabari[13] and the Yoruba peoples. Allowing for slight variations in tribal practice, mimesis, as seen in ancestor worship, usually follows this format:

It is night-time, and early warnings have imposed a curfew on the community. A member of the secret cult concerned is fully masked. He is supposed to represent the deceased whose memory is being honoured. Accompanied with drumming and chanting by fellow-members of the cult, he emerges from the cult house or sacred grove and approaches the home of the deceased. Reaching there, chanting and drumming abate or stop completely while the cult elder or cult priest calls the name of the deceased loudly, invoking him to return to life and visit with the children he left behind. He intones repeatedly, supported by drum or choral accent. Finally, the masker speaks. His voice is sufficiently disguised to sound like that of the deceased himself, or dehumanized to reflect the ethereal eeriness of Spirits' voices. He then addresses his children within, giving words of advice, of reassurance, of blessing, or of harsh reprimand. The children within may respond where need be. Some other ritual may follow, like formally accepting or rejecting the gifts that have been placed on the threshold by the children. This done, he withdraws with his followers to the 'land of the dead'.

But even this exchange, like the mime, is skeletal, much in the same sense as the Quem Queritis 'colloquy'[14], which, while affirming the deathlessness of the Christian life force, was but a sideshoot in the elaborate proceedings of Mediaeval England's Easter worship.

Mimesis and/or dialogue of an invocatory nature can thus be taken to be the touchstone for testing the presence or absence of drama in Nigerian ritual displays. And it is by this test that the presence of drama is found in the Egungun ritual of the Yoruba, or the Duen ceremonies of the Kalabari peoples. On the other hand, using this test, such ancestral displays as the Eyo masquerade of Lagos, and the Ahate masquerade in the Ekwechi-Anokehi ceremony of the Igbirra tribe in Northern Nigeria, are entirely lacking in what can be described as drama. When mimesis does occur in any of these, it is found wanting in definiteness as to the object being imitated, and is not ritual drama.

In any case, mime thrived where it could as a testimony of our forbears' early attempt to understand or to master the immediate, visible world about them. Correspondingly, religion waxed on as a conscious invention that acknowledged a dominant life force which bound our forbears to other co-tenants of the universe: the beasts of the field, the birds of the air, the fishes of the sea, the hills, the mountains, the heavenly bodies, the phenomenal sounds of wind and thunder, the mystery of earth itself, the crossroads, and, most importantly, the memory of the dead.[15]

Placide Tempels touches upon an idea that is in no way alien to yet another aspect of the Nigerian traditional world-view. This is the idea that, by using certain means that have come to be called 'black magic', man is quite capable of controlling these 'forces of nature which God places at man's disposal'.[16] With this conviction, our forbears saw themselves responsible for the maintenance of order and good will within their community. But accord within the the community alone was not enough. They became, again in the words of Professor Lambo, 'fundamentally concerned with establishing good relations with man in the sense that it means not only man here and now (that is the empirical man), but man when he has ventured from mortal sight'.[17] Our Nigerian forbears were also aware, as implied in sacrificial rites,[18] that, as Elsy Leuzinger puts it: 'ill-will obstructs the exercise of force, and disturbs the cosmic order'.[19] It was imperative, therefore, that at least their human world—the tribe, the village or the community—co-operated toward ensuring the fulfilment of this responsibility to maintain order and good relations. The outcome of such co-operative effort is the widening of previously confined ritual codes, proven taboos and sacred rites, formerly practised by an initiated few, into broader sociological mores that affected a whole community or tribe. The community as a whole must know something about the mysteries of the world. Not only that, it must also appreciate the sure justice which awaited any breach of the ground-rules for communal peace and well-being.

With these extended moral demands the way was now set for the ritual to move out from confined conclaves, from sacred groves and from hallowed shrines, and meet the masses on the king's special forecourt, in the chief's backyard, in village squares, and in the more general market-place. The elders and initiates, having consolidated their knowledge of the world's mysteries in the secrecy of cult worship, were now ready to educate their fellow-men; ready to, as it were, 'justifie the wayes of God'[20] to them. But how such knowledge could be imparted liberally without at the same time compromising the austerity of cult worship was another problem.

One approach was to instil fear into the minds of the community, first as a way of curing evil intentions. Hence, for instance, the nightly displays of cult worship which must be preceded by stern warnings to all non-initiates to remain indoors and never attempt to peep out at the spirits as they passed. As further reinforcement to this occult approach, idealized representations of these spirits came into being in the form of masked actors or impersonators. This innovation, the masked actor or actors (the masquerade), marked the final stage for a new development in the Nigerian dramatic heritage: the traditional drama.

But the birth of truly traditional drama, free, as it ought to be, from the demands of worship, and orientated more toward entertainment[21] and open communal participation, must wait for one other cultural adjunct: oral literature. Myths, legends, tales, riddles—these can be said to have paved the major passageway from the occult to the secular world of theatre. Reik, in a study on ritualism, holds that the mythological world is 'older than religion'.[22] On the contrary, it seems logical that religion, which is an expression of 'recognition of a super-human controlling power',[23] came before mythology, which is a way of interpreting, of explaining, the enigma of this superhuman controlling power. It follows that oral literature, which helped create traditional drama in our society, came into being at a time when the mysteries of the universe were being unravelled in the idiom of man's daily experience. The ways of gods were now much nearer to man's understanding of his own ways. Sociological codes proved to be not only a means of preserving peace and accord within the community, but also a challenge for the attainment of the ideal life. Our Nigerian forbears began to aspire to 'the good' expected of the individual within that community. Men who made themselves living examples of this attainable ideal later passed away. But songs extolling their examples, and stories recalling the virtues and courage of their actions, lived after them, and became the main root for the blossoming of traditional drama. In order to bring these examples or actions of the past closer to the present, it was inevitable to exploit a vehicle of ritual drama: the mime.

With this type of community-orientated, rather than occult, approach to learning, the trend of this new form of drama was now towards entertainment. The major components of traditional drama were now at hand: learning and entertainment. Under this framework, of course, remained such borrowed footholds of ritual tradition as the dance, rhythm (music), chants and worship. Latterly came the following evidences of communal interest: pageants, processions, contests. Traditional Nigerian drama had now arrived.

It is only appropriate at this point to treat, individually, the most salient characteristics of traditional drama: dance, mime, music, masquerade, procession, worship, and the lesson or moral theme. The dance is an advance on mime. Varied in form and tempo, it is not only a visible expression of rapport between rhythm (music) and movement, but a manifestation of a state of mind whose farthest stretch is trance.[24] In the Nigerian society, the dance is more important than the drama or mime which, in the case of traditional drama, is present only as a 'framework upon which to hang the dance sequence'.[25] The only time that mime can retain a prolonged hold on the audience is when props are called into the act. The Delta tribes of the Rivers State of Nigeria are noteworthy in this regard. An example is the Erema Segi Ogbo[26] presentation during a 'Water-Spirit' ceremony. This spectacle employs any variety of props, common among which are the handkerchief, the paddle, the umbrella, the walking stick and even the broom. Each item is applied to its normal, everyday usage in the dance sequence. The Wuruye or 'invitation to drink' dance item of the Itshekiris of the Mid-West State is another instance. In this dance sequence, actual breakable drinking-glasses lend themselves to as many drink improvisations as the dancers' movements can portray. Another example in which a prop is called upon to heighten the dramatic substance of mime in a dance sequence is the Ukwa war dance of the Efiks of the South-Eastern State. This dance, unlike its counterpart— the Tarkai war dance[27] of the Borgu in Northern Nigeria—derives its thrill and suspense-value from a far more menacing prop: the cutlass. At points of intense involvement, dancers challenge one another to a mock duel which has all the fury of actual fight.

Dancing is also the medium for the display of yet another important aspect of the Nigerian cultural heritage: acrobatics. The world-renowned Igheleghe dance of Ishan, in the Mid-West State, is dominated by acrobatics deftly performed to achieve climaxes of brisk somersaults and varying tableaux of body contortions. Within the structure of traditional Nigerian drama, acrobatics are a prominent feature. Instances in the Egungun Alarinjo display of the Yoruba,[28] the ikaki[29] and the angalaiyai[30] of the Delta tribes in the Rivers State come quickly to mind. Here, again, the somersault, performed with variation in style and complexity, is a common feature. Whereas, for instance, the Yoruba Egungun type of somersault is generally executed vertically— frontwards or backwards—the approach of the Delta tribes is horizontal and sideways—very similar to the style of the Igheleghe display of the Mid-West. The dancer takes off, first with a vertical leap into the air, and levels his body horizontally in a spin aloft, then lands on the opposite foot to that which set him off into space; up again, level, spin, down; up, level, spin, down—repeatedly and with increasing speed, covering a sizeable distance in the process.

Nowhere in the world can there be dance without music, or dance without some kind of rhythmic accompaniment. In Nigeria, music and dance or mime must blend in the sense that mimetic movements in a dance are not only accompanied by, but are also punctuated with, drum accents. Dance, in other words, is the medium through which mimetic impulses are carried.

The term 'Nigerian music', or for that matter 'African music', may at once conjure up, in the mind of the foreigner, the image of an assemblage of objects being beaten—in particular, drums. But the sound of Nigerian music, in so far as it concerns traditional dramatic presentation, is dependent on a wide variety of instruments which may be classed under four principal heads:

beaten objects[31]	drums, wood, metal, bamboo
wind instruments	horn, trumpet, flute
vocal	chants, songs, tremulo, hoot, grunt, hum, yell
effects	rattles, bells, bull-roarer

Of all these, beaten objects are most important for dramatic expression. In traditional drama, as in the ritual and folk opera, dialogue or speech is conveyed not only by the human voice but also by the drum. The Yoruba 'lya-lu' in the 'dundun' ensemble is widely known as the 'talking drum'. But this talkative knack is by no means the preserve of the 'lya-lu'. In the Rivers State, for instance, drum-dialogue[32] vis-à-vis the performer (masker) is a pronounced characteristic in the structure of any traditional dramatic display. Known as the 'ekule' or 'salute', its importance in the traditional drama format of the Rivers State culture is similar to the entrance song of the chorus or 'parados'[33] in Greek drama.

Dialogue, in the conventional sense of oral give-and-take, generally holds a position of less magnitude in the format of traditional Nigerian drama. Rather, mime and song serve as major handmaids to story-line in such display. This dependence on song as a method of plot exposition has been further developed in the folk opera genre to a point where the folk opera is distinct. In this genre, song also comes readily to hand in moments of 'parabasis'[34], when the moral theme or lesson of the play needs to be driven home.

Nigerian culture conceives mask not just as 'a covering for the face or part of it'.[35] In association with costume and headpiece, mask forms part of a cultural triad that constitutes the masquerade. Masquerade, in turn, is a concrete evidence of the Nigerian's world-view that asserts the union between man and the powers—the mortal and the immortal. It is a testimony of the continuity of the life force. But, whereas the Nagarassa, the Pratnakuta and the Gurulurassa masks of Senhalese traditional Kolam drama,[36] and the Pao Kung[37] mask of traditional Chinese theatre, depict the faces of divine or supernatural beings, masks in traditional Nigerian drama limit the extent to which the faces of gods can be exposed to public view. Mannerisms of the gods can be attempted in mimesis with an intent that borders on genial humour,[38] in the same way as Dionysus' inebriated exploits served the needs of Hellenic comedy; however, masks that bear the actual visage of a god are a rarity in the tradition of Nigerian craft. The type of union which the Nigerian masquerade aims at depicting is generally one between man and the departed ancestors who have invariably assumed eternal life through death. It is one that, in the words of Jomo Kenyatta, flaunts our 'communion with Ancestral Spirits'.[39]

Complementary to, but even more popular than, ancestral masks is the other type which depicts animal features in unique or combined forms. Apart from animal characteristics, there are borrowings also from the bird, fish and even vegetable world. The Egbukere mask of Ahoada in the Rivers State displays a symbol of modern technology: an aeroplane. These two types, taken together, show a pattern in our cultural development. Animal masks tend to represent the legacy of ritual drama which gained roots at a time when man's immediate concern was with understanding the ways of the beasts of the field, the birds of the air, the fishes of the sea, in order to ensure his own survival. Ancestral masks, on the other hand, were a later development which came at a time when maintenance of good relations between man present and man past was considered a prerequisite to survival. As has been mentioned earlier, this was the time that marked the beginnings of the traditional Nigerian dramatic form. For the Egungun ancestor cult of the Yoruba, this time was, according to Joel Adedeji,[40] between c. A.D. 1590, in the reign of Alafin Egunoju, and 1610 under Alafin Ogbolu. This was when Olugbere, the hybrid son of the Ologbin, as a masked performer, broke away from the formalism of Egungun ritual display, and took liberties in dance, in acting, and in acrobatics, thus initiating the entertainment motif of Egungun worship. It was from these beginnings that the Alarinjo masked theatre developed to become a classic example of traditional Nigerian drama as we know it today.

Even in the Alarinjo repertory, popular and sometimes lavish as the performers tend to be with characterization, respect for the persons of gods is preserved. There is hardly any facial mask or headpiece representing a god. In the Yoruba town of Ede where Sango is the patron deity, there was a fierce protest from elders of the cult and community when a troupe once overstepped ethical bounds by presenting a caricature of Sango in mime.

It could be argued that presentations which concern the gods are not traditional but ritual drama, in which case worship and not entertainment is the prime purpose. On the other hand, traditional drama thrives on impersonation of the animal world, and of man either at the zenith of moral and physical courage, as Obunjigba[41] in Opobo traditional drama, or at the nadir of disrepute, as the thief in Kalabari traditional drama[42] or the courtesan of the Alarinjo repertoire.[43] (In

43

between these extremes is a stock of personages subject to caricature for the purpose of evoking something like the Aristophanic type of humour, which thrives on recognition rather than on passing a moral or social comment.)

According to Constantin Stanislavski, the key to good acting lies in the subjection of inhibitive forces of the self to the resources of the senses, the memory and the psyche.[44] It is for the realization of this ideal that the role of costume (either alone, with mask and headpiece, or headpiece alone) is important to Nigerian cultural presentations. Invariably, the masker, in any form of Nigerian display, is the focus of the event. It is expected that the actions, dance steps, voice and general stance of the masker not only conform with rhythm (music) but also attain the superhuman ideal being acknowledged in the display.

In traditional drama, where caricature is rife, precision in mimesis is essential. Here the role of the mask is fully utilized. The mysteries and strange forces long identified with mask in traditional thought become real at the moment of ceremonial performance. This is when the power of the god or spirit of the ancestor comes forth and enters into the masked performer with the aid of the masking medium. The feel of the presence of these powers affects the masker's state of mind. Absolute belief in this presence results. In time, often aided by sacrifice or prayer to the powers, self-identification by the masker with the power being pleased becomes total, and the caution of self-regard is submerged. Sometimes, further stimulated by sounds of rhythm (music), this feeling of mystical eminence is heightened and stretched beyond the level of the purely physical to affect the psyche, precipitating a state of trance.[45]

The other role of mask, which is more pronounced in traditional than in ritual display, is aesthetic. To ensure visual appeal, traditional Nigerian drama constantly experiments with form and colour. In ritual display, employment of form and colour is more often than not geared toward the bizarre. This tendency is not unconnected with, and in contrast to, the need for austerity in worship. Traditional drama, orientated as it is toward entertainment, uses form and colour for comedy, as well as for purposes of sheer beauty. Examples are the bulbous-jowled 'elekedidi' of the Alarinjo stock, and the parti-coloured aeroplane masquerade of the Egbukere ceremonial in Ahoada, Rivers State.

The Nigerian's innate love of form and colour is not restricted to mask and costume alone. It aspires to grandeur and magnitude in procession, which is a common spectacle in the ritual as well as in traditional ceremonies. Ceremonies such as these which allow for communal participation point to another important feature of the Nigerian cultural heritage. They mark the meeting point between ritual and the traditional dramatic forms. It is not uncommon to observe, at the end of a ritual ceremony, an afterpiece in the form of a play with a clear entertainment intent. The Amagba ceremony is a good example of such generic synthesis. Performed about mid-November in the Delta regions of Nigeria, this ceremony serves the dual purpose of purifying the community of malevolent forces and of ushering in the local New Year. The ritual begins at night with the 'akuma' or drum call sounded at regular intervals. Libation, feasting and supplication to the gods of the tribe then follow at dawn, climaxing in the gathering of the whole community to witness the symbolic embodiment of the ills of the past year. These are portrayed in the shape of a figurine seated in a small canoe. After more invocation to the gods by the chief priest of the community, a carrier comes forward, starkly attired in a white loin-cloth, a feather stuck in his hair, and chalk marks outlining the eyes and nose. Affected by the rhythm and ever-increasing tempo of the 'akuma', and overwhelmed by the immense religious importance of the occasion, the carrier becomes possessed, shivering to the rhythm of the beat. Suddenly, he whirls round, hoists the figurine and canoe on to his shoulder, and hurries to the riverside, the whole community trailing fast behind him, chanting, urging him to go on, hurry on, with the evils, the illnesses, the bad luck and allied misfortunes that have troubled the land for the past twelve months. Reaching the riverside, he transfers his ill-fated burden on to a large canoe manned by some able-bodied youths of the village. They then race downstream to dump the evils far away from the new purity of the community. This serious ritual is soon followed by dancing, masquerading and plays put on purely for the entertainment of the 'cleansed' community. Among the Yoruba, the occult Egungun ceremony is followed by more festive events mounted in the spirit of sheer fun and games, with no barrier whatsoever to communal participation. Since this type of display is meant for communal appreciation, prominent in the play-content is always an all-pervading moral lesson.

Perhaps the outstanding dramatic link between traditional drama and such later developments as the folk opera and Nigerian drama in English is this concern with moral values. Springing from the old world-view that upholds the merits of virtue and wisdom, a moral vision has spread through the heroic ordeal of a Moremi[46] in the legend, suffused the wily escapades of the tortoise in the folktale world, seeped down into the entertainment plot of traditional drama, inundated the folk opera and showed up subtly in Nigerian drama in English. A concern with morality is so characteristic of the folk opera that a symbolic Nigerian gesture has been incorporated into folk opera histrionics to signify a moment when a moral lesson registers on stage.

45

For instance a defeated, miserable character will convey his emotion of grief, remorse, compunction, or plain undeserved suffering, in this sequence:

a. A clenched fist is raised toward the chin.
b. The thumb is stuck out and bitten between the foreteeth.
c. The hand, still clenched, is propping the chin.
d. The head is lowered.
e. As a final relay of the magnitude of the emotion being experienced, a slow shake of the head from left to right (or vice versa), another right to left, any number of times. The longer, the more painful the experience is supposed to be, the slower, the graver.

The moral lesson can be seen as evidence of the philosophy and virtuous ideals of the Nigerian yesterday and today, and as evidence of the lnik between the drama of worship and later dramas of entertainment and free learning.[47]

Notes

1 Joel Adedeji, *The Alarinjo Theatre*, a Ph.D. thesis, University of Ibadan, 1969.

2 Ulli Beier, 'Yoruba Folk Operas', *The Journal of the African Music Society*, Vol. I, No. 1, 1954, p. 32.

3 For example, *Akeju* (The Spoilt Child) by Oyin Adejobi.

4 As in *Moremi* by Muritala Olowoomojuoere, which is in authentic Ife dialect.

5 Ogunmola's *The Palm-Wine Drinkard* experimented with classic English in parts of the original Yoruba text of this play at the Algiers Festival Production of the play.

6 T. A. Lambo, *African Traditional Beliefs*, Ibadan University Press, 1963, p. 4.

7 Professor Lambo bears this out with this story about a twentieth-century West African: 'An English University-trained West African patient . . . got promoted in the Administrative Service by superceding quite a number of able West African contemporaries by virtue, it was alleged, of his highly placed social position and contact. A few weeks after his promotion, he had an accident in unusual circumstances and became somewhat terrified. He thought his colleagues were trying to get at him in a mysterious way. During this time of stress, the patient dreamt and saw his grandfather who assured him of long life expectancy, and also asked for a goat. He bought a goat the following day and carried out this

"instruction", and he quickly recovered from his severe anxiety state.

'Even though he did not like to discuss this matter, presumably as it casts a shadow on his entire educational background, he conceded the point that he believed there was something in this "native thing".' (Lambo, *op. cit.*, p. 8.)

Another example that reflects this widespread belief in 'homeopathic magic' among Nigerians is in this extract from the Problem Page of a recent issue of the Nigerian *Sunday Times* (Lagos, August 17, 1969, p. 8): 'I am a girl of 21 and in love with a boy of 20. We both finished our secondary education the same year and we are both looking for jobs. My boy has just told me that he needed my menstruation pad because a moslem preacher (alfa) wanted to use it to make juju for him so he could get a job.'

8 Genesis 1:24-25.

9 Mulk Raj Anand, *The Indian Theatre*, Dennis Dobson Ltd, London, 1950, p. 16.

10 Robin Horton, *The Gods as Guests*, a *Nigerian Magazine* special publication, 1960, p. 27.

11 Mulk Raj Anand, op. cit., p. 17.

12 'The most crucial psychological point of all cult worship.' Lambo, op. cit., p. 5.

13 The Duen ceremonies performed by the initiates of the Ekine Society.

14 Allardyce Nicoll describes this as 'a piece of four-lined dialogue', *The Development of the Theatre*, George Harrap, London, 1965, p. 63. Also see A. M. Nagler, *A Source Book in Theatrical History*, Dover, New York, 1952.

15 'The certainty of the individual's extinction as a human being contradicts so outrageously the value and effort of living that most culture minimizes the confrontation with this certainty, or cushions it with assurances of some immortality.' Peter Morton-Williams, 'Yoruba Responses to the Fear of Death', *Africa*, Vol. XXX, No. 1 (January 1960), p. 34.

16 Elsy Leuzinger, *The Art of the Negro People*, Methuen, London, 1960, p. 22.

17 Lambo, op. cit., p. 6.

18 Ulli Beier and Peter Morton-Williams see the purpose of sacrifice as essentially purgatory: an instrument for the cleansing of human thoughts and of evils in the human body or in the community.

19 Leuzinger, op. cit., p. 22.

20 John Milton, *Paradise Lost*, Book I, l. 26.

21 i.e., arousal of joyous sensation in the spectator.

22 Cited in Lambo, op. cit., p. 5.

23 H. W. Fowler and F. G. Fowler, *The Concise Oxford Dictionary of Current English*, fourth edition, Clarendon Press, Oxford, 1950.

24 More evident in ritual than in traditional dramatic presentation.

25 Robin Horton, 'Changing Year', *Nigeria Magazine*, No. 67, 1960, p. 294.

26 Women's dance troupe of the Ijo tribes.

27 Said to date back to the days of prophet Mohammed, it is now considered the dance of the Borgu aristocracy. Wooden truncheons form the prop.

28 Joel Adedeji, op. cit.

29 Robin Horton, 'The Tortoise Masquerade', *Nigeria Magazine*, No. 94, 1967.

30 Stilt dancer. See E. J. Alagoa, 'Ijo Origins and Migrations', *Nigeria Magazine*, No. 92, 1967.

31 The term 'percussion' is being avoided here, since beaten objects may not necessarily vibrate. In Ogun worship, only metallic objects are struck.

32 See Robin Horton, *The Gods as Guests*, op. cit.

33 Allardyce Nicoll, op. cit., p. 37.

34 A section in Greek dramaturgic format in which the author comes forward and addresses his audience directly.

35 A. S. Hornby, E. V. Gatenby, M. Wakefield, *The Advanced Learner's Dictionary of Current English*, second edition, O.U.P., London, 1963.

36 See Sir Gunasinghe, *Masks of Ceylon*, Department of Cultural Affairs, Ceylon, 1962.

37 Faubion Bowers, *Theatre in the Far East*, Grove Press, New York, 1960.

38 For more about the idea of Nigerian masquerades 'playing with gods', see Robin Horton, *The Gods as Guests*; and Joel Adedeji, op. cit.

39 Cited in Lambo, op. cit., p. 6.

40 Joel Adedeji, op. cit.

41 The legendary slayer of the water monster, Mingi Oporopo. See Onuora Nzekwu, 'Carnival at Opobo', *Nigeria Magazine*, No. 63, 1959.

42 Robin Horton, *The Gods as Guests*, op. cit., p. 44.

43 Joel Adedeji, op. cit.

44 Constantin Stanislavski, *Building a Character*, Max Reinhardt, London, 1965. See also John Gassner, *Treasury of the Theater: From Ibsen to Ionesco*, Simon and Schuster, New York, 1960.

45 It is possible that trance can affect an ordinary spectator, in which case empathy with the masked performer or power being pleased is considered as the source.

46 A memorable Yoruba heroine who sacrificed her son for the survival of the people of Ile-Ife. This legend has been dramatized in varying versions in the folk opera genre by Duro Ladipo, Oyin Adejobi, and Muritala Olowoomojuore of Ododuwa College, Ile-Ife.

47 John Gassner calls this 'enlightenment'. See 'Catharsis and the Modern Theatre', in *European Theories of the Drama*, ed. Barrett H. Clark, Crown Publishers, New York, 1961.

A Survey of Modern Literature in the Yoruba, Efik and Hausa Languages

by Adeboye Babalọlá[1]

To celebrate the achievement of political independence by Nigeria in 1960, a special issue of the magazine *Nigeria* was published in that year. This contained an article entitled *Nigerian Literature* written by Ulli Beier and entirely devoted to Nigerian literature in English. The existence of a worthwhile body of Nigerian literature in the various Nigerian languages was ignored in the article. In this book of essays, the editor intends that such misrepresentation of the scope of Nigerian literature should be avoided. Hence the collection includes not only essays on traditional oral prose and poetry in Nigerian languages, and on Nigerian traditional drama, but also this survey of modern printed literature in three of Nigeria's numerous languages, these three serving as representatives.

Modern Yoruba Literature

A standard orthography for the Yoruba language was established by the missionaries of the Church Missionary Society of London working in Yorubaland in the period 1842-82. The climax of the deliberations on this orthography was the Conference of Missionaries held at C.M.S. Mission House at Faji, Lagos, early in the year 1875. Thereafter, literacy in Yoruba was an ability greatly sought by adult members of the Yoruba Christian congregations and it was the initial main aim of the instruction given to the children in the elementary schools.

One of the earliest best-known books in Yoruba was *Bíbélì Mímọ́*, the Holy Bible translated from the original Hebrew and Greek texts, as well as from the existing English versions, by Bishop Ajayi Crowther and first published in 1900. Read aloud in the churches every Sunday and in the Christian homes every day, morning and night, *Bíbélì Mímọ́*, impressively massive with its sixty-six books, set a particular style of the Yoruba language as a standard for all Yoruba-speaking people to use in such places as mixed gatherings where dialect Yoruba would be out of place.

50

The translation of the Bible was followed in 1911 by the publication of *Ilọsiwaju Ero-Mimọ*, a Yoruba version of John Bunyan's *Pilgrim's Progress*, which was as popular as *Bíbélì Mímọ́*. The translation was done by the Reverend David Hinderer.

To provide reading material for Yoruba schoolchildren, the Lagos headquarters of the Church Missionary Society brought out a series of Yoruba Readers (First, Second, Third, Fourth and Fifth) *Ìwé Kíkà Yorùbá Èkíní* (1909), *Èkejì* (1910), *Èkẹta* (1912), *Èkẹrin* (1911) and *Èkarùn* (1915). Each of these contained a miscellany of prose and poetry, on subjects of a wide variety. The narratives in these, some traditional, others translations from English, are the most striking contents.

The first anthology of 'original' Yoruba poems to be published was *Ìwé Kinni Ti Àwọn Akéwì* by Adetimkan Ọbasa, the editor of a weekly newspaper called *Yoruba News*. It was launched at Ibadan in 1927. In the preface, the author stated that his labours on the book began as far back as 1896 and he explained that the originality to which he could lay claim in the poems ceased at assemblage, the words in the poems being mostly traditional Yoruba sayings of a proverbial nature embodying the philosophy of life of the Yoruba people. Typical poems in the anthology are 'Ìkà Èké' (Treacherous Wickedness); 'Ìlara' (Envy); 'Ọmọ' (Offspring); and 'Ọgbọ́n' (Wisdom). A second anthology of poems by this author on the same general theme of Yoruba philosophy was published in 1934, entitled *Ìwé Kejì Ti Àwọn Akéwì*. Ọbasa's third anthology of poems, *Ìwé Kẹta Ti Àwọn Akéwì*, in continuation of his series on Yoruba traditional principles of conduct, was published in 1945. Ọbasa's books of poems were very well received at the time of their publication and from then on have been held in high esteem especially because they make available in written form Yoruba wisdom lore, classified in an interesting way.

Another well-known creative writer in Yoruba in the 1920s and 1930s was Kọlawọle Ajiṣafẹ of Abẹokuta. His books included anthologies of original poems from his pen and prose discourses on problems of human life. The most important of his poetic works were *Aiyé Àkámarà* (1921), a meditation on the vicissitudes of human life, and *Gbadebọ Alake* (1934), a dirge on the then recently deceased King of Abẹokuta. His chief prose work was *Enia Ṣoro*. In this period *Iwe Arofọ Orin* (1929), an anthology of original poems in Ẹgba Yoruba dialect by J. S. Ṣowande (alias Sọbọ Arobiodu), received widespread acclaim.

The first novelette in Yoruba was *Ìgbẹhìn á dùn* (tàbí) *Ọmọ Òrukàn*, written by E. A. Akintan, the editor of the bilingual weekly *Eleti Ọfẹ*, and published in Lagos in 1931. It is a realistically written story about a girl who was orphaned in her tender years but who grew up to become a queen.

It was not until 1938 that the first Yoruba novel appeared. This was *Ògbójú Ọdẹ Nínú Igbó Irúnmalẹ̀* written by Ọlọrunfẹmi Fagunwa, a Church primary school headmaster, and published by C.M.S. Bookshop, Lagos. It is a fantastic novel featuring monsters and men, with characters bearing allegorical names and with weird incidents in mysterious forests and in wonderland outside the real world of Yorubaland. The story is about a brave hunter's experiences in his wanderings in a tropical jungle, including a dangerous expedition successfully undertaken on a king's orders. This type of outline proved to be the pattern for Fagunwa's later novels, each of which is a fantasia novel. The stories start in real life but very quickly plunge into a forest world of supernatural beings and become vehicles for the author's sermonizings. At the end of the novel, the moral in each story is explicitly drawn and this is repeatedly along the lines of 'Labor omnia vincit'.

So well did the first edition of *Ògbójú Ọdẹ* sell that a new edition was brought out in 1950 by new publishers, Thomas Nelson and Sons. A year before this, the firm had published Fagunwa's second novel *Igbó Olódùmarè* and his third *Ìreké Oníbùdó*. In 1954 his fourth novel *Irinkerindo* was published, after which ten years were to elapse before his last novel *Àdììtú Olódùmarè* came out.

Other literary productions by Fagunwa are in prose and they include collections of traditional Yoruba folktales and reports of his experiences during his eighteen-month stay in Britain.

Adekanmi Oyedele is important in the growth of modern literature in Yoruba because in 1947 the Western Nigerian Literature Committee at Ibadan published his novel *Aiye Rèé!*, which is a clear departure from Fagunwa's trail. It is a realistic novel, a fictitious autobiography, based on the traditional way of life of the Yoruba people before the coming of the Europeans. It is only in the style of narrative that we have the Fagunwa touch in numerous didactic digressions in the course of the story and in an explicit statement of the moral of the story at the end. It is regrettable that this writer has not produced another novel after this promising beginning.

In 1955 Chief Isaac Oluwọle Delanọ, already well known then as an officer of the Yoruba cultural society Ẹgbẹ Ọmọ Oduduwa, joined the band of Yoruba novelists with the publication of his first novel *Aiyé d' Aiyé Òyìnbó*. This is a fictitious autobiography with a time span ranging from before the Europeans' arrival in Yorubaland right up to contemporary times. The author employs a descriptive, documentary style which is somewhat destructive of the novelistic element in this work.

A few years later Chief Delanọ left the employ of the Yoruba cultural society mentioned above. This was a blessing for the development of the Yoruba language and its literature, for this gifted writer now decided to devote all his time to this cause. He wrote a monolingual

Yoruba dictionary and several books on Yoruba usage and Yoruba grammar. It was in 1963 that his second novel, *L'Ójọ́ Ọjọ́un*, was published. This is an historical novel, a narrative constructed round the events which led to the passing of the Liquor Licence Ordinance in Lagos to control the consumption of strong drinks by the people of Yorubaland. The narrative is both an adventure and a pageant of Abẹokuta and its farmlands in the 1920s.

A return to the fantasia novel was made in 1956 when *Ibu Olókun* was published. Written by Ogunṣina Ogundele, a schoolteacher, this novel has as its chief character Ọrọgodoganyin, a man gifted with supernatural powers right from his birth and involved in all sorts of fantastic situations in which he performs various feats. Much along the same lines is Ogundele's second novel *Èjìgbèdè Lọ́nà Ìsálú Ọ̀run* (1957), in which the hero, Ejigbede, is portrayed in several adventures in his wanderings on the way to heaven from earth. After the publication of this book the fantasia novel did not have any new exponent until D. I. Fatanmi wrote his *K'Orimalẹ Ninu Igbo Adimula*, which was published in 1967.

The General Publications Department of the Ministry of Education at Ibadan was established in 1954 to encourage Yoruba authors by facilitating the publication of their original works. Thanks to its staff and its Advisory Committee this department has published several books of Yoruba modern literature, featuring poetry and prose. Among the most striking of the poetry books are Ojo's *Ọlọrun Ẹ̀san* and Fagbamigbe's *Ogun Kìrìjì*, both of which are long narrative poems. In this connection also must be mentioned the periodical called *Olókun*, a journal of modern Yoruba literature, which the department in association with the Ẹgbẹ́ Ìjìnlẹ̀ Yorùbá, a society for the promotion of Yoruba culture, launched in 1957.

To celebrate Nigeria's attainment of independence in October 1960, the department organized a competition in which every writer was invited to compete for a special prize by submitting a realistic novel of about 60,000 words in Yoruba. It was this competition which brought into the limelight Fẹmi Jẹbọda, who won the first place with his novel *Olówólaiyémọ̀*, subsequently published in 1963. In this work, a chronicle of contemporary life and manners, Jẹbọda attacks the seamy side of urban life in Yorubaland. His *Afínjú Àdàbà* (1964), a novelette, is on the same theme.

Only four other authors remain to be mentioned: Chief Fọlahan Ọdunjọ, Adebayọ Faleti, Ọlanipẹkun Ẹsan and Afọlabi Ọlabimtan. The actor-playwrights Ogunde, Ogunmọla, Ladipọ, Onibọn-Okuta, Adejọbi and other writers and performers of Yoruba musical plays have still to get their works published.

Chief Ọdunjọ's *Àkójọpọ̀ Ewì Aládùn* (1961) is an anthology of his poems, which are mostly didactic. There is in these poems the traditional ring of Yoruba poetry with its lofty phrasing and calculated tones at pauses. Like Adeboye Babalọlá's *Pàṣán Ṣìnà* (1956), Chief Ọdunjọ's play *Agbàlọ́wọ́mèèrì* (1958) is in five acts. The characterization is slight but there is a lot of action in the plot which borders on the supernatural towards the end. Chief Ọdunjọ has already produced two novels, *Ọmọ Òkú Ọrun* (1963) and *Kúyẹ* (1964). Each of these is a realistic novel on the theme of the long ill-treated child who ultimately enjoys good fortune.

Adebayọ Faleti is a poet and a playwright. His published poetry includes not only the poems in the journal *Olókun* but also some long narrative poems published in booklet form, notably *Ẹ̀dá Kò L'Áròpin* (1956). The humour which abounds in his poems is also amply evident in his novelette *Ogun Àwìtẹ́lẹ̀* (1965) and in his play *Nwọ́n Rò Pé Wèrè Ni* (1966). Whilst the former is pure comedy, the latter is comedy with a large dose of tragic tension in a situation involving attempted sacrificial murder. Faleti's Yoruba prose is of the classical *Ọ̀yọ́* type, rich in idiomatic expressions and appropriate proverbs.

Ọlanipẹkun Ẹsan, a classics scholar of the University of Ibadan, has contributed to modern Yoruba literature three books of note, all of them being reproductions of Latin or Greek literary works, not word-for-word translations but recasts in Yoruba mould, with Yoruba names for the characters and the places. The books were all published in 1965: *Ẹṣin Atiroja* (written in verse and embodying the Trojan Horse story in Virgil's *Aeneid*), *Tẹlẹdalaṣẹ* (written in verse and based on Sophocles' *Oedipus*) and *Òrékelẹwà* (a play in prose reproducing Plautus' *Mercator*).

The latest arrival on the scene of Yoruba creative writing is Afọlabi Ọlabimtan, schoolmaster, whose short play *Olúwa L'Ó M'Ejọ́ Dá* (1966) depicts in a closely-knit plot the disreputable areas of the lives of bad specimens among contemporary priests of various religions and among other professional groups. His *Kékeré Ẹkùn*, published in 1967, is a realistic novel in which he gives an exquisitely accurate portrayal of the notorious type of the polygamous Yoruba home, with its intrigues between co-wives, and also of the Yoruba church and church school in a rural community.

The contemporary creative writer in Yoruba has a relatively small audience among the adults because of the still high percentage of adult illiteracy and the continuing indifference of many educated Yoruba citizens to their mother tongue. It appears that the further development of Yoruba literature will depend on the determination of talented writers to continue to produce Yoruba literary works in obedience to the dictates of their genius, and not merely to meet the demands of the market existing in the primary and secondary schools.

Modern Efik Literature

Efik is one of the many dialects spoken by the various ethnic groups that occupy the basin of the Cross River in Eastern Nigeria. The people, generally referred to as Efiks, Ibibios, Anangs and Ekois, number about 3,500,000. But Efik has gradually become the principal language of the area because for nearly two centuries now it has been the language of commerce and of the Christian religion from Ikom near the Cameroons border to Calabar at the mouth of the Calabar River.

On the arrival at Calabar of the Rev. Hope Masterton Waddell and Mr Samuel Edgerley, a printer and catechist, on the 10th day of April, 1846, under the auspices of the Jamaica Mission of the Church of Scotland Mission, a well-planned study of the Efik language began. The first major publication in the language was the Holy Bible in Efik (1868).

With the commencement of the serious study of the Efik language by Christian missionaries and the encouragement they gave to the Efik people in order to get them to be able to read the Efik Bible, some authors started to write down the traditional fireside tales of Efik oral literature. They also wrote down the romantic poems and the tales of courage and trickery usually told at the meeting and parting of lovers, at community get-togethers on moonlit nights and on the way to the farm or to the spring. Here is a classic example of a verse from a love song written by E. N. Amaku in praise of a lover whose name begins with the letter 'E'.

> 'E' mi—o—o,
> Mmaha nditi,
> Nti nduŋke,
> Nduŋ idige k'ima.

This means:

> My Love 'E'
> I don't like to remember
> If I do, I wouldn't like to be here
> (without him/her).
> If I am here, it wouldn't be voluntarily.

In similar vein these authors wrote on a large number of secular topics. New ideas brought by contact with Europeans led to the coining of new words in Efik which enriched the Efik language and subsequently gave birth to Efik literature of the new age. Then emerged a nobler breed of writers, some of them very versatile in prose, poetry and drama—the Amakus, the Ŋkaŋas, the Elizabeth Asiboŋs, the Edyaŋs, to name a few. Their themes were no less varied and enchanting.

The most dignified prose writers are E. N. Amaku and E. E. Ŋkaŋa. In Mr Amaku's greatest prose work, *Edikot Ŋwed Mbuk*, the author depicts Efik culture in all its variety. The principal animal characters in this six-volume series are Ekpe (Leopard), famous for his agility and bravery, and Ikut (Tortoise), notorious for his craftiness. From here the author proceeds to paint an exquisite picture of the grandeur of Etinyin Abasi (which literally means 'Our Father God') and the splendour of his domain, including Esop Nditↄ Isↄŋ (the Court of the Elites or Aristocrats) and the exploits of Abasi Ekpenyↄŋ, an illustrious prince in that kingdom. After Amaku comes E. E. Ŋkaŋa, whose name has become a household word among the Efik-speaking peoples because of his fascinating novel *Mutanda Oyom Namondo*. Here he makes the gods and goddesses of traditional belief come alive in the adventures of a king, Mutanda, who went in quest of his lost son, Namondo.

The most notable Efik poet is the versatile E. N. Amaku, whose name has already been mentioned above. Prominent among his poetic works are *Ufↄk Uto Ikↄ Efik* and *Enem Inua Ikↄ*, both of which are anthologies of Efik poems—some serious, others lighter; some secular, others religious; some plaintive, others romantic. In one of his best-known poems he eulogizes Idorenyin (Hope). Another worthy contributor to Efik poetry is Elizabeth Asibↄŋ, whose poems are broadcast daily from Calabar over the network of the Nigerian Broadcasting Corporation. Her most popular work is an epic poem composed in 1956 to commemorate the visit of Queen Elizabeth II to Calabar.

Written Efik drama dates back to the early days of Christian missions in Calabar when religious plays were written for special Church ceremonies. From these developed the production of secular plays, partly romantic and partly historical, for the entertainment of kings as well as the general public. Foremost among the playwrights is Ernest A. Edyaŋ. His major plays are *Asibↄŋ Edem, Sidibe, Akpamↄŋ Idim* and *Bↄkit Ekↄŋ Mbaŋ*. *Asibↄŋ Edem* is generally acclaimed the most fascinating and the most dignified of Edyaŋ's plays. This play is a tragedy depicting historical events in the political and social life of the great prince Asibↄŋ Edem of old Calabar. It portrays vividly various aspects of Efik life and culture ranging from the luxurious life of the princes in the royal court to the commoners' hard life on the plantations; from the influence of the diviners to the absolute authority of the 'Ekpe' society. The play depicts how, in spite of the apparent harmonious blending of the plans of the deities with those of human beings, the gods can at will thwart a man's ambition to become a king even on the eve of the man's coronation.

What does the future hold in store for Efik literature? It appears that with the creation of the South-Eastern State of Nigeria additional emphasis is likely to be laid in the schools' curricula on the study of

Efik, which now serves as the main vehicle of communication among the various ethnic groups of the State. This should lead to a rapid development of Efik literature through the exertions of budding writers who evidently abound among the new generation.

Modern Hausa Literature

Although the Hausa people must have had the knowledge of writing before 1800, it was evidently put to use only by a close circle of Muslim leaders (who mostly wrote in Arabic and for religious purposes), and it was only at the start of the twentieth century that written Hausa literature came into being. The first Hausa novel to be published is in fact barely a generation old. Many of the modern works are clearly in the line of direct and immediate continuity from the older, oral Hausa and Arabic forms. Not only do some of these works give fresh renderings of old tales but also some modern Hausa novels draw upon certain characteristic elements of motif, setting and style in the older forms, and in poetry the influence of an earlier Arabic verse form is often very visible. Nevertheless, certain works, together with the birth of the drama, point to new trends and developments in the literary tradition.

To appreciate fully modern Hausa prose fiction one must first recognize the influence on it of Hausa folklore and Arabian tales. The world of Hausa folklore is prominently, though not exclusively, peopled with animals having human characteristics and tendencies. It is in fact a significant reflection of human society in which, however, seniority is determined not by age (as in real Hausa society) but in most cases by sheer physical size and strength. In such a world, therefore, the tiny creatures would be easily victimized but for the fact that their greater intelligence protects them and even turns the tables in their favour. This theme, the victory of brain over brawn, runs through most of the animal stories. Thus the spider, the hare and the jackal often exploit the stupidity of the hyena, or even the elephant, to their advantage. In other tales where human beings figure, certain other qualities, such as keen and upright moral conscience, become the weapon of the otherwise helpless. Another popular feature is the stereotyped figure of the ogre, the incredibly gigantic and strong man-eating monster who lives in the solitary wilds or in caves, hoarding wealth and keeping as maid or wife a young human beauty. Set against him is the figure of the human hero, whose additional weapons include courage, strength, a fatal sword or some supernatural charm. And in the spirit world proper, we come across all kinds of djinns and fairies, evil and good. The human hero fights his way, against them or with their help,

57

always to victory. From a more political view, the figure of the Waziri, invariably wicked, cunning, disloyal and power-hungry, passes on unchanged.

Although published later than *Gandoki*, *Magana Jari Ce* is the first work that should be examined against this background, not only because the setting is clearly older but also because it demonstrates a direct affinity with indigenous Hausa folklore and with Arabian sources. Imam, in the three volumes of this magnificent work, imaginatively blends traditional narrative vigour with the charm of Arabian romance. The fountain of these tales is a parrot, not a beautiful princess as in *A Thousand-and-One Nights* which evidently is Imam's source of inspiration. Imam does not merely borrow certain tales from the Arabic work; he also borrows, and transmutes, the overall plot. The stories the parrot narrates vary widely in nature and appeal, but they all more or less point to some moral, and in the first volume serve to make Musa, the Emir's son, forget his intention to ride to the battleground to meet his mate. The affinity of *Magana Jari Ce* to folklore does not lie only in the tales narrated by the parrot, but also in the basic plot of the book itself. The parrot at first is simply a common bird, useless except as a pet. But he soon turns out, owing to his infinite wisdom and perception, to be indispensable to the King not only privately but also officially. It is the parrot that tells of approaching enemy troops, and advises on how they can be surprised and routed, and discloses the plots made by the Waziri against the Emir, the Emir's only son, and the state. Against his superior knowledge the human beings appear as pathetic puppets under the benign shadow of a god-figure. This is essentially the theme in the animal stories; the supremacy of intellect and knowledge over other kinds of power. Some of the stories include only animals, others feature both animals and humans, while others have humans only. Humour, pathos and excitement flow through the tales. The basic setting seems to be an essentially pre-Islamic one, although some of the tales are clearly Islamic. In any case, it takes us back much earlier than most other works of the time.

A later work, Ingawa's *Iliya Dam Maikarfi* (1965), seems much more definitely to be Islamic in setting. Probably influenced by the earlier *Gandoki*, this epic is marked by a strong supernatural content. Iliya is born of a peasant couple who had for long been praying for a child. This opening illustrates a very popular theme in modern as well as traditional Hausa literature. People marry to beget so that in their old age there will be someone who will show them love and kindness and will also perpetuate their kind. Childlessness is the King's initial problem in *Magana Jari Ce* and recurs in many a later work. Often, in literature as in real life, it leads to quite ridiculous beliefs and practices which might otherwise never be contemplated.

Iliya, born to this couple after years of wedlock, falls ill at two years old and subsequently becomes paralysed in both arms and legs. One day after he has grown into manhood, alone in bed in the compound, Iliya suddenly receives and entertains as guests three men in Arab attire, each counting a rosary. They have come, we are told, to test and heal him; they are angels:

Then one of them fetched water in a calabash, said a prayer, and handed it to Iliya, saying, 'Wash your face and your body'. Iliya received [it] with his healthy right hand, and washed all over. In the twinkling of an eye, lo, Iliya's body became right again, as if it wasn't his. His paralysed legs and arms all straightened up so much so that unless one knew beforehand, one would not say that Iliya had once been lame.

And when they have finished their ministration on him and infused him with superhuman strength, one of them warns him to continue to believe in God and serve him meticulously, and then reveals to him that he will be famed throughout the world and that he will be victorious over all except a certain human called Wargaji, whom he is therefore not to fight but to befriend. Iliya's mission, a rather obscure one, is to journey to Kib City without wasting any time on the way. 'And as soon as they finished talking, Iliya sought those learned men but could not find them.'

It is in the course of this journey that Iliya fights battle upon battle; he is victorious in each and on meeting Wargaji he befriends him. At last he accomplishes his mission, and as he has nothing else to do, he sits on a rock holding his sword, his horse standing behind him, and prays to Allah to transform him and his horse into stone. His prayer is answered and here ends the story—a rather unusual ending in that it appears to immortalize man although it is written in an Islamic vein. Is it perhaps the pre-Islamic pagan belief in legendary heroes rearing its head up against all odds? Or is it a possible pointer to future literary developments?

While *Iliya Dam Maikarfi* is pure legend, *Gandoki* blends history and legend. It is a narration by the hero of his experiences during the difficult period of European colonization of Northern Nigeria. In this thrilling novel, Bello essentially follows history which he uses as a sort of springboard to plunge from a war with the white man to wars with djinns and giants. Gandoki, the hero, is perhaps the greatest adventurer in modern Hausa fiction. His whole life centres upon an almost obsessive love for war. He will not hesitate to intervene anywhere where a battle is likely to occur; rather, he will go to any extent to invite trouble. When news reached him at Kwantagora that the

C

English had captured Bida, he immediately went thither leaving his wife and son at home. Whenever any daring act is to be done, and men are slow to act, it is Gandoki who leads. When the colonial wars were almost over, he felt that he was getting rusty and was therefore ill at ease; so he set out together with his brave son, Garba, on a pilgrimage to Mecca, but the white men again scattered their caravan and foiled their aim. One day, after a fierce battle in which all but the two of them were killed, they fell asleep while resting in the wilds. They awoke to find themselves flown over to the spirit island of Sayalana in India. It turned out that the battalion they had fought previously belonged to the ruler of that island. It is from here that their tough, incredible experiences with the spirit world really begin.

As in *Iliya Dam Maikarfi*, the more contemporary world of *Gandoki* is strongly controlled by the supernatural. The great adventurer and his son are able to perform their military feats not only because they are strong and courageous, but also because they have armed themselves to the teeth with charms. Gandoki, for instance, has some charms and amulets that protect him from missiles or bullets or sharp edges and others that confer invisibility on the user and, above all, he possesses the how-on-earth-did-you-manage-to-escape charm. Here, as elsewhere, in modern Hausa literature, the reader is led to a willing suspension of disbelief.

While it stands out among other works in being firmly rooted in history, *Gandoki* is nevertheless somewhat typical of those works closely influenced by the older literary forms. Like the heroes of old, Gandoki survives incredibly narrow escapes fighting battles not only with ogres but also with djinns and white men. Through his sense of humour, his humanity and his narrative power, his account of his life, tough as it is, is redeemed from the uneasy vagueness overhanging the horizon of Iliya's world.

Dau Fataken Dare (now out of print) and *Tauraruwar Hamada* are two interesting and similar stories of notorious but prosperous thieves. In the latter, Ahmed Daura satirizes current superstitions. M. Danye is charged with the formidable task of stealing 'the Star of the Desert', the peerless beauty after whose name the novel is titled, and bringing her to the Emir of Langeri. He consults an astrologer before he sets out, but nevertheless he undergoes much suffering in enforced servitude and imprisonment. In the course of his varied adventures he is reformed and at the end becomes not only an immortal but also a king. Thus, while Iliya is simply eternalized by being transformed into rock, here M. Danye and his friend Dabo are immortalized, and, the reader is told, 'Right now if you go to Damas you will find them. And the snake visits them every week.' Thus the immortality theme is developed here.

While *Tauraruwar Hamada* is akin to *Iliya* and the other stories which may be said to constitute one phase of a tradition, it appears to point to a new trend such as satire of the contemporary habit of consulting so-called *mallams*, who claim to have the power to foretell the future. Instead of going back to a past rich in superstition and the supernatural, modern Hausa fiction is here beginning to look at and comment on contemporary realities. In a small way, therefore, *Tauraruwar Hamada* may be regarded as introducing new ideas which develop in the later novels and receive fuller treatment in drama and in later poetry.

Earlier Hausa poetry, on the other hand, belongs to a different phase. As might perhaps be expected, the early modern poetry is heavily didactic and religious, like early Islamic Arab poetry. Perhaps all of this poetry has been written by artists who are to a greater or lesser degree conversant with Arabic and Arabic verse form, for apart from the fact that quantity is a feature common to both languages, and also that Hausa poetry has followed Arabic in the bare stylistic arrangement of the verses, rhyme seems to be one clear area of direct influence and some poems show traces of Arabic verse metre.

Perhaps the longest religious poem is the ode '*Imfiraji*' of the blind ascetic Aliyu Namangi. In this poem, written in eight volumes, he devotes a substantial portion to the praise of the Prophet; moral and religious teaching; vivid descriptions of Heaven and Hell; the life of man from the moment of his conception in the womb to the hour of death; and a criticism of contemporary social evils.

The vast religious poetry of this phase includes works by Alhaji Muhammadu Givandu, Baba Maigyada and several later poets such as Muazu Hadeja. In Muazu Hadeja's anthology of poems (published by Gaskiya) there are five poems on religious and moral teachings. The other poems in the anthology are social rather than religious. All through the volume the reader is treated to the remarkable spontaneity of Muazu Hadeja's lyricism.

From the predominantly religious phase we pass on to the more social, in which the literary works are concerned with contemporary society and examine and diagnose the strengths and weaknesses of social habits and customs from a wider viewpoint than the religious. Some of this poetry also takes on a strong political twentieth-century outlook. From purely religious teaching modern Hausa poetry can be seen as gradually covering wider moral fields. Society is thereby often satirized and out of this some sort of political and nationalistic literature is somehow born. Thus a general condemnation of adultery from the Islamic viewpoint develops into a social, even sociological, study of the prostitute by, first, Hamisu Yadudu Funtuwa in 'Uwar Mugu' (= lit. 'mother of the evil one') and, later, by Muazu Hadeja.

The poetry of this phase is full of indignant attempts to rouse society from its slumber. Saadu Zungur and Muazu Hadeja in their political poems warn the Hausas that they must awake and catch up with the rest of Nigeria. Zungur condemns, as indignantly as Hadeja does, prostitution, mendicancy and other social evils.

In another poem Zungur celebrates the illustrious exploits of the Nigerian Army during the Second World War:

> O, how proud and happy we are, the
> Nigerians have made a name.
> To the troops of liberation and trust,
> O Lord, for the sake of the son of Amina,
> Give your lasting reward.

In yet another poem contemporary with this one, the poet warns against rumour-mongering during war. This preoccupation of literature with contemporary realities is also illustrated by the few works of drama published. In *Zamanin Nan Namu* and *Jatau Na Kyallu* Makarfi attacks the social life of the day. The former dwells on the evils resulting from lax and inattentive upbringing of children, especially daughters, and the latter shows up the vices of prostitution. Jatau, once a wealthy, respectable man with three wives, makes Kyallu, a notorious example of a prostitute, his fourth. He ends up by divorcing his other wives and losing all his property. Then Kyallu leaves him, a poor wretch who only then realizes how foolish he has been.

In *Mallam Inkun Tum*, Dogondaji cleverly caricatures the all too credulous dependence of the ignorant on *mallams*; and Tunau in *Wasan Marafa* takes us back to an earlier period when the value of Western education was still unknown. The theme of the play is the importance of personal hygiene as well as the usefulness of sending children to school.

While the literature of the first category generally draws upon older forms in style and even theme, that in the second tends to free itself from them. The late Sir Abubakar's *Shaihu Umar*, set in an older world of slavery and the slave trade, is essentially a work showing the new trend. An account of a man's hard life from childhood to middle age, *Shaihu Umar* is essentially realistic and devoid of the fantasy that fills and sometimes overflows novels from the earlier period. No ogres are present, the supernatural content is minimal, and there is no obvious moralization. It is a very taut and imaginative work which is marked by a serious awareness of human suffering and human goodness. Umar, the hero, is impressively portrayed. In the shifting patterns of suffering and joy, in the struggle with physical pain and keen sense of bereavement, this work is essentially a record and, in a deeply religious sense, an optimistic one, of man's struggle with the vicissitudes of his life.

Shaihu Umar is thus clearly a major development in the literary tradition of modern Hausa fiction. Its poetic counterparts are the politically prophetic poems by Zungur and Hadeja. Furthermore, the new trend in poetry is represented by Namangi's last-published religious poem *Kasbur Ragaibu*, as well as by the poems of Mudi Sipikin, and those of Abubakar Ladan, Akilu Aliyu, Baba Maigyada, Yusufu Kantu and Aliyu (a Zaria Emir). With regard to drama, the very fact of its birth is a result of the new promising development in Hausa literature.

Note

1 I am indebted to Mr N. U. Ekefre and Mr D. Muhammad for valuable information given me on modern literature in Efik and Hausa, respectively.

Amos Tutuola: The Nightmare of the Tribe

by O. R. Dathorne

Amos Tutuola narrates his four novels almost in the manner of a folktale artist, but the allegorical implications are implicit rather than explicit. This is the real achievement of *The Palm-Wine Drinkard* (1952), about which Wole Soyinka has commented:

> Of all his novels, *The Palm-Wine Drinkard* remains his best and the least impeachable. This book, apart from the work of D. O. Fagunwa, who writes in Yoruba, is the earliest instance of the new Nigerian writer gathering multifarious experience under, if you like, the two cultures, and exploiting them in one extravagant, confident whole.[1]

Tutuola has therefore removed the presentation of attitudes from the sociological level on which Chinua Achebe presents them, and has taken the quest out of the *genre* in which Gabriel Okara works.

Because of this, Tutuola stands at the very forefront of Nigerian literature and, by inference, African writing in English. He was not only among the first black African writers to be published and to win a measure of international recognition, but he was also quite definitely the first writer to see the possibilities of the imaginative translation of mythology into English. But it would be equally correct to add that he was misunderstood for these very reasons: Dylan Thomas, writing a review in *The Observer*, saw Tutuola's first novel, *The Palm-Wine Drinkard*, as having a 'brief, thronged, grisly and bewitching story' and added that 'nothing is too prodigious or too trivial to put down in this tall, devilish story'.[2] In the British National Bibliography it was classified under 'Literature', not, however, with 'Modern fiction in English' but with 'English Miscellany'.[3]

Tutuola was well received in England and in Europe,[4] but for the wrong reasons, and in West Africa he was, and is still, not accepted, for reasons equally mistaken. In an article on 'Nigerian Literature', Ulli Beier stated possible causes for Tutuola's non-acceptance in West Africa:

> Nigerian readers complained, on the other hand, that Tutuola wrote 'wrong' English, that his books were a mere 'rehash' of

grandmother tales they had all heard before. They alleged that Europeans were mainly attracted by the quaint exotic qualities of the book and that they did not judge the work on literary merits.[5]

A young Ghanaian, writing in 1963, asked the question, 'Has Tutuola anything besides a good imagination and bad grammar?'[6]

Somewhere between these two extremes—Tutuola the 'natural', teller of the fantastic account of an individual's nightmare and Tutuola the syllogist, infringer of the copyright of folklore—lies Tutuola's true significance. And it is this: Tutuola is a literary paradox; he is completely part of the folklore traditions of the Yorubas and yet he is able to modernize these traditions in an imaginative way. It is on this level that his books can best be approached. His characters are not *on* the threshold of a cultural dilemma as in Chinua Achebe and Onuora Nzekwu—they are involved *in* it. They have no *rationale* like Okolo in Okara's *The Voice*, for their spiritual dichotomy is expressed in the vacillatory manner in which they move between bush and town, between the rigours of the inner demands of a superstition they cherish and the necessities of an external materialism to which they must conform. This is how in *The Palm-Wine Drinkard* myth grows into man.

Tutuola's first novel is the story of how a man, much addicted to drinking palm-wine, goes in search of his dead palm-wine tapper. He undergoes a number of adventures, including one in which he captures Death and another in which he overcomes the Skull and brings back a lady whom the Skull had held captive. The protagonist subsequently marries this woman. In both cases his victory proves that he was 'Father of gods' and because of this he is therefore worthy of attempting the discovery of the whereabouts of his tapper. Later the couple have a child who plays all kinds of harmful pranks and they attempt to kill him; but out of the ashes a 'half-bodied' baby emerges. They are forced to carry him with them on their journey but get rid of him when they meet Drum, Song and Dance. Being by now penniless, the protagonist changes himself into a canoe, and his wife operates a ferry. Eventually they have enough money to continue their journey and manage to escape from the long white creatures and the field creatures. They experience kindness from the creatures of 'Wraith-Island', find the horrors of the inhabitants of the 'Greedy Bush' too much for them, narrowly escape from the Spirit of Prey and, after being tortured, escape from 'unreturnable Heavenly Town'. They are then looked after by the 'Faithful Mother in the White Tree'. Before they leave, they have sold their death but retained their fear. Later they meet the 'Red-people in the Red-town', enter a 'Wrong Town' by mistake and finally come to the 'Deads' Town' where the dead palm-wine tapper is. He explains that he cannot return with them, but gives them an 'Egg'.

On the way back they are pursued by dead babies and captured by a man and put in a sack. After their escape, they find themselves in the 'Hungry Creature's' stomach and meet the 'Mountain Creatures'. But the protagonist arrives back in time to help save his town from famine with the aid of his magic egg. The famine arose because of a misunderstanding between Land and Heaven. Eventually a sacrifice is taken to Heaven and rain begins to fall.

Tutuola deserves to be considered seriously because his work represents an intentional attempt to fuse folklore with modern life. In this way he is unique, not only in Africa, where the sophisticated African writer is incapable of this tenuous and yet controlled connection, but in Europe as well, where this kind of writing is impossible. J. P. Sartre, contrasting poetry in French by Frenchmen and Africans, had this to say:

> It is almost impossible for our poets to realign themselves with popular tradition. Ten centuries of erudite poetry separate them from it. And, further, the folkloric inspiration is dried up; at most we could merely contrive a sterile facsimile.[7]

The more Westernized African is placed in the same position. When he does introduce folklore into his writing it is more in the nature of a gloss; in Tutuola it is intrinsic.

The *raison d'être* for Tutuola's hero is as beguiling in its simplicity as it is suggestive of larger interpretation. He sets out to find his dead palm-wine tapper in the Deads Town—he wants to perpetuate the transient, to give to the sensual qualities of spiritual longevity. The language which expresses the decison of the hero to set out has just this combination of the legendary and the more immediately material, the impulsively supernatural and the compulsively natural:

> When I saw that there was no palm-wine for me again, and nobody could tap it for me, then I thought within myself that old people were saying that the whole people who had died in this world, did not go to heaven directly, but they were living in one place somewhere in this world. So that I said that I would find out where my palm-wine tapster who had died was.[8]

Tutuola's hero then begins on his long series of adventures. But in choosing to put the palm-wine tapper in a town in the world, Tutuola is not blindly incorporating mythology. He has intentionally perverted the Yoruba belief about death, or rather he has merged and re-interpreted two beliefs on the subject. In *Olódùmarè: God in Yoruba Belief* (1962), the Rev. Idowu has this to say of after-life:

Generally one may say that there are slightly varying opinions on the matter. There are those who believe that to die is only to change places on this earth. The deceased continues in existence in another country or region far away from his former home. He settles down in his new environment by beginning life all over again . . . *until he either dies again or moves because his whereabouts have been discovered by people who knew him in his former life* [my italics].[9]

Tutuola intentionally suppresses this last point, since he wants his palm-wine tapper to be found by the drinkard, and if he disappears as soon as he is found (as he ought to), then there would be no purpose whatever in the journey. Furthermore, as Idowu adds:

A slightly modified form of this belief is that *only the wicked and those whose days on earth are not yet fulfilled,* and, therefore, cannot be received back into heaven, continue like that in some part of the earth [my italics].[10]

Tutuola's palm-wine drinkard is in search of his tapper who symbolizes physical and spiritual purity. Therefore what he stands for is almost an inversion of the legend.

As the protagonist progresses on his journey, his adventures become significant for two main reasons. First, they help him grow spiritually, so that after his meeting with Death and his experience of dying (by entering into the village of the palm-wine tapper), his eventual apotheosis (his egg gives him the power of life and death over mankind), comes as no surprise to the reader. Secondly, his adventures, which are all closely integrated into the pattern of the narrative, give Tutuola the opportunity to integrate folklore and myth into his novel. The way in which this is cleverly interwoven into the texture and pattern of the writing shows Tutuola's mature craftsmanship. But here again Tutuola does not hesitate to distort, expand or summarize. An examination of how he does this in two cases will show his ability.

Both instances are concerned with the protagonist acquiring, quite early in the novel, the *sine qua non* of the myth-hero—what Gerald Moore calls 'the ever-faithful and helpful female companion (Dante's Beatrice, Theseus's Ariadne, Jason's Medea)'.[11] First the protagonist rescues her from the Skull, who is disguised as a 'complete gentleman', and later she bears him a child. In the straightforward account of the tale, published in a collection of Yoruba legends which appeared in 1929, the details are given as follows:

There is a certain country where the inhabitants have heads but no bodies. The Heads move about by jumping along the ground, but they never go very far.

67

One of the Heads desired to see the world, so he set out one morning secretly. When he had gone some distance, he saw an old woman looking out of the door of a hut, and he asked her if she would kindly lend him a body.

The old woman willingly lent him the body of her slave, and the Head thanked her and went on his way.

Later he came upon a young man sleeping under a tree and asked him if he would kindly lend him a pair of arms, as he did not appear to be using them. The young man agreed, and the Head thanked him and went on his way.

Later still he reached a river-bank where fishermen sat singing and mending their cone-shaped net. The Head asked if any one of them would lend him a pair of legs, as they were all sitting and not walking. One of the fishermen agreed, and the Head thanked him and went on his way.

But now he had legs, arms and a body and so appeared like any other man.

In the evening he reached a town and saw maidens dancing while the onlookers threw coins to those they favoured. The Head threw all his coins to one of the dancers, and she so much admired his handsome form that she consented to marry him and go and live with him in his own country.

Next day they set out but when they came to the river-bank, the stranger took off his legs and gave them back to the fisherman. Later they reached the young man, who still lay sleeping under the tree, and to him the Head gave back his arms. Finally they came to the village, where the old woman stood waiting and here the stranger gave up his body.

When the bride saw that her husband was merely a Head, she was filled with horror, and ran away as fast as she could.

Now that the Head had neither body, arms, nor legs, he could not overtake her, and so lost her for ever.[12]

In the extract from Tutuola's book, no emphasis is placed on the superhuman abilities of the Skull to take on human form, as this is largely irrelevant to the narrative. Instead Tutuola poetizes on the dichotomy between appearance and reality and so immediately establishes a sympathetic relationship between his hero and the woman he is shortly to marry. Tutuola revitalizes the legend, re-invigorating it through imagery with the equipment of modern experience (and so making it more directly relevant), introduces the tragedy of unrealizable ideals (which is not in the legend) and shortens the mere mechanics of the Skull's transformation (which is the core of the legend). Tutuola writes:

I could not blame the lady for following the Skull as a complete gentleman to his house at all. Because if I were a lady, no doubt I would follow him to where ever he would go, and still as I was a man I would jealous him more than that, because if this gentleman went to the battle field, surely, enemy would not kill him or capture him and if bombers saw him in a town which was to be bombed, they would not throw bombs on his presence, and if they did throw it, the bomb itself would not explode until this gentleman would leave that town, because of his beauty. At the same time that I saw this gentleman in the market on that day, what I was doing was only to follow him about in the market. After I looked at him for so many hours, then I ran to a corner of the market and I cried for a few minutes because I thought within myself why was I not created with beauty as this gentleman, but when I remembered that he was only a Skull, then I thanked God that He had created me without beauty, so I went back to him in the market, but I was still attracted by his beauty. So when the market closed for that day, and when everybody was returning to his or her destination, this gentleman was returning to his own too and I followed him to know where he was living. . . .

When I travelled with him a distance of about twelve miles away to that market, the gentleman left the really road on which we were travelling and branched into an endless forest and I was following him, but as I did not want him to see that I was following him, then I used one of my juju which changed me into a lizard and followed him. But after I had travelled with him a distance of about twenty-five miles away in this endless forest, he began to pull out all the parts of his body and return them to the owners, and paid them.[13]

Tutuola has made of the legend what he wanted, omitting elements that were irrelevant to him.

In another written version of the legend, the moral side is emphasized at the end:

But spies were around her and had not been sleeping. They saw all that transpired; they were biding their time, simply because they would want her to learn a little more lesson.

Accordingly, as she went three miles along her experience-path, four men came out from the two sides of the road and carried her away. Away and away from the dangerous spirit, until they reached home.

The girl asked them how they foiled the spirit, they replied that they hypnotised him. In their turn they demanded from her: 'What do you learn from this?'

'Yes,' she answered shyly, 'I now believe that parents can be right.'[14]

In his re-creation of the story Tutuola omits this as well.

It is perhaps pertinent to add that in Tutuola 'Head' and 'Spirit' had become 'Skull', as he wishes to emphasize the utter emptiness of mere appearances. Also the transfer of folktale into modern imaginative literature involves a curious necessary acceptance of Christianity. This fusion of pagan myth and Christian belief occurs naturally and easily in Tutuola and is part of his much wider and more universal literary cosmorama. In him the paradoxes of culture are evened out.

In another instance, the legend is only lightly touched on. The legend of Child-Wiser-Than-His-Father is found in *Folk Tales and Fables* (1953) collected by Phebean Itayemi and P. Gurrey. The beginning of this legend reads:

Once a childless woman went to the Deity to beg a child of him. He said that he had none left, for they had all gone on errands, except one who would be wiser than any father, and who was very disobedient. The woman said she would have him, and the Deity told her to go home. On the way she stumbled and her big toe became swollen, and when she entered the house, again she stumbled, and out of the swelling of her toe came a tiny child. He walked and talked almost as soon as he was born, and the next morning told his father that he wanted to go to the farm and work with him.

His father refused to take him along to the farm because he was so young; so Mogbonjuba, which is omo-gbon-ju-baba, meaning Child-Wiser-Than-His-Father, took the bag which his father always strapped on his back when he was going to the farm, and having filled it with ashes, cut a tiny hole in the bag. The father went to the farm knowing nothing of the hole in his bag. Then soon after he had left, his little child, Child-Wiser-Than-His-Father, followed the white trail which had been made by the wood ashes dropped through the hole.

He soon came up to his father at the farm, who was very surprised to see his little son. The child told him he had found the way through his wisdom, and then he told his father that they must play a game. His father was at the top of a palm tree cutting a bunch of ripe palm nuts, and he wanted to know what the game was. Child-Wiser-Than-His-Father then covered himself with a basket and stood at the foot of the palm and asked his father to throw down one bunch on him and see what would happen.

His father, thinking this a rather dangerous game, did not want to do it at first, but Mogbonjuba persuaded him, and he threw down a heavy bunch on to the basket. But while he was preparing to throw it, Mogbonjuba had slipped out of the basket, so that when the bunch came down and crushed the basket, he was not under it; but then, rolling the bunch aside, he pretended that he had been, and told his father that he was unhurt. He then said it was his father's turn to stay under the basket, and when he had climbed the palm tree, he threw down a big bunch on the basket, and the poor father was crushed to death.

Mogbonjuba came down, uncovered his dead father, and then, after he had cut him up, took out his liver, and took it home to his mother. She asked for his father, and he replied that he was still coming behind, and he gave her the liver and said that it was part of an animal they had killed in the farm. The mother thanked Mogbonjuba, cooked it and ate it, Mogbonjuba refusing to eat any of the soup. Then, when she had eaten it all, he sprang out and said she had eaten his father's liver.[15]

In Tutuola's story the child is also born in an unusual manner, and just as wise as the child in the legend, but his birth is related to Tutuola's theme: he is born when his mother's swollen thumb touches a palm-tree thorn and he drinks vast quantities of palm-wine. In addition his exploits are infused with all the rich vigour of Tutuola's humour and exaggeration, and his death is not the end of an interlude but a further step forward in the apotheosizing of the drinkard himself. As Tutuola writes :

I spent three years with him in that town, but during that time, I was tapping palm-wine for myself. Of course I could not tap it to the quantity that I required to drink; my wife was also helping me to carry it from the farm to the town. When I completed three and a half years in that town, I noticed that the left hand thumb of my wife was swelling out as if it was a boy, but it did not pain her.

One day, she followed me to the farm in which I was tapping the palm-wine, and to my surprise when the thumb that swelled out touched a palm-tree thorn, the thumb burst out suddenly and there we saw a male child came out of it and at the same time the child came out from the thumb, he began to talk to us as if he was ten years of age.

Within the hour that he came down from the thumb he grew up to the height of about three feet and some inches and his voice by that time was as plain as if somebody strikes an anvil with a steel hammer. Then the first thing that he did, he asked his mother: 'Do you know my name?' His mother said no, then he turned his face to me and asked me the same question and I said no; so, he said that his name was 'ZURRJIR' which means a son who would change himself into another thing very soon. But when he told us his name, I was greatly terrified, because of his terrible name, and all the while that he was talking to us, he was drinking palm-wine which I had tapped already; before five minutes he had drunk up to three kegs out of four kegs. As I was thinking in my mind how we could leave the child in the farm and run to the town, because everybody had seen that the left hand thumb of my wife only swelled out, but she did not conceive in the right part of her body as other women do. But immediately that I was thinking so, this child took the last keg of palm-wine which he drank through the left of his head and he was going to the town directly, but nobody showed him the road that led to the town. We stood in one place looking at him as he was going, then after a little time, we followed him, but we did not see him on the road before we reached the town. To our surprise the child entered the right house that we were living in. When he entered the house, he saluted everybody that he met at home as if he had known them before, at the same time, he asked for food and they gave him the food, he ate it; after, he entered the kitchen and ate all the food that he met there as well.[16]

By now it ought to be apparent that Tutuola is no mere plagiarist of folklore.

Part of Tutuola's success at this imaginative re-ordering of folklore is due to his use of language. Those who argue that he writes 'wrong' English do not take two factors into consideration. One is that they forget that the story is written in the first person and is about a palm-wine drinker. Were he to speak standard English this would be ludicrous to anyone acquainted with the realities of West African speech. Secondly, Tutuola's English is a sensible compromise, between raw pidgin (which would not be intelligible to European readers) and standard English.

The effect of this compromise is to enliven the story, to project it beyond the level of sociological documentation. Tutuola is therefore neither 'quaint' nor 'semi-literate', neither a 'natural' nor a 'sophisticate'. He is a conscious craftsman, who knows where his own talents lie. In a recent interview he expressed a desire to collect world folklore and use it in his novels,[17] and he told me recently of his wish to travel through Nigeria gathering folklore for use in his work. Indeed, in an age when Africa is to a large extent in the process of cultural evolution, it is more important than ever to ensure that written literature should carry over from the past some aspects of the oral traditions. As Jacob Drachler says of Tutuola in *African Heritage* (1957):

He undoubtedly adds something to the old themes by his extraordinarily graphic style, which is helped and not hindered by his limited education. We can only speculate about the forms that this traditional material will take in the work of the more sophisticated literary artists in the future; but Tutuola's success is a sign that very old themes and motifs of African oral literature will not be completely cast aside.[18]

After *The Palm-Wine Drinkard,* there is a falling off in Tutuola's work, but *My Life in the Bush of Ghosts* (1954) and *Simbi and the Satyr of the Dark Jungle* (1955) are not written on the 'fairy-tale' level of *The Brave African Huntress* (1958) and *Feather Woman of the Jungle* (1962). *My Life in the Bush of Ghosts* and *Simbi and the Satyr of the Dark Jungle* both pose problems of ethics. The boy of the former undergoes various experiences to discover the meaning of 'good', and in the latter a spoilt rich girl passes through a number of gruelling tests in order to discover the meaning of poverty.

However, Tutuola has failed to relate the disorganized adventures of either protagonist within the ethical significance of a novel. In *My Life in the Bush of Ghosts,* the young boy who is the hero is the victim of jealousies among his father's wives. He has to run away from his town when raiders come looking for slaves and he stumbles into the Bush of Ghosts where his adventures begin. Tutuola relates the various experiences of the boy, how he is changed into various objects and animals, how he marries twice, first to a ghostess and then to a Super Lady. He had entered the Bush of Ghosts when a boy of seven and, after twenty-four years there, he is given the chance to escape by a weird creation, half-mythical, half-ordinary—the Television-Handed Ghostess. He has a number of other misfortunes before he finally returns to his village.

Simbi's adventures are in one of two of Tutuola's novels which have women as their central characters. Simbi herself is a more active character than the protagonist of *My Life in the Bush of Ghosts,* in that her adventures do not just simply happen—she wills them upon herself. As she is later to remind the satyr, she is the most beautiful girl in her village, her voice could wake 'deads' and she is the daughter of the wealthiest woman. The Ifa priest whom she consulted had suggested a way in which she could embark on her adventures, and following his advice, she makes a sacrifice at the crossroads. There Dogo comes and carries her off on the Path of Death. She experiences great tribulations before she meets with two of her friends who had been similarly kidnapped. They wander on for some time, barely escaping from various threats to their lives and, finally, Simbi and one of her friends reach home. Her experiences have brought her into contact with sinners, tigers, birds, a snake, a Siamese twin Bako who changed into a cock, and the satyr himself. She escapes from him by changing into a fly and flying up his nostril.

Both the adventures of the protagonists in these two novels illustrate a means of growing up. Both of them return as adults to their villages and Tutuola's fantasy can be seen as one of the mind, where the phantoms of childhood battle in a last desperate effort with the concrete realities of the adult world. On another level, they represent a transition —from the innocence of a traditional way of life to the turbulence of modernity. While both interpretations may be read into these novels, they never obtrude as in Okara's *The Voice*. But even though use is still made of the folktale and the *personae* of mythology and legend, the force of *The Palm-Wine Drinkard* is not there. It is true that *My Life in the Bush of Ghosts* and *Simbi and the Satyr of the Dark Jungle* are about 'the initiation of a child'[19] and 'initiation into the trouble and adventure of living'[20] as Anne Tibble argues, but they are only ephemerally so. They do not demonstrate these stated themes in action, as *The Palm-Wine Drinkard* does.

Tutuola's next two books are solely concerned with the more sensational side of adventure. It is as if one is suddenly let out from the closed villages of Achebe into Ekwensi's open towns. In *The Brave African Huntress*, a girl masters the hunting skill of her father and rescues her brothers from the Jungle of the Pygmies. And though *The Feather Woman of the Jungle* has a male spokesman in the person of an old chief who tells stories for ten nights to his people, the fantasy of *The Brave African Huntress* is paramount. In actual fact these are simply short stories weakly linked together by a central narrator. Although Tutuola attempts to capture the atmosphere of an African story-teller, the work fails as a coherent piece of writing.

In these last two books the language has altered: instead of the semi-pidgin and the solecisms which contributed to the effect of *The Palm-Wine Drinkard* there is a biblical style, which is sometimes equally as effective:

It was the 'Day of Confusion' Wednesday, that I entered this Jungle of the Pygmies, at about eleven o'clock in the morning. After I travelled in this jungle for a few minutes—the great fears, wonders, and uncountable of undescriptive strange things, which I was seeing here and there were stopped me by force. When I was unable to travel further because of these things then I thought within myself to climb a tree to the top so that I might see these things to my satisfaction. And at the same time I climbed a tall tree to the top. I sat on one of its branches and as it was a leafy tree therefore these leaves were covered me and I peeped out very seriously as when an offender peeped out from the small window of his cell. Then I was looking at these handiworks of God with great wonder.[21]

Also, it will be observed from the above extract, an element of nature-description has entered into the work and, incidentally, into the West African novel. As Prudence Smith has written, Tutuola's language is 'constantly invented, constantly unexpected'[22] and this is a virtue that pervades all the novels. The above extract is very different from the episode in *The Palm-Wine Drinkard*, where Tutuola writes:

When the debit-collector asked for the £1 which he (borrower) had borrowed from his friend since a year, the debitor (borrower) replied that he never paid any of his debits since he was born, then the debit-collector said that he never failed to collect debits from any debitor since he had begun the work. The collector said furthermore that to collect debits about was his profession and he was living on it. But after the debitor heard so from the collector, he also said that his profession was to owe debits and he was living only on debits.[23]

The reason for the difference in language lies in the nature of the experience. In the first instance Tutuola is describing a moment of awareness, whereas in the second he is being intentionally abstruse, since the incident he recounts is the extension of a riddle. Indeed, in the final resort Tutuola succeeds because his works remain enigmatic intrusions of the inexplicable past into an inquisitive present.

Notes

1 Wole Soyinka, 'From a Common Backcloth: A Reassessment of the African Literary Image', in *The American Scholar*, Vol. 32, No. 3 (Summer 1963), p. 360.

2 Dylan Thomas, Review in *The Observer*, No. 8405, 6 June 1952.

3 *British National Bibliography Annual*, Volume 1952, Council of the British National Bibliography Ltd, London, 1953, p. 636.

4 *The Palm-Wine Drinkard* has been translated into French, German, Dutch and Italian.

5 Ulli Beier, 'Nigerian Literature', in *Nigeria: A Special Independence Issue of Nigeria Magazine*, Federal Government of Nigeria Publications, Lagos, October 1960, p. 213.

6 Christina Aidoo, Letter in *Transition*, Vol. 4, No. 10 (1963), p. 46.

7 J. P. Sartre, *L'Art Nègre*, in *Black Orpheus*. Aux Editions du Seuil, Paris. In *Présence Africaine* No. 10-11 (1951), p. 231. Originally this was J. P. Sartre's Preface to *L'Anthologie de la Nouvelle Poésie Nègre et Malgache de Langue Française*, ed. Leopold Sedar Senghor, Presses Universitaires de France, Paris, 1948.

8 Amos Tutuola, *The Palm-Wine Drinkard*, Faber, London, 1952, p. 9.

9 Boluji E. Idowu, *Oládùmarè: God in Yoruba Belief*, Longmans, 1962, p. 196.

10 Idowu, op. cit.

11 Gerald Moore, *Seven African Writers*, O.U.P., London, 1962, p. 196.

12 M. I. Ogumetun, *Yoruba Legends*, The Shelden Press, London, 1951, Legend No. XXI, p. 86.

13 Tutuola, *The Palm-Wine Drinkard*, op. cit., pp. 25-6.

14 Kolawole Balogun, *The Crowning of the Elephant*, Oshogbo, Nigeria, n.d., p. 34.

15 Phebean Itayemi and P. Gurrey (eds.), *Folktales and Fables*, Penguin, London, 1953, p. 46.

16 Tutuola, *The Palm-Wine Drinkard*, op. cit., pp. 31-2.

17 Interviewed with other Nigerian writers for Transcription Centre, London.

18 Jacob Drachler (ed.), *African Heritage*, The Cromwell-Collier Press, New York, 1963, p. 144.

19 Anne Tibble, *African-English Literature*, Peter Owen, London, 1966, p. 100.

20 Tibble, op. cit.

21 Tutuola, *The Brave African Huntress*, Faber, London, 1958, p. 55.

22 Prudence Smith, Review in *Ibadan*, No. 7, Nov. 1959, p. 30.

23 Tutuola, *The Palm-Wine Drinkard*, op. cit., pp. 111-12.

Cyprian Ekwensi

by Douglas Killam

Cyprian Ekwensi belongs to the first wave of modern Nigerian writers. He has produced a significant number of books by which his achievement as a novelist may be judged. He is concerned with the quality of modern Nigerian life, specifically with the ways in which traditional values and institutions were redefined as a result of the presence of Europeans in West Africa during the colonial period. His theme, then, broadly defined, is concerned with the conflicts which the colonial presence promoted in Nigeria and the cultural, social and political changes which resulted. Finally, he writes in English and uses the language to encompass his Nigerian inspiration and experience. In accepting English as a medium of literary exchange he suggests a criterion by which his work should be judged.

The modern Nigerian novel is at once similar to and yet different from novels written in English in other parts of the world. It follows the main historical development of the English novel and makes an addition of its own which springs from the chance encounter of Europe and Africa during the imperial-colonial period. Thematic material is various among writers but generally falls within this large context. Differences between the emerging African literary tradition and English literary tradition are obvious (and find correspondence in the literary traditions of other former colonial areas—India, the West Indies, Malaysia, as well as in the white colonies, Australia, Canada and perhaps even America). These differences are the result not of innate racial differences—although often racial themes are an important element in modern Nigerian writing. They stem rather from a group past with its bitter and often ambiguous experience of colonialism and from the group present which seeks to define the relevance of the colonial experience to the present. They stem from the contact (in some cases collision), both historical and immediate, between the traditional folk and/or myth past of various indigenous ethnic groups and European modernity. They stem from a relatively brief, nevertheless intense, experience with separate and dominating institutions—political, social, cultural—and express a desire to modify these to suit local and national needs by incorporating what is valuable in the colonial legacy whilst retaining a Nigerian identity. Nigerian writing to date has been concerned exclusively with the reality of Nigerian life (as contrasted, say, with Indian or West Indian writing) and no Nigerian novelist to date has sought his thematic material in a larger and more cosmopolitan culture. Nigerian novelists have not turned their backs on their own culture; rather, they have faced up to cultural problems and sought solutions for them in imaginative form. Their fiction is a literary echo of a general cultural reality.

Like any other artist, the Nigerian novelist must achieve universality through a sensitive interpretation of his own culture and, in a very real sense, the Nigerian novelist has not one but two cultures to interpret. He is concerned with and must be conversant with Western culture and especially with the traditions of English literature of which he declares himself a part, at the same time as he affirms the Nigerian quality of his experience, exploiting his Nigerian heritage as a legitimate contribution to the larger culture. There are real dangers implicit in this situation: often the writer's art will suffer because of his desire to explain, interpret and expound the values and virtues of his society. Often his art is subverted to polemical purposes. Often the Nigerian novelist sees himself in what must be generally described as an educative role. This is understandable and inevitable, as Achebe points out when he says: 'The writer cannot be excused the task of re-education and re-generation that must be done. In fact he should march right in front. For he is after all . . . the sensitive point in his community.'[1] And in another place he observes:

> I believe that the writer should be concerned with the question of human values. One of the most distressing ills which afflicts new nations is a confusion of values. We sometimes make the mistake of talking about values as though they were fixed and eternal—the monopoly of Western civilisation and the so-called higher religions. Of course, values are relative and in a constant state of flux.[2]

Achebe puts these comments into a legitimate perspective from the point of view of the imaginative writer when he says: 'The writer's duty is not to beat this morning's headlines in topicality, it is to explore the depth of the human condition. In Africa he cannot perform this task unless he has a proper sense of history.'[3]

As Professor Eldred Jones has remarked, 'Modern African literature in the general pattern of other literatures may be said to have settled down after a period of intense activity.'[4] The aim of this brief commentary on the writing of Cyprian Ekwensi is to measure his contribution to the Nigerian literary tradition which is beginning to emerge clearly.

Cyprian Odiatu Duaka Ekwensi is Nigeria's most prolific writer and the first Nigerian novelist to have a book published in England. He was born in Minna in Northern Nigeria in 1921 of Ibo parents. He got his secondary education at Government College in Ibadan and attended Yaba College in Lagos and Achimota College in the then Gold Coast. He went to the Forestry School in Ibadan (1944-5) and for a short time was lecturer in Biology, English and Chemistry at Igbobi College, Lagos. In 1947 he began his studies in pharmacy and taught that subject for a period before going to England in 1951, where he undertook further studies at the Chelsea School of Pharmacy. Back in Nigeria he worked as a pharmacist with the Nigerian Medical Services. Then his career changed. He joined the Features Department of the Nigerian Broadcasting Services (which was to become the Nigerian Broadcasting Corporation) and in 1958 became head of the Features Department. In 1961 he became Director of Information for the Federal Ministry of Information.

His novelette *When Love Whispers* was published in 1947 but it was with *People of the City,* published in 1954, that he established his reputation. Since that point a great amount of work has been published.[5] His fiction falls into two broad categories—serious adult fiction (*People of the City, Jagua Nana, Beautiful Feathers* and *Iska* and the short stories of the *Lokotown* volume), and shorter works aimed at children and adolescent readers. The concern here is with writing in the former category although the works in the latter are not without interest.

Ekwensi's limitations as a novelist are many and it is as well to mention them at the outset. He has often declared that he considers himself a writer of popular fiction, and if we define popular fiction to be that which pleases or is read by a class of reader commonly indifferent to literature, we understand that Ekwensi directs his work to a wider audience than, say, Achebe, Clark or Soyinka, and suggests, as well, the limitations that work may possess. His novels do not possess the unique qualities which are inherent in works of literature—a formal beauty of design and execution which lead the reader on to a new awareness of the greater potentialities of self. Rather, Ekwensi's work is concerned with the external features of modern Nigerian life, especially the life in and of the city. His heroes seek for but never make profound discoveries about themselves. Perhaps this accounts for the fact that in each of the full-length novels we find the same kind of hero—almost a stereotype—who, progressively lacking energy, becomes unconvincing as a character.

His plots suffer in the same way: just as we find the same kind of hero in each of the novels, so we find him (or her) in more or less the same circumstances. Moreover, Ekwensi pays little attention to his plots and his novels are full of inconsistencies and contradictions. The books,

79

therefore, possess a perverse logic in terms of the art of the novel: because the motives of the characters are not explored in any depth, because their behaviour is based on the novelist's whim rather than on the circumstances of their lives about which the novelist forces them to reflect and accordingly revalue and adjust their behaviour, the plots of the novels reflect this confusion and irresoluteness, and organic unity is lacking in them. Added to this is an insistently melodramatic approach, the presentation of sensation for its own sake.

A final delimiting feature which must also be mentioned is Ekwensi's uncertain use of English. Achebe remarks on the problems which confront an African writing in English. He says the writer 'can try to contain what he wants to say within the limits of conventional English or he can try to push back those limits to accommodate his ideas',[6] and he enjoins his fellow-novelists that, whatever method they adopt, those 'who can do the work of extending the frontiers of English so as to accommodate African thought-patterns must do it through their mastery of English and not out of innocence. . . . It is important first to learn the rules of English and afterwards break them if we wish. The good ones will know how to do this and the bad ones will be bad, anyway.'[7] These comments are timely and relevant to all Nigerian writing, and while they nowhere relate specifically to Ekwensi's writing, they do apply. Ekwensi has not mastered the rules of English and the bad English which is often used in his novels, taken together with the inconsistencies of plot and characterization we have mentioned, and the insistent melodrama in his treatments, militate against his fiction achieving the first rank in importance as art.

Yet despite these limitations—which are considerable—Ekwensi is a serious novelist whose writing reflects his serious concern with some of the most pressing problems facing modern Nigeria. Ekwensi's fiction represents, almost exclusively, an attempt to come to terms with the chaotic formlessness and persistent flux of the modern Nigerian city— that is, with Lagos. His novels arise out of his acquaintance with and involvement in the complexities of city living and his attempt to probe with an unflinching realism the superficial delights and real terrors of the city places his work in a twentieth-century tradition of novel writing. The tension in his major novels derives from the attempts of their heroes—Amusa Sango, Jagua, Wilson Iyari and Filia Enu, all of whom live on the borderline between success and failure, triumph and collapse—to extract as much pleasure as they can from city living whilst constantly confronted by the fear of poverty and failure.

In *People of the City* are found the themes, structure, characters, style and values which characterize all of Ekwensi's attempts at serious fiction.[8] *People of the City* is a novel of city manners. The plot is loose and episodic. It has a certain style without structure. It has a rich verbal texture without dramatic form. The novel tells the story of Amusa Sango, born in the 'Eastern Greens' of Nigeria, and, when the story opens, a crime reporter with the *West African Sensation* and, in his spare time, the leader of a dance band playing in various Lagos clubs. The opening paragraphs encompass the whole of the novel's meaning.

> Most girls in the famous West African city . . . knew the address Twenty Molomo Street for there lived a most colourful and eligible young bachelor, by name Amusa Sango.
>
> In addition to being crime reporter for the *West African Sensation*, Sango in his spare time led a dance band that played the *calypsos* and the *konkomas* in the only way that delighted the hearts of the city women.
>
> Of women Sango could have his pick, from the silk-clad ones who wore lipstick in the European manner and smelled of scent in the warm air to the more ample, less sophisticated ones in the big-sleeved velvet blouses that feminized a woman.
>
> Yet Sango's one desire in the city was peace and the desire to forge ahead. No one would believe this, knowing the kind of life he led: that beneath his gay exterior lay a serious nature and determined to carve for itself a place of renown in this city of opportunities.[9]

The two needs which Sango, and indeed all of the other characters in the book, experience—the need for success on the one hand and the need for peace on the other—are presented as a necessary condition of city living. Yet the two things are not compatible: the need to compete and survive at one level and to succeed at another destroys the possibility of finding peace, as the novel shows through its description of Sango's career as a reporter and in revealing his affairs with various 'people of the city'. By developing those aspects of plot which relate to Sango's career as a crime reporter, Ekwensi is able to offer criticism, sometimes implied, sometimes direct, on general social issues which characterize modern Nigerian urban life. By delineating Sango's affairs with a variety of women Ekwensi is able to dramatize general problems as they are consolidated in the lives of specific individuals, at the same time broadening the scope of the novel.

When we first meet him Sango is a crime reporter. By giving Sango this activity Ekwensi is able to assume the role as his hero and report on various events and issues of public, social, political and national importance. The events which Sango reports range from the macabre and occult activity of the *Ufemfe Society*, to a coal strike which creates a sense of national identity and purpose, to a national election campaign. Each event affords Ekwensi the opportunity of making social and political criticism of contemporary Nigerian society. The incident involving the *Ufemfe Society*, for example, relates to one Butaihmah Ajikatu who for years worked as a clerk in a department store and who, at thirty-five years of age, is without prospects of receiving the promotion which will allow him to take care of his wife and children. He joins the *Ufemfe Society* (the exact activities of which are hinted at although never revealed) and his fortunes are immediately repaired. He achieves promotion and an increase in salary. And then:

> One night the blow fell. This was the unexplained portion of the pact. They asked him in a matter-of-fact manner to give them his first-born son. He protested, asked for an alternative sacrifice, and when they would not listen threatened to leave the society. But they told him that he could not leave. There was a way in, but none out —except through death. He was terrified, but adamant.
>
> He had told no one of his plight, and that was when he vanished from home. Now that the good things of life were his, he would not go back and tell his wife. All this Sango learnt, and much more besides. For him it had great significance. By uncovering this veil, he had discovered where all the depressed people of the city went for sustenance. They literally sold their souls to the devil.[10]

Ekwensi's reactions to the presence of this kind of evil in society appear ambiguous when at the end of the chapter he has Sango muse on his own situation and say:

> Even so, when things became much too unbearable for him, Sango often thought it would not be the worst thing in life to join the *Ufemfe*. And he would remember the swollen body with its protruding tongue and bulging eyes, a body that had been rescued from the devil's hands and given a decent Christian burial. And yet the tragedy remained.[11]

The ambiguity is not, however, a mark of inconsistency in Ekwensi's approach to his theme; rather, it is a reflection of the ambiguous position of the generality of people, Sango among them, who struggle for survival in the city.

The coal strike in the 'Eastern Greens' is reported in a direct fashion and Ekwensi's message is palpable. Sango is sent to cover the strike which saw, in its initial phase, 'twenty-one miners shot down by policemen under orders from "the imperialists" '.[12] The police who had put down the strike were 'not the friendly unarmed men he had been used to in the city, but aggressive, boot-stamping men who carried shot guns, rifles and tear-gas equipment. There were African police and white officers and they all had the stern killer look on their faces'.[13] Sango is at the airport to see

> the arrival of dark troop-planes from Great Britain. His report on the arrival of these reinforcements drew forth an immediate denial from the Government. The troops had nothing to do with the coal crisis, they said. And now the coal city was drained of women and children, black and white. Only able-bodied men remained to face the terror.[14]

Sango's reports emphasize that

> this shooting had become a cementing force for the nation. The whole country, north, east and west of the Great River, had united and with one loud voice condemned the action of the British Government in being so trigger-happy and hasty. Rival political parties had united in the emergency and were acting for the entire nation.[15]

And his accounts are 'loud in praise of the new movement and caustic in their attitude of the British'. Through constitutional means, and not through violence, will a way be found for the solution of national problems and for achieving independence. This view typifies Ekwensi's attitude towards political action, as his evocation of the election campaign in the novel reveals. (He can be and often is ironic and condemning of the abuses to which political means are subject as *Jagua Nana* and *Beautiful Feathers* both reveal.)

His despatches from the 'Eastern Greens' (doubtless the locale is the Enugu area), though militantly anti-British, gain him promotion and the promise of a bright future with the *Sensation*. This promise is confirmed by his reports of the election campaign.

The description of the Town Council election is one of two central episodes in the second part of the novel. Two parties—the Self-Government Now party (the S.G.N.) and the Realisation Party (R.P.)—contend the election. Both parties spend lavishly, give entertainments, offer help and promises to anyone who will give them their votes. The S.G.N. promises 'better working conditions, improved medical services, more and better houses'. The R.P. offers 'more houses, more food, more water, and more light for the people'. That is, each offers more or less the same things. What is important is not the humanitarian motives of the politicians but the achieving of power. What is important to Ekwensi and renders his irony of secondary importance is that an African mayor will be elected for the first time and this is seen as a triumph for Africans. Readers must remember that the book was produced in 1954 long before Nigeria's independence had been achieved. But the general application of the events to considerations of self-determination is still of some interest.

The second central episode in the second part of the novel, and perhaps the most effective piece of imaginative writing in the book, relates to Sango's friend, Bayo. When we first meet him Bayo is a dandy, a wide boy, an opportunist. One of his habitual activities is to bring teenage girls to Sango's room and seduce them. When we next meet him he is involved in a penicillin racket and again uses Sango's rooms for his illicit and criminal activity. Still later, we learn that Bayo has decided to 'become a serious man and move with the times'. It is at this point that he meets and falls in love with a Lebanese girl, Suad, who returns his love. The affair ends tragically when Zamil, the girl's brother, shoots both Bayo and Suad and then attempts suicide. Sango, a witness to the killings, makes them the occasion for an article on the 'Lebanese menace', a controversial exposé of the social tension attached to a powerful social and economic minority in the community. Where his accounts of the coal strike, though anti-European in tone, gained him praise and promotion, his reports of the Suad-Bayo affair get him fired from his job because, as the editor points out, 'the *Sensation* does not stand for playing one section of the community against the other'.[16]

Sango's fortunes are at their lowest ebb: the best he has been able to do is win a precarious living in the city. And this is true of all those with whom Sango comes in contact—Aina, a girl from the slums who when we first meet her is arrested and sentenced to prison for stealing a length of cloth and who returns to coerce Sango throughout the book; Beatrice I, the tubercular common-law wife of an English engineer and mother of his three children, whose life depends on 'high-life and drinks and music' and who dies finally in the arms of a tough but tender timber merchant from Ghana.

These are the people of the city and they are its victims. The city is more than a central image in the book. It assumes, as it were, the role of another character, controlling, defining, organizing and often destroying the lives of her people. Ekwensi establishes the role of the city at the outset. The corporal who arrests Aina says: 'You see person who's not careful, the city will eat him.'[17] A few pages later when Aina is led into court, Ekwensi comments: 'As it was she stood against a city determined to show her no mercy'.[18] The city is held to account for the debased morality of youth, of Bayo and his teenage mistress Miss Dupeh Martins who is described as

> a girl who belonged strictly to the city. Born in the city. A primary
> education, perhaps the first four years at a secondary school; yet she

knew all about Western sophistication—make-up, cinema, jazz. . . . This was the kind of girl who Sango knew would be content to walk her thin shoes in the air-conditioned atmosphere of department stores, to hang about all day in the foyer of hotels with not a penny in her hand-bag, rather than live in the country and marry papa's choice.[19]

When Sango is thrown out of his lodgings he muses on his fate:

> He had been given notice to quit. This could be more than serious. A man thrown out of his lodgings in the city could be rich meat for the ruthless exploiters: the housing agents and financiers, the pimps and liars who accepted money under false pretences.[20]

The irony of all this, so far as Ekwensi is concerned, is that the victims care nothing for their fate: 'What do the People of the City care? Nothing whatever. They have created the flitter and they are content to live in it. The irony of Fate. The strange turns of justice. . . .'[21]

Contrasted with the victims of the city are those, few in number, who in one way or another survive. Prominent among these are Lajide, Beatrice II and her father. Lajide is the most fully drawn portrait in the novel. He is the landlord of Twenty Molomo Street where Sango lives when we first meet him. Lajide is an unscrupulous dealer in a variety of things, a mean and avaricious landlord whose eviction oɪ Sango causes the latter to say 'Brotherhood ends where money begins'. Lajide is a type representative of the man who succeeds in the city through exploiting his fellow-men by whatever nefarious means come to hand. And he dies in a drunken stupor, a victim of an obsessive fear that his evil will be punished.

Beatrice II is the good woman whom Sango meets when he has reached his lowest ebb and who becomes his redeemer. When Sango meets her she has a fiancé studying in England. This man eventually commits suicide when he achieves low grades, thus paving the way for Beatrice II's marriage to Sango. Her father, a respectable patriarch, feels that marriage to Sango is beneath his daughter's dignity but he eventually yields. While a successful member of the middle class, the father's respectability is brought into question since his success has been dependent upon his membership in the *Ufemfe Society*, the signs of membership of which are ostentatiously displayed on the walls of the sitting-room.

The novel ends with Sango, having seen Aina through a dangerous abortion, having learned of the death of Beatrice I, marrying Beatrice II and setting forth for the Gold Coast, there to win a new and more successful life. The wedding is a tableau of middle-class respectability 'without even the sound of a drum to liven things up'.

The novel's close is a rationale for postponement. Unable to come to terms with Nigerian life, Sango will fly from it—but only for a time.

> 'Let's go to the Gold Coast. I have always wanted to go there.' There was a plea in Beatrice's voice.
>
> 'Yes. We want a new life, new opportunities. . . . We want to live there for some time—but only for some time! We have our homeland here and must come back when we can answer our father's challenge! When we have *done* something, *become* something!'[22]

Perhaps in 1954 opportunities were better in the Gold Coast. One wonders what Sango's reaction would be today.

Ekwensi's limitations as an artist are plain. The episodic nature of the plot precludes the emergence of a satisfying overall pattern in the book. Characters are not drawn in any depth—while they possess a certain individuality, they are types who represent a cross-section of the people who live in the city and seek to come to terms with it. In this respect the novel can claim an importance. Through a deliberately realistic approach Ekwensi seeks to lay bare and call attention to various evils in society—to corruption in high places and low, in politics, government, civic administration; to debased morality both public and private. The obvious polemical and reformatory purposes dominate the novel. There are passages of descriptive and dramatic power and Ekwensi does have genuine insight into the complexity of problems which attend modern urban living in Nigeria. But he is unable to develop and sustain these insights in novelistic terms and the book, in the end, is a series, however valid and worth while, of random vignettes and impressions.

Jagua Nana, Ekwensi's second full-length novel and probably his best, bears many resemblances to *People of the City* but here the author pays more attention to the formal problems of fiction writing and the effect is more satisfying and convincing than the first book. An early review of the book called Ekwensi a 'Nigerian Defoe [who] chronicles the fierce life of the city of Lagos' and describes its heroine, Jagua Nana, as 'a Nigerian Moll Flanders'. The comparison is valid in several respects. The novel has, for two-thirds of its length, the loose, episodic structure of the picaresque form with unity supplied by the central relationship of the heroine to the events described and dramatized. Jagua, like Moll in Defoe's book, is a woman who struggles for survival in a tough, competitive society which threatens to engulf her at any moment. In the first novel the hero, Amusa Sango, sought to earn his living through socially acceptable means—journalism and band-leading. But Jagua, like Moll, though she has an awareness of moral standards, will sacrifice them without hesitation to the necessities of the moment. And like Defoe, Ekwensi has a strong moral purpose (not as overtly declared as Defoe's): he displays Jagua's moral turpitude in order to expose and condemn those forces which make her behaviour necessary.

Jagua Nana, like *People of the City*, offers a view of urbanized Nigerian life. Ekwensi evokes a convincing portrayal of the variety of Lagosian life—its poverty and squalor, existing side by side with glamour and riches; its pimps, prostitutes and politicians and their greed and lust. As Ulli Beier observes, this is not every Nigerian's Lagos but 'everybody will come into contact with this aspect of the city's life at some time or other—people from the most diverse walks of life form an integral part of it'.[23]

The story centres on Jagua Nana—'they called her Jagua because of her good looks and stunning fashions. They said she was Ja–gwa, after the famous British prestige car.'[24] Jagua is an independent woman from eastern Nigeria, a woman of easy virtue who although no longer young when we meet her, clings to a life of drinking and dancing, fine clothes and many lovers. Though she indulges in a bewildering series of casual love affairs, living on the 'dashes' of the men she sleeps with, her real love is for Freddie, a young, idealistic and impecunious student. Eventually Freddie leaves Lagos to study in England and Jagua travels to her village in the east, where she has a brief affair with a powerful chief, Obufara, and seeks wealth in an unsuccessful venture among the market queens of Onitsha. When Ekwensi moves from the intense and familiar urban life of Lagos he is likely to go astray. It is a feature of modern Nigerian writing that at some point in the story a character returns to his village at a place remote from the city. This affords the author the opportunity of contrasting the alleged simplicity of village life with the sophistication and complexity of life in the city. Many novelists—Nzekwu, Achebe, Aluko and Nwanko—manage this with conviction. Ekwensi's account of Jagua's affair with Chief Obufara is the least successful part of the book.

At last Jagua returns to Lagos, continues her casual, immoral life, becomes involved with an unscrupulous politician, Uncle Taiwo, who in an election campaign stands against and is responsible for the death of Freddie, now returned from England. Uncle Taiwo is eventually murdered and Jagua, because of her association with him and his campaign, is forced to flee to her village, a broken woman. She loses a child born of an affair with a lorry driver and, in a contrived happy ending, finds peace (and fifty thousand pounds given, unknown to her at the time, by Uncle Taiwo and stolen from party funds).

The episodic form and picaresque treatment of the first two-thirds of the novel give way to a firm and developing narrative in the final third, the part of the novel devoted to the election campaign, a campaign centred on the two principal competitors for Jagua's affection. Whereas Ekwensi's treatment of politics in *People of the City* is ironic and flippant, here it is bitter and characterized by an invective and presented with a brutality which preclude irony or humour. Jagua says to Freddie when he announces his intention to contest the Obanla riding, held by Uncle Taiwo:

'No, Freddie, I no wan' you to win.' She saw him sit eagerly forward and frown. She went on. 'Politics not for you, Freddie. You got education. You got culture. You're a gentleman an' proud. Politics be game for dog. And in dis Lagos, is a rough game. De roughest game in de whole worl'. Is smelly and dirty and you too clean an' sweet. I speakin' frank to you Freddie.'[25]

And she goes on to explain the methods by which elections are won:

Elections in Lagos were not won by wearing smart clothes and appearing distant from the people. You had to show them what you could do for them, before you won. You must associate with everyone, particularly the lowest ones, and regard them as your friends. You must give them the freedom of your time and thought, your car and your room. In such a manner only would you learn how they thought and acted. Uncle Taiwo was working very hard indeed, she told him. Uncle Taiwo was distributing money presents to the people. She told what happened only last week. She went with him to the court in Obanla and when anyone was fined, Uncle Taiwo promptly paid up the fine. . . . The whole of Obanla was plastered with pictures of Uncle Taiwo and all women had received match boxes and cooking stoves with his portrait on them and the school children exercise books with his portrait.[26]

This represents Ekwensi's appraisal of contemporary Nigerian politics and the rest of the book dramatizes the prosecution and consequences of the campaign in which both Freddie and Uncle Taiwo lose their lives. The story of Uncle Taiwo's end, told to Jagua by her friend Rosa, is presented with a starkness unmatched in contemporary African writing.

And on the second night, Rosa told the story of Uncle Taiwo: a terrifying one indeed, and one that taught Jagua that politics was dirtiest to them that played it dirty. Rosa told how she was going to

market and she heard that a dead man was lying at the roundabout
in the centre of the city. She was terrified. It was said to be lying
near the market-place, in front of the Hotel Liverpool. People
going to work saw it from their cars in the early morning as they
came up the hill. The policeman at the control point had the cape
of his raincoat up and white cap was sodden with the endless rain.
The roads were all muddy and pitted; the gutters were full, the
farms in the suburbs were overgrown with weeds. Lagos was in a
state of chaos that day. It seemed as if the ghost of that corpse had
gone abroad among them. The body was lying there twisted and
swollen; one knee was drawn up against the chest, the arms were
clutching at the breast, rigid like a statue.

In Africa you see these things, Rosa reminded her. Rosa said she
circled round the body three times. She saw some dogs circling too.
Perhaps they were waiting for nightfall to feast on the body of the
famous man. This was in Lagos, nowhere else. Then she went up
into the Hotel Liverpool and stood looking down from five floors at
the chain of red, blue, green, scarlet, yellow and cream cars; at the
slow jerk and stop of the traffic flowing into the island. But it was
the body of Uncle Taiwo, lying in the rain, that seemed to rivet all
the attention and to spread terror among the drivers. . . . They said,
however, that he had been murdered by his party and abandoned
at the roundabout. He had broken faith with them and they had
blamed him for losing the elections.

Jagua was horrified by the story. She had never loved Uncle
Taiwo. She had been a mere tool in his hands, an elderly man who
knew what he wanted and did not complain when asked to pay for it.
She had never realized that he was so deeply enmeshed in political
ties and societies he would never mention in public. How different
he was from Dennis, with his pulsebeat of life and his daring disregard of convention, his youthful urgency, a young man who had
stirred her deep down and made her restless and inadequate.[27]

Ekwensi's insistent and genuine concern over the political life of
his country accounts for the power and conviction of the writing in this
part of the novel. His prose rises to the level of his concern and the
sensation of the life the novel creates is convincing. Notice the power
of the rhetoric and the appropriateness of the language in this part of a
speech delivered to the Lagos market-women by Jagua which sums up
Ekwensi's awareness of the inequalities of modern Nigerian social-
economic life:

'I am still coming to the end of my story.' They listened, and she
went on: 'You see the sort of people you will be voting for, if you

vote O.P. 1. You will be voting for people who will build their private houses with your own money. But if you vote for O.P. 2, the party that does the job, you will see that you women will never pay tax. Don't forget that. O.P. 2 will educate your children properly. But those rogues in O.P. 1? They will send their children to Oxford and Cambridge, while your children will only go to school in Obanla. No: Obanla is still too good for your children, because—oh!—how can your children find the space to be educated in Lagos schools, if O.P. 1 ever comes into power? No, your children will be sent to the slummy suburbs. These people will open a hundred businesses using the names of their wives. But you? You will continue to sleep on the floor with grass mats while their wives sleep on spring mattresses. You will carry your things to market on your head, and while in the market, you will be bitten by mosquitoes, and your children will be bitten by mosquitoes and develop malaria. And you will console yourselves that you are struggling. Tell me, what are you struggling for? Or are you going to struggle all the time? Now is the time to enjoy! On Saturdays you will kill a small chicken and call your friends. You will shake hips to the *apala* music and deceive yourself that you are happy. But look! The roof of your house leaks when it rains. The pan roofs are cracking with rust. There is no space in the compound where your children can play. The latrine is the open bucket, carried by nightsoil men who are always on strike, so the smell is always there. The bathroom is narrow and slimy and it smells of urine. You call that life!'[28]

The novel ends on a sentimental and sanctimonious note with Jagua, having lost her child, setting out for Onitsha, Uncle Taiwo's 'blood money' in her possession. She says:

> I goin' to Onitsha. I want to become proper merchant princess. I goin' to buy me own shop, and lorry, and employ me own driver. I goin' to face dis business serious. I sure dat God above goin' to bless me.[29]

Many Nigerians have condemned both *People in the City* and *Jagua Nana* for presenting modern Nigeria in a bad light. They claim that Ekwensi exaggerates events for the sake of sensation. Present events would seem to confirm that his evaluation of the political life of the country in the time he describes was not far wrong. Moreover, and more important, he convinces us that the world of *Jagua Nana* is authentic. Jagua and the people around her are vital and memorable. Their lives are the legitimate material for novels. As Ulli Beier points out, 'nobody in his right senses would assume that all people of Lagos are like Jagua'[30] and her circle. They are, however, a prominent feature of Lagos life, members of the lower reaches of society, people who influence and shape the quality of the life of the city.

Beautiful Feathers, Ekwensi's third novel, is an attempt to provide a fictional assessment of Pan-Africanism. The book has the same virtues (a strong sense of place, a plethora of incident, a moral earnestness) and faults (careless plotting and an uncertain use of language) as the earlier books. The novel has two related plots suggested by the title, itself taken from an Ibo proverb which says: 'However famous a man is outside, if he is not respected inside his own home, he is like a bird with beautiful feathers, wonderful on the outside but ordinary within.'

Wilson Iyari, the proprietor of the Independence Pharmacy, is the leader of the Nigerian Movement for African and Malagasy Solidarity, a Pan-African movement formed because of Iyari's recognition that, although all of the political parties in Nigeria—the N.C.N.C., Action Group and Northern People's Congress—were 'Striving towards the same end, freedom from Colonial rule', the dream would not be realised because none of the parties 'could put aside the bitterness, frustrations and jealousies and realize that the end in view was the same'.[31] Iyari enjoys the respect of the masses, and among leaders of Nigerian political thought his name and movement have significance. But inside his own home he has no authority. His wife, Yaniya, rejects him, finds satisfaction in the arms of various lovers and eventually leaves him, taking their children with her to her father's home in the forests near Benin. The eldest son, Lumumba (all Iyari's children are named after leaders of anti-colonial Independence movements), dies and she returns to Lagos where she lives for a time on the fringes of the underworld before becoming a hostess with Nigerian airlines.

Iyari, after leading an abortive protest demonstration on Independence Day (the exact purposes of which are never clearly defined) which results in a riot, is enlisted by the Prime Minister (modelled on Nigeria's first Prime Minister, Sir Abubakar Tafawa Balewa, to whom the novel is dedicated) to represent Nigeria at a congress on self-determination at Dakar. While accord is seemingly reached between whites and blacks at the conference table, the underlying enmity between races is pointed up in a hunting episode. A shooting party comprised of Americans, Russians, British, French and delegates from various African countries, come upon and kill 'a beast shaped like a rhino, but infinitely more elegant'.[32] An argument arises—'some of the hunters wanted the horns, some wanted the whole beast preserved in a museum'—followed by confusion and shooting:

> Wilson saw the white men carrying off the beast and running down the slope. He aimed at the retreating white men, but a shot

struck him in the ribs and he fell. He lay there in a shot-riddled mist, choking for breath, while his body floated in endless circles, weightless.[33]

The symbolism is palpable and underlined by the Prime Minister's comments when he speaks to Iyari on the latter's return from Dakar after spending two months in the hospital:

'My dear Mr Iyari. You are a young man.' His voice fell one octave. 'A very young man, and therefore impatient. You led a strike here because you thought Nigeria was this, Nigeria was that. Now you've seen for yourself how a very little thing can upset unity. But we must keep trying.'[34]

Iyari's experiences in Dakar, together with the death of his Ghanaian friend, a political agitator exiled in Nigeria and significantly named Kwame Amantu, chastens his enthusiasm for African and Malagasy independence and he learns that unity of the kind he envisages is comprised of more complex factors than he at first supposed. This leads him to seek and achieve reconciliation with his wife and family. In the end he settles for the more modest role of successful pharmacist and husband.

Wilson was touched by the new attitude of Yaniya. He could not believe his eyes or his ears. They had truly come together now. It could be said of him that he was famous outside and that at home he had the backing of a family united by bonds of love. Wilson's beautiful feathers had ceased to be superficial and had become a substantial asset.[35]

The novel reveals political concern without political awareness. It reveals, as well, Ekwensi's desire to offer a serious treatment of his subject. But because he fails to define exactly what the N.M.F.A.M.S. really stands for and what its aims really are, the novel ultimately lacks convincingness.

Iska, the most recent novel, is in many ways the least satisfactory of the four books mentioned and displays in excess the faults in Ekwensi's approach to writing fiction. This is the story of Filia Enu, a beautiful young Ibo girl born in Northern Nigeria who, on the death of her father and her Muslim Hausa lover, Dan Kayiba, moves to Lagos, becomes involved with 'fashionable' literary and political cliques, becomes a model, attracts many lovers and eventually dies, overwhelmed and defeated by the city.

The title of the book, *Iska*, is the Hausa word for 'wind' and the symbolic analogies which this title affords Ekwensi are obvious. Filia Enu (as indeed are all of the characters in the novel) is a 'child of the wind', subject to its caprices and at its mercy. The publisher's blurb for the novel says that the wind symbolizes the change which 'blows strongly through Africa, destroying the old, preparing the way for the new'. Doubtless this is less satisfactory as a summary of his achievement.

The novel is formally divided into five parts, each named after a character with whom Filia is closely associated. Filia's story is the subject of the first section but then it is subordinated to that of each of the characters for whom the other sections are named. The movement of the novel is linear: themes are introduced and developed independently, then woven together in rather skilful counterpoint which evokes the complexity of Lagos living. The first two parts of the novel are the best because they offer, unlike the others, fresh material. Here Filia's life in Northern Nigeria is described. Here the Hausa-Ibo quarrel is an important part of the theme. Against the background of tension and rioting, the tribal quarrel is given focus in the tragic story of Filia and Dan Kayiba. The young Hausaman is killed by a group of Ibomen in a dispute over an entirely trivial matter. The convincingness of these sections of the novel is marred to some extent by the author's moralizing and his preaching of the need for national unity and federalism, a worthy enough motive in itself.

The reader, in trying to assimilate Filia's experience and assess its central meaning, is directed to the closing pages of the novel, to the musings of Dapo Ladele, Filia's latest lover, as he travels for the first time into Iboland.

> His impressions were quick and sharp. He quickly noted the industrialization and eagerness of the East. The new roads. The new progress. The impressiveness and love of the people of Eastern Nigeria. It was startling to him and quite unbelievable. Having for so long earned his living by writing articles inciting the hatred of a people, he had almost reached the stage where—temporarily at least—he was inclined to believe what he wrote. Now he knew that he had been living in a dream world. Once across the Niger he understood the background of Filia's life and struggles, her pride and independence.[36]

The conclusion is an impasse: corruption and dissipation of human and emotional resources will continue; side by side with these, we are told, the desires of people like Filia and Dapo may ultimately be attainable.

Lokotown and Other Stories, also published in 1966, is a collection comprised of two long stories—the title story and 'Glittering City'—and seven short pieces. Of these the longer ones are the best, although 'The Ivory Dancer' and 'Timber Merchant' display the control and economy of statement, and the irony in their endings, which characterize successful short-story writing. The stories here, as in the novels, deal with city life. Their plots follow the familiar theme of the innocent from the village caught up in the competition for survival in the hard, bright city, sometimes successfully, but generally disillusioned and broken. Ekwensi evokes his characters and situations with economy and precision, and the moralizing too often blatant in the longer works is here implicit in the fabric of the stories. While the characters in these stories are familiar, they possess an urgency and vitality which carry readers through the segments of their lives which the stories dramatize.

Finally, brief mention must be made of *Burning Grass*. One commentator has said that the book is of 'purely anthropological interest'.[37] This is to do the book less than justice. This novel—perhaps tale is a better description—reveals Ekwensi's knowledge of and affection for the Fulani cattlemen of Northern Nigeria and tells the story of Mai Sunsaye, a patriarch who is afflicted with the *sokugo*, the wandering sickness, his adventures and those of his herdsmen and sons. The opening paragraphs establish the tone of the story:

> When they begin to burn the grass in Northern Nigeria, it is time for the herdsmen to be moving the cattle southwards to the banks of the great river. And the hunters, lurking on the edge of the flames with dane gun, bow and arrow, sniff the fumes and train their eyes to catch the faintest flicker of beasts hastening from their hiding places.
>
> It is time too for the harmattan to blow dust into eyes and teeth, to wrinkle the skin: the harmattan that leaves in its wake from Libya to Lagos a shroud of fog that veils the walls and trees like muslin on a sheikh.[38]

Ekwensi's control of his materials is nowhere more secure as he blends facts and fantasy, reality and illusion. The characters suggest typical figures in the landscape and carry great conviction. The story closes on the same note as it opens. Mai Sunsaye, worn out by his long and eventual wanderings, dies, the name of his beloved son Rikku on his lips. Ekwensi records this with simplicity and tenderness:

> Sunsaye was indeed well beloved and they buried him in great pomp on the spot where his first camp had been. Then they cleared away in great haste. For legend holds that the place where a man has died is bad luck.[39]

Burning Grass is Ekwensi's most successful book from the point of view of its achievement as art. But it is not typical. He is the chronicler of city life, of the morality of the city and its influences and effects on the lives of city dwellers. We have commented on the excesses and inefficacies apparent in his use of the novel form. His success often proceeds from his topicality—he is always up to date. The faults and excesses arise from the reflection of the chaos of life in the modern urbanized Africa the novels seek to create. We recall Achebe's comment that the novelist's duty is 'not to beat the morning's headlines in topicality'. This statement clearly specifies the difference between writing which is likely to endure and that which achieves brief popularity and then passes. Ekwensi's fiction falls within the realm of popular art. And this is not without its importance. Popular fiction is always significant as indicating current popular interests and morality. Ekwensi's work is redeemed (although not saved as art) by his serious concern with the moral issues which inform contemporary Nigerian life. As such they will always be relevant to Nigerian literary history and to Nigerian tradition.

Notes

1 Chinua Achebe, 'The Novelist as Teacher', *New Statesman*, 29 January 1965, p. 162.

2 Chinua Achebe, 'The Role of the Writer in a New Nation', *Nigeria Magazine*, June 1964 (No. 81), p. 158.

3 Ibid., p. 159.

4 Eldred Jones, *African Forum*, Vol. 3, No. 1 (Summer 1967), p. 24.

5 His works are: *When Love Whispers* (1947); *The Leopard's Claw* (1947); *Okolo, the Wrestler* (1947); *For a Roll of Parchment* (1951); *Beware of the Bight of Benin* (1951); *People of the City* (1954); *The Drummer Boy* (1960); *The Passport of Mallam Ilia* (1960); *Jagua Nana* (1961); *Burning Grass* (1962); *An African Night's Entertainment* (1962); *Beautiful Feathers* (1963); *Murder at the Yaba Roundabout* (1963); *Lokotown and Other Stories* (1966); *Iska* (1966).

6 Chinua Achebe, 'The Role of a Writer in a New Nation', op. cit., p. 158.

7 Ibid.

8 *Burning Grass*, ostensibly a children's story, is unlike Ekwensi's other work and will be mentioned below.

9 Cyprian Ekwensi, *People of the City*, Heinemann, London, 1954, p. 3.

10 Ibid., pp. 70-71.

11 Ibid., p. 71.
12 Ibid., p. 72.
13 Ibid.
14 Ibid., p. 75.
15 Ibid., p. 74.
16 Ibid., p. 127.
17 Ibid., p. 13.
18 Ibid., p. 18.
19 Ibid., p. 29.
20 Ibid., p. 45.
21 Ibid., p. 146.
22 Ibid., p. 155.
23 Ulli Beier, *Black Orpheus*, No. 10, p. 68.
24 Cyprian Ekwensi, *Jagua Nana*, Panther Books (Hutchinson), London, 1961, p. 5.
25 Ibid., p. 103.
26 Ibid., pp. 102-3.
27 Ibid., pp. 139-40.
28 Ibid., pp. 109-10.
29 Ibid., p. 144.
30 Beier, op. cit.
31 Cyprian Ekwensi, *Beautiful Feathers*, Hutchinson, London, 1963, p. 29.
32 Ibid., p. 135.
33 Ibid.
34 Ibid., p. 137.
35 Ibid., p. 160.
36 Cyprian Ekwensi, *Iska*, Hutchinson, London, 1966, p. 219.
37 Oladele Taiwo, *An Introduction to West African Literature*, Nelson, London, 1967, p. 61.
38 Cyprian Ekwensi, *Burning Grass*, Heinemann, London, 1962, p. 1.
39 Ibid., p. 150.

The Novels of Chinua Achebe

by John Povey

Chinua Achebe is very clearly the best novelist in that group of writers who at Ibadan in the fifties contrived the birth of West African literature in English. He may lack the easy grace and wit of that urbane dramatist Wole Soyinka, yet his work has a structural strength and architectural coherence unmatched by other novelists. Too often other West African novelists, experimenting with their first novels, disregard structure; so that the pattern ceases to be a series of organized aesthetic choices and becomes merely the shapeless sequence of one thing after another. So close are many African novelists to the events they record that there is none of that artistic distance which is the basis for the writer's art. Plots mirror the autobiographical information proffered in the fly-leaf of the book's dust-jacket and this causes the balance of events to be seen only through the single self-satisfied vision of the protagonist, and the end, unless it has the shock of unexpected melodrama, can be a mere finish, for the novel has failed to develop any impetus more structural than that of the author's own life. None of these criticisms can be levelled at Achebe. The mere fact that he is one of the few novelists from Africa to write his stories with an historical setting is in itself indicative of the way he has been able to separate his own immediate experience from that of his protagonists, and thus achieve artistic rather than personal expression.

There is a sense in which this very virtue, which has received so much praise, may have imposed upon him an order so tight as to have become restrictive. Undoubtedly one of the reasons for Achebe's great success as a text in schools has been the relative orthodoxy of his handling of the genre of the novel. Teachers of literature have found that although the novels are written by an African they retain a structure that allows the established tools of European literary criticism to be applied. When one can so readily make cross-comparisons with the work of Achebe and, say, Thomas Hardy or Joseph Conrad, one has the satisfying sense that the African writer can be conveniently set within the context of the much wider field of English language writing: the whole 'Great Tradition' of which F. R. Leavis so persuasively writes. Not for Achebe those bold, though not necessarily successful, experiments in the novel such as have been attempted in that provocative first work *The Voice* by Gabriel Okara. There is rather a rigour in Achebe's planned development that gives his novels an extraordinary sense of inevitable power, a monolithic culmination of events, that is suitable to the inescapable disasters which he describes, especially in the two novels concerning the earlier period of Nigeria.

Yet Achebe cannot be dismissed in this way as a minor branch on the tree of modern British writing, for he has a very real individuality. His immense competence as a writer has allowed him to tackle and largely solve the two major problems that face the African writer who chooses to employ his second language for his creativity and who recognizes that for all his popular audiences in Africa he has to be published abroad and write at least partially for an international and therefore foreign readership. The first problem is the difficulty of bridging the gulf between the cultural assumptions of the writer and a part of his readership, without the intermediary assistance of a translator. The second is the establishing of a suitable English-language diction that will reflect the syntax and tone appropriate to the range of African characters the writer presents, while yet retaining that international standard of English which is required if his work is to be other than merely local in its effects.

Since the writer is aware of a foreign audience, he must too often explain things which his own local readers can take for granted. He must act, as it were, as both anthropologist and artist. Thus there is the paradox that the more he explains to outsiders the less interest is retained for the readers who share his culture; and yet to refuse explanation at crucial points is to deny the international readership any understanding of the beliefs which sustain the characters' actions and establish their motivations. Clearly some explanations are essential and the difference between, say, Achebe and Onuora Nzekwu is the degree of skill employed. Nzekwu sometimes makes his plots appear only the frame upon which he can lodge his long explanations of the Igbo customs of bride price and funeral rituals, and the story is broken off while the information is aired. Achebe manages to convey the essential elements of belief, of the importance of the yam festival in *Arrow of God* for example, without there being a sense that one is reading a series of notes in parenthesis. He makes them an integral part of the structure of his story, so that we are informed, almost, as it were, without recognizing it and our attention is not directed away from the essential elements which give the novels their power and concentration.

In the formation of a new diction Achebe is just as successful. If he does not play with exciting variations with words as Okara does in his Ijaw variants of English, he concentrates with all his great professional competence upon solving the question of how you indicate the speech styles of the African characters, all of whom must use English. He achieves an impressive range of styles, from the extremely formal appropriate to the most educated, to the rather dislocated English of the less educated. He also employs pidgin English where appropriate, retaining sufficient comprehensibility for the works to be readily inter-preted and yet retaining all the flavour of pidgin itself. This may best be seen in the speech of the characters in *A Man of the People*. One notices the range of Nanga's idiom and how exactly it reflects his sense of the degree of formality of the occasion.

If this is in a sense a common skill which must be acquired by any good novelist, it is worth observing that only Achebe amongst the African writers has achieved it consistently. Others too often use language which could be redistributed impartially among the char-acters for all the degree of individual differentiation achieved. Achebe's language matches his people, from the somewhat shallow intellectual-ism of Odili to the powerful command sustained by the speeches of Ezeulu. His deliberate use of Igbo proverbs, at times a mannerism, more often lends density and distinction to the style and flavours it with the African speech which he knows from the vernacular of his locality. To read Achebe is to feel a deliberate and effective selection at work moulding verbal patterns to achieve specific artistic aims, while others occasionally give the impression of a single style con-structed without any attempt to obtain that variation without which there can be no realism in character presentation.

Now that Achebe has completed the promised tetralogy which records the history of his family locale it will be interesting to see where he next turns his significant skill. With the developed ease and variety of language, with the powerful handling of structure by change of pace and tone, through carefully developed sequences of events, he has all the equipment needed to become one of the major novelists of this period. The four novels discussed at further length in this essay make the most important prose achievement yet in African literature in English.

The title of Achebe's first book, *Things Fall Apart*, is a line taken from Yeats' poem 'The Second Coming'. Its continuation 'mere anarchy is loosed upon the world' indicates the pessimistic theme which Achebe develops within the context of this novel.

The story tells of the people in an Ibo village during the 1890s at the period of the first confrontation between the tribal organization and the British colonialism introduced by the missionaries and the civil and military administrations. With loving and precise detail, Achebe records the customs of traditional tribal ritual. It is to a world rigorously restrictive, yet orderly and secure, that the white men come. At first these legendary creatures are discussed with incredulity, and Achebe skilfully structures it so that the whites appear on the very fringes of recognition. Only gradually do they intrude themselves more closely into the life of the village. Fearsome stories come first from the nearby village of Abame recording the power of the white men. A white missionary arrives and the elders consult the oracle for guidance. With that ironically inverted truth by which the classic Greek oracles lured their unlucky consulters to destruction, the oracle told them that the strange men would break the clan and spread destruction among them. To escape this fate they murder the missionary and tie the bicycle to a tree 'because it looked as if it would run away to call the man's friends'.[1] When the search is made the tethered bicycle becomes the very evidence that condemns them and a punitive expedition destroys the village and kills the inhabitants. This incident contains all the elements of many others which Achebe describes. There is the same irony which underlies the same disintegration when the beliefs of missionary and determined African conflict with one another.

When more missionaries come to other areas at first their appeal is rather beautifully, like the Christians of early Rome, aimed at the outcasts and rejected of the society, 'the excrement of the clan',[2] but then the son of the great title-holder Okonkwo also joins the new faith. 'Okonkwo felt a cold shudder run through him at the terrible prospect, like the prospect of annihilation.'[3] That prescient recognition is precisely what this novel is about, 'annihilation', of Okonkwo, his family, his clan, and the entire system by which he has lived. The village 'falls apart'. There are occasional outbursts of tribal solidarity as when the mission church is burned down, but the victory of the outside forces is seen in the disintegration of the tribal solidarity. 'Our own men and our own sons have joined the ranks of the stranger.'[4] The tribe can no longer act as one.

Perhaps I have emphasized too strongly the element of change in this novel. As in Achebe's other books, the tragedy arises less out of change, harsh as its results may be, than out of a sense of conservatism. Artistically speaking, Achebe's concern is less with the Christianizing of the young than with the destruction of the old who abide by their traditional values. The central situation in this book is the unlucky and largely undeserved downfall of Okonkwo. But undeserved (if I may make this comparison without inflating his significance) in the sense that the fall of Oedipus is undeserved. With Okonkwo one recalls the Greek contention that character equals fate. In spite of our general sympathy Okonkwo is not a lovable man; there is an energetic but ultimately debased motivation in ambition that requires the rejection of his engaging old father, the beating of his wife and son as he labours to obtain status in his community. Like the American self-made man, such as the father in Arthur Miller's *All My Sons*, success becomes elevated to a virtue in its own right. Strength becomes the only principle by which he will live.

Okonkwo's spirit is unyielding and continues to be so even when all other men have recognized the good sense of some discretion. In this way Okonkwo matches other tragic heroes who in their extremes are simultaneously the most heroic and also the most unreasonable of men. He kills the young boy who had lived with him like a son, scorning as mere evasive hypocrisy the rationalism of his friend Obierika, 'the oracle did not ask me to carry out its decision'.[5] His heroism is based upon his unyielding sense of rectitude. He becomes the target for the conflict of events because for him no compromising appeasement is possible. One recalls the words of Bernard Shaw, 'The wise man adjusts himself to the world, the fool tries to adjust the world to himself.' Okonkwo's integrity has a certain nobility in its fixity of spirit, but it includes an element of folly, for no man can be so assured of his own rightness. Such an attitude brings destruction to Okonkwo as surely as it does to the old priest Ezeulu in *Arrow of God*. There is much to be said for rational adaptation to irresistible circumstances, but Okonkwo will have nothing of this. To him compromise is cowardice. For him there is not honour but weakness in adjustment which he regards not as progressive good sense but abdication of principle. 'Let us not reason like cowards. If a man comes into my hut and defecates on the floor what do I do? Do I shut my eyes? No, I take a stick and break his head. That is what a man does.'[6] There is much characteristic about Okonkwo's choice of metaphor and the violence and rapidity of his reaction. His moral view is ultimately a very simplistic one, that, if someone offends you, you fight him or die in the attempt.

He returns to his village after a disastrous seven-year exile resulting from the accidental commission of a female crime. His absence is an important structural device to divide him from the people of his home village and he is shocked to see the changes. 'What has happened to our people? Why have they lost the power to fight?'[7] One notices his immediate assumption that the fighting will solve the complex events which are undermining the traditions to which he had pledged his own life. Obierika, always reasonable, explains without excessive regret, 'It is too late. Our own men and sons have joined the ranks of the strangers.'[8] But Okonkwo is incapable of seeing the force of that 'too late' and acts in the way appropriate only to earlier time. Okonkwo is angered by the woman-like softness of the clan's behaviour. Yet in a sense the tribal tragedy is only a generalization of the issues that were already fought out within the individual psyche of Okonkwo, as he battled the womanliness he assumed he had inherited from his father with further displays of violence. The tribe, in adjusting to change in the manner which Okonkwo so bitterly laments, has, paradoxically, avoided that other more final destruction which, in the microcosm of his own acts, Okonkwo brings upon himself. Okonkwo's suicide shows the death that would have fallen upon the whole tribe if they had remained as unyielding as he did. More rationally than weakly they have bent before the irresistible force of change—and they at least survive.

The climactic battle where the issues are fought out is the extra vehemence which comes when extreme principles are arrayed in opposition. The challenging forces which face Okonkwo are no longer represented by the moderation of the older missionary, Mr Brown, but by the bigoted ardour of Mr Smith. Mr Smith is as uncompromising and narrowly tenacious in his faith as Okonkwo is in his own belief. Between these men there can be no middle ground, for there is no room for manœuvre when two such forces seek their naked exclusive authority. From this point the novel accelerates into a rhythm that drives towards its inevitable violent climax. 'There is a saying in Umuofia that as a man danced so the drums were beaten for him. Mr Smith danced a furious step and so the drums went mad.'⁹ The same madness soon possesses both protagonists, Okonkwo readily matching Smith's vehemence and determination.

Okonkwo is arrested for his destruction of the local church, and jailed. It is revealing that the suffering he receives, though deriving from British authority, is not directly at the hands of the British. It is the assimilated, those who have greedily seized the opportunity for power upon the bottom rungs of the system, who are so cruel. It is the court messenger who shaves and knocks their heads so humiliatingly. At the village meeting that follows the ransomed prisoner's return, the debate clearly centres upon the need for an acceptable formula to cloak the inevitable acceptance of superior force. Under the circumstances this is a sensible and responsible attitude. To Okonkwo it is a betrayal; treason to the past. In bitterness he observes, 'I shall leave them and plan my own revenge.'¹⁰ Now his sense of self-righteousness is so vast, that it stands even against the decisions of the tribe whose unity had been originally the most urgent motivator of Okonkwo's act. Ironically his determined decision adds further to the elements which will destroy the old ways. If Okonkwo is successful they can look forward to nothing but sharing in his destruction. But in demanding the old cohesion of the past now he is also splitting that remnant of necessary coherence that remains—and thus he becomes not a force for continuance but another tool that creates disintegration.

As Okonkwo makes his powerful appeal for total unity, the hated court messenger arrives, the quisling who most immediately symbolizes administrative oppression and tribal disintegration. One notices how skilfully Achebe has arranged it that all the moral issues have been brought to the point of a personal confrontation. Hate cannot readily be focused upon an abstract principle, but when that principle is apparently contained within a person who stands before you, delusively you begin to imagine that you can destroy, with a murderous blow, the complex elements that have enraged you. The men of Umuofia watch with dismay the violent act as Okonkwo kills the messenger with his machete. Okonkwo contemplates the inaction of the clan and the final understanding is revealed—they will never again act cohesively against an enemy. He goes out and commits suicide, an act doubly horrible in the African context and therefore an ironic repudiation of the principles by which he was supposed to set such violent store. His body hangs on a tree and the tribe cannot even cut him down without violating all the taboos which his acts were supposed to perpetuate.

There remains only the profound irony of the last line. The new British commissioner decides that this death will make another item in the book he is completing about his African experiences. 'He had already chosen the title of the book after much thought. The pacification of the primitive tribes of the lower Niger.'[11] The insight and subtle irony of this scathing remark in the face of the powerful tragedy enacted is the mark of real maturity. It echoes the end of a novel by Thomas Hardy yet it holds little of his easy defeatist pessimism. This situation has moved beyond optimism and pessimism into the very painful heart of human experience where human honour and determination seem to be the toys of immeasurable forces that play with mankind's pretentions and struggles, turning heroism into villainy and honour into folly.

In his second novel Achebe moves to a more modern setting of Nigeria in the fifties, but his theme remains similar; the divided response to change initiated by Europeans as found in the local society. At the political level the battle is all but won. Though not yet independent, Nigeria is moving its young educated Africans up into responsible government positions. But the results of the English intervention into the economic and social life of the country seem as intrusive and threatening as ever. There are still no easy adjustments for the been-tos who return with their English degrees. This time Achebe turns to T. S. Eliot for his title, *No Longer at Ease*. Again the line should be seen in its fuller context which predetermines the author's attitude:

> We returned to our places, these kingdoms,
> But no longer at ease here, in the old dispensation,
> With an alien people clutching their gods . . .

The sense of alienation is significant because it refers to the young men who are, after all, returning to their own country and the alien people are not the British but their families and acquaintances. For such people the necessary change is no less serious than for those men who faced the white man's intervention in the earlier periods. *No Longer at Ease* is modern in subject but not less powerful in theme. The book is structured around a flash-back, leading us to the terminal irony which is to become an Achebe trademark. The whole series of painful incidents is bracketed by the court case and the remarks of the judge, whose dimness is initially mere arrogance, 'I cannot comprehend how a young man of your education and brilliant promise could have done this.'[12] Achebe demonstrates to us that these results are exactly inevitable given the social context which Obi must face. Obi's bribe-taking, in Achebe's presentation, is just another variant upon the necessary submission and adjustments which the African has to make in the face of all-powerful intervention, and Obi's failure is as inescapable as those of his more powerful ancestors in earlier times. Obi has his own proud sense of integrity, but it is not enough to resist the forces of change and he is not even allowed the gesture of death which concluded the heroic struggle of Okonkwo; for him there is only the jail term accompanied by the scorn and derision of those who know nothing of the struggle to retain integrity which he has attempted.

The plot concerns the fall of Obi Okonkwo from the eager promise of the first government job that crowns an excellent academic career to the penalty of jail for the taking of bribes. The issues may be scarcely heroic enough in any way to constitute a tragedy and yet the events happen with that same inescapable inevitability that brings a tragic hero to his downfall. The demands made upon him by his commitments to family and clan and his necessary standard of living in Lagos make Obi desperate for money, even when his salary is such unimaginable largesse to the villagers who have so cruelly taxed themselves to educate him to this standard. Their misunderstanding is not only in the financial demands; it rests upon the most fundamental discrepancies implicit in their belief in the results of education. Just as the mission school in *Things Fall Apart* was seen as useful because it brought information about the white man, the village has taxed itself to gain from its most intelligent youth a return of both prestige and cash. They seek to combat the intruding European ideas, to protect themselves against the administration. They now expect results for their expensive training. But there is another irony; an educated man in these circumstances is as potentially dangerous as the wooden horse of Troy. Such a person will be utterly unable to avert the disintegration of the tribe but will in fact spur its more rapid destruction. If in the first novel 'things fall apart', in the second perhaps we see things being welded together again, albeit the join is botched and weak. But the changes are based upon an acceptance of inevitabilities which would in fact have prevented the disaster that came to both the earlier heroes. 'Today greatness has changed its tune. Titles are no longer great, neither are barns or large numbers of wives and children, greatness is now in the things of the white man.'[13]

Again the nebulous theoretical elements of this debate become dramatically focused in the individual situation Achebe creates. Sometimes Achebe can handle his confrontation as mere comedy. There is the beautiful scene of Mr Stephen Udomo on the ship waiting till Lagos is sighted and then on a humid October day dressing himself up like an English banker with bowler hat and rolled umbrella. But for Obi the confrontation is necessarily more serious. His desire to marry Clara, an 'osu', exposes the continuing conflict between traditional beliefs and Christian teaching. No appeals to his father's conversion can make him acquiesce to this abominable relationship.

'We are Christians but there is no reason to marry an osu.'
'The bible says that in Christ there is no bond and free.'
'My son, I understand what you say, but this thing is deeper than
    you think.'[14]

For Obi the moral issue, whatever the more general causation, centres upon the 'dash' that accompanies many West African trans- actions. Whatever place the custom took in past society, under contemporary circumstances it corrupts the very fabric of economic organization. This issue may seem slight compared with the pressures that afflict Achebe's earlier heroes, but it makes a symbol of social change for which Obi has to formulate a new, acceptable moral code. Against Obi's gradually corrupting spirit is set the absolute integrity of his British boss, Mr Green. He is not an agreeable man to represent a moral standpoint. He is sad, bitter and cynical, anticipating universal dishonesty. By this cynicism he insulates himself against disaster with the luxury of being able to say 'I told you so'. There are manifold ironies that such a man, who despises Africa and the Africans, should be so personally honest, while Obi is a crook. This appears to follow from Green's confident statement, 'The African is corrupt through and through'. Yet although he thinks this is confirmed by Obi's crime, it is not true or there would be no struggle at all, simply a story of villainy and its punishment. Some of his acquaintances pretend to see in Obi's fall only inexpert technique; he should have had his house-boy handle the money. But Obi himself never sees the temptation with such moral obliquities. He knows his acts are wrong, deplores them, but is forced to go on doing them, recognizing his total guilt. It is a low-level Macbeth story of inevitably increasing villainy granted the first step has been taken. He exists upon a financial treadmill. Only continuing bribery can hold off his fall, yet the fall will be the more catastrophic when it finally inevitably occurs. The sad thing is the destruction of Obi's fine theory that the civil service is corrupt because it is staffed by old, experienced men. He really believed that when the places were filled with young educated people like himself corruption would disappear. With his personal downfall there is an immense pessimism implicit—a view that finally culminates in the sardonic anger of the last novel, *A Man of the People*.

Obi lacks the fine courage of Okonkwo and Ezeulu though he has his own integrity. His very weakness perhaps prevents the kind of cataclysm that the older heroes faced, for they were stronger and their disasters more shattering. In this novel Achebe first makes the assertion of corrupt society that sustains his *Man of the People*. The people have never been worthy of their heroes. But before that there was to be another novel on the great heroic mould of *Things Fall Apart*, *Arrow of God*.

Many critics considered *No Longer at Ease* a less powerful novel than *Things Fall Apart*, which was probably because they took an historic event as being more epic in its significance than a modern dilemma such as Obi's, much as we think that modern tragedy is less impressive than that set in historic times. There was a superficial assumption when, for his third novel, *Arrow of God*, Achebe returned to the historical, that this represented his admission of failure in handling a contemporary theme. In fact Chinua Achebe, in a conversation, indicated that he had from the very beginning planned his tetralogy; had simply rearranged the order for variety in his own task of writing the sequence. Certainly the theme of *Arrow of God* has much in common with his first novel. There is the same powerful protagonist representing all that is strongest and best in the old traditions and yet so uncompromisingly harsh, by very definition of his belief, that he must of necessity be crushed by circumstances which require adjustment rather than firmness. His heroism becomes obstinacy in times that require change rather than arbitrary attachment to old ways. In this novel the clash is rendered more powerful by the fact that the representative of the external European power, the British administrator Winterbottom, is not the kind of fatuous man as in *Things Fall Apart*, who wrote his memoirs about 'pacifying primitive tribes', but a man of courage and ability whose strength and integrity only match those of the old chief priest Ezeulu. The profound theme of the book recognizes that personal strength and integrity are as nothing when unimaginable social forces develop their own impetus towards uncontrollable change. No honest integrity can resist these powers and this becomes the pessimistic conclusion of the novel.

The story is set in the period around 1910 when British power, only initially foreshadowed in *Things Fall Apart,* had become a powerful reality; novelty now exchanged for administrative continuance. The plot concerns the fine old priest Ezeulu who controls the harvesting of the vital yam crop of the village. Exactly, Achebe records the monthly ritual as Ezeulu each month eats one symbolic yam to mark the passing of the moons towards the festival of harvest. He rejoices in his position of authority. He is flexible enough to send his son to join the white men that he may learn, but firm enough to resist the many changes the English attempt to bring. A man of legendary honesty and moral commitment, Ezeulu treats himself as the equal of the administration. When Winterbottom seeks an honest chief and finds only corruption in the mission-educated James Ikedi, he tries to make Ezeulu the new chief in keeping with the brash ordinance for administration handed down from London. It is characteristic that Winterbottom, although strongly opposed to the new system of appointing local chiefs, should attempt so conscientiously to carry it out. He is the administrator accepting his necessary duties as, in a way, Ezeulu accepts the duties required of him by the god whom he serves.

Ezeulu is angered at being offered the chieftainship, for though it is made in good faith, it is an act which shows appalling lack of understanding of his powerful position in the community. His resentment is aggravated by administrative bungling during Winterbottom's absence, through which Ezeulu suffers the humiliation of jail for failing to co-operate with the British administration. He returns to his village, burning with anger at the villagers who have not attempted to resist this humiliation done to the high priest of the god Ulu. He sees the villagers, not the white man, as his first enemy. He believes that the god must now punish the villagers. Ezeulu feels himself 'an arrow in the bow of his god'. A vision comes to him asking:

> We told you that this was your own fight which you could arrange to suit you. Beware that you do not come between me and my victims or you may receive blows not meant for you. . . . After that there was no more to be said. Who was Ezeulu to tell his deity how to fight? . . . It was a fight of the gods. He was no more than an an arrow in the bow of his god. This thought intoxicated Ezeulu like palm wine.[15]

The last comment is important, for until this point it has always been Ezeulu's rationalism and dignified moderation that have been his great qualities; now in his exhilaration he can ignore the warning of the spirit and become not the arrow but the bow that decides the direction of the shaft. Power has begun its inevitable corruption, and with a series of ironies which Achebe handles in a superbly gathering crescendo, he begins to design his god's vengeance in order to reaffirm Ulu's power. Yet ironically every act he makes ensures the old god's downfall, every penalty he imposes upon the village becomes a penalty against the god and what is aimed at the god's final triumph becomes his final humiliation.

Returning from prison, Ezeulu continues his traditional task of eating one symbolic yam at each new moon. But three moons have lapsed while he was in prison and so at the expected time of harvesting he chooses to insist that there are three more months to go before Ulu will bless the crops. This act in a less moral man would be diabolical. The old supplies run out, the new crops dry up in the ground and the people suffer wretchedly until they are informed by the missionaries, whose blandishments they have for long resisted, that their god Jesus Christ can bless crops. With relief the first Christian harvest festival is held in the village, the long resistance to the missionaries is ended and their triumph is the direct result of Ezeulu's penalty that was aimed to bring them repentant back to the traditional god. The last line has a complex irony unmatched even by Achebe. 'Thereafter any yam that was harvested in the man's fields was harvested in the name of the son.'[16]

The battle lines between the gods were drawn up throughout this book and *Things Fall Apart*; the end is painful and not, granted Achebe's context, an optimistic promise of future Christianizing. It is but a record of a disaster to the tribe and all that has achieved coherence in it. The death of his son is impossible for Ezeulu to accept because it seems as if everything points to his being punished by the gods, and how could that be when he was the arrow carrying out the gods' orders? For the first time he is unable to comprehend events. The sense of personal disintegration matches his sense of the tribal destruction too. 'What was his offence? . . . What could it point to but the collapse and ruin of all things.'[17] He finally goes mad contemplating this intolerable and irresolvable situation. Achebe sympathetically observes:

> But this final act of malevolence proved merciful. It allowed Ezeulu in his last days to live in the haughty splendour of a demented high priest and spared him the knowledge of the final outcome.[18]

What a dramatic comment it is upon the appalling situation that Ezeulu has created that mad ignorance is seen as an absolute blessing! In a sense Achebe is carrying on yet further the painful diagnosis of *Things Fall Apart*. Ezeulu is an even more honourable figure than Okonkwo and more significant within the tradition. The destruction is more total both for the individual and the tribe. This powerful work, perhaps Achebe's best, brooks no compromise with its conclusion, in which internal disintegration sped by external and foreign pressures accelerates the total loss of continuity with the past, and the death of a way of life.

A Man of the People, the last novel of Achebe, completed the sequence of his planned tetralogy. It was published within a month of a Nigerian military coup. From the viewpoint of the reception of the novel, this was most unfortunate, as few reviewers went beyond the amazement created by the discovery that Achebe had apparently anticipated the actual political event in the conclusion of his novel. In fact, of course, not only was speculation about such change commonplace in Nigeria, but there is an inevitability purely within the context of the novel itself which requires that resolution. To measure Achebe's work only by exterior event is to denigrate the artistic skill of its construction.

A Man of the People is another book in which a very simple story is turned into a complex revelation, as when poor Obi's taking of bribes proved within the context of the novel, *No Longer at Ease*, not to be the simple greed cynically anticipated by Mr Green and the judge, but a response to a series of events too powerful to resist. It would have been very easy for *A Man of the People* to have been drawn as a simple battle between good and evil, with the villainous Chief Nanga pitted against the honest integrity of the young intellectual Odili. But the book does not advance in that melodramatic way. It begins with Odili taking all the fire-brand stands of idealistic youth, yet it is very soon apparent that he is much further removed from common people than Nanga. The culminating renunciation of this book is the recognition that Nanga really is a 'Man of the people', exactly reflecting and epitomizing their greed and vulgarity on the infinitely grandiose scale made possible by his position.

When Odili first meets with Nanga he feels bitterness at 'silly ignorant villagers' who admire him, but the villagers with an easy rationalism would have readily asked if 'a sensible man would spit out the juicy morsel that good fortune placed in his mouth'.[19] It is this selfish rationalism which is the ugly basis for all actions within this novel. Odili is temporarily deluded by Nanga's gross but warm charm. He *knows* Nanga is corrupt and we are told of his viciousness and his persecution of yet another minister in the early chapters, but we do not *feel* this knowledge any more than Odili does. Indeed, Chief Nanga really is generous in his ready invitation to his home. Nanga has something of the brash, open affability we find in Cyprian Ekwensi's politician, Uncle Taiwo in *Jagua Nana*. Even the reader finds it sometimes difficult to resist the confident virility of the man. The descriptions of Nanga ruthlessly on the hunt in parliament have to be constantly recalled to avoid making too great an apologia for the man. This is also the result of our finding too little to admire in young Odili that would enforce a balance.

The motivation of the plot does not derive from political principle but begins in jealous reaction to Nanga's seduction of Odili's girl-friend. There is no evidence of great reluctance on her part and Nanga is openly shocked and then angry at Odili's honourable but naïve reaction. Odili is young and rather silly but not so silly that he cannot see the unalterable corruption of every part of Nanga's nature. Yet his denunciation terms, 'bloated by the flatulence of ill-gotten wealth', have an absurd ring which fits well with the political simplicity of Odili. His revenge too is an inextricably entwined mixture of sexual and political. Odili decides to counter Nanga's seduction by winning Nanga's intended new parlour wife to 'give her the works good and proper', and by joining with Common Peoples' Convention, the articulate band of ardent leftists led by Max. Yet he is never really a dedicated politician in their sense, he is both too innocent and too idealistic. Odili's reaction of horror when he hears Max has accepted a bribe in order to use the money to support his new honest politics, and Max's rationalization that all means must be used against the entrenched powers, demonstrate the fundamental differences in their attitudes.

'I know how you feel,' said Max rather patronizingly. 'I felt like that at first . . . but we must face certain facts.'[20]

Odili, being an intellectual, seeks the luxury of the perfectly just cause, Max is closer to the realism of politics.

In fact, the theme of this book is the corruption inherent in the system, intensified by Achebe to such a vehement degree that it virtually constitutes an attack on the entire political process. The title is with deliberate irony proved to be the exact truth. Nanga is a 'man of the people'. He does win votes and is more admired than condemned for his swindles and wealth. It is disturbing from a literary viewpoint, and no doubt more generally, that the fine rapier of Achebe's irony here appears like the bludgeon of sarcasm. Bitterness has soured the novelist and it is indicative that the most urgent condemnation comes not from characters but where the author himself most obviously intrudes.

The people themselves, as we have seen, had become even more cynical than their leaders and were apathetic into the bargain. 'Let them eat,' was the people's opinion, 'after all when white men used to do all the eating did we commit suicide?' Of course not.[21]

The selfishness of 'you chop, me self I chop palaver finished'[22] expresses all. This simple creed has at least directness to recommend it and Odili faces the ultimate problem that affects every intellectual involved in politics.

> Men like Nanga [became] successful politicians while starry-eyed idealists strove vaingloriously to bring into politics niceties and delicate refinements that belonged elsewhere.[23]

One might quibble that these are merely the extremes of the debate; but that the idealists are seen as inevitably 'starry-eyed' is an admission that politicians like Nanga are inescapable, which lends another dimension to Achebe's view of cynicism. Odili is aware of the attractions. Surveying the lavish bathroom appointments of Chief Nanga's house he remarks, 'I had to confess that if I were at that moment made a minister I would be most anxious to remain one for ever.'[24] Such minor political success as Odili does have derives from the small way in which he measures up against the people's measure of success. His father is impressed that he already has a car from his party and village support comes because Odili offers them the path to the lavish government trough. 'The village of Anata has already eaten, now they must make way for us to reach the plate.'[25]

There is an extra note in the pessimism in this novel, in that Odili ends in a sense as he began, there is no recognition, even a painful one such as Obi's painful self-confrontation. The dismal diagnosis Odili has made of his world in the early pages of the book is dramatically confirmed; proved to be fundamental truths rather than the exaggerated dismay of the intellectual with his simplified principles. For Odili there is no resolution. At the ending of this book he is not in any manner an older but wiser man, he is confirmed in his initial diagnosis and this is the measure of change in Achebe's last novel. The contemporary situation defeats intellectual resolution and Odili is granted neither the success nor destruction the earlier protagonists had met. He is forced merely to continue, and if that resolution is not a tragic one it may be the most painful of all. Okonkwo died with his self-grandeur confirmed, Ezeulu had the luxury of ignorance derived from madness. Odili knows and understands that there is nothing to be done. This ultimate self-suicide kills belief in action itself. This theme is more painful than the direct sneer of the last statement for it touches on all attempts at social organization; rationalism pressed to this depth may appear realistic but it bears despair as its only message in a manner avoided by the earlier novels.

Notes

1 Chinua Achebe, *Things Fall Apart*, London, Heinemann (African Writers Series), 1962, p. 125.

2 Ibid., p. 130.

3 Ibid., p. 139.

4 Ibid., p. 159.

5 Ibid., p. 60.

6 Ibid., p. 145.

7 Ibid., p. 159.

8 Ibid., p. 159.

9 Ibid., p. 169.

10 Ibid., p. 180.

11 Ibid., p. 187.

12 Chinua Achebe, *No Longer at Ease*, London, Heinemann (African Writers Series), 1963, p. 2.

13 Ibid., p. 54.

14 Ibid., p. 133.

15 Chinua Achebe, *Arrow of God*, London, Heinemann (African Writers Series), 1965, p. 240.

16 Ibid., p. 287.

17 Ibid., p. 286.

18 Ibid., p. 286.

19 Chinua Achebe, *A Man of the People*, London, Heinemann (African Writers Series), 1966, p. 2.

20 Ibid., p. 93.

21 Ibid., p. 161.

22 Ibid., p. 167.

23 Ibid., p. 12.

24 Ibid., p. 42.

25 Ibid., p. 141.

The Essential Soyinka

by Eldred D. Jones

If Wole Soyinka had never written another line, he would probably always be remembered in one version or another of his duiker-duikritude, tiger-tigritude, Negro-negritude quip. In many minds, particularly minds unfamiliar with his work, Soyinka is permanently installed as the arch opponent of negritude, while in fact his work exhibits all that negritude was essentially about, bar the shouting. Few writers have used the totality of African experience to greater purpose or with more effect. No African writer has been more successful in making the rest of the world see humanity through African eyes.

Using his African background, he explores the human condition. His experience—even as it appears in his work—is not entirely confined to his local environment, but this is his main inspiration and his starting-point. He makes the fullest use of Yoruba mythology, the Nigerian landscape—mountain, stream and forest—as well as its steel bridges, power stations, night clubs and tenement houses. The local pantheon of deities, the shrines in which they were and are worshipped, the animals, the plants, the rocks, all form the environment against which Soyinka treats his essential subject, *homo sapiens*, in his constant struggle of adjustment to this changing environment. *Homo sapiens* may be dressed for the nonce in a black skin and live in the sun and rain of Africa, but being essentially human he would still be recognizable if he decided to change both habit and habitat.

Soyinka is a conscious but not a self-conscious artist—this explains his impatience with too much philosophizing about being an African. That he can afford to just be himself is the result of two things. The first, which has to be stated with some care since it has been stated so often without enough definition, is that Soyinka is the product of British colonialism which differed from French colonialism, particularly in the area of education. The differences between the two systems have been exaggerated. Neither system was designed to produce an African who would be proud of being African. In this contempt for the African heritage, no Briton in the nineteenth century, when it most mattered, would have yielded an inch to a Frenchman. The British, because they are a reticent people, not given to clear-cut

113

pre-definitions, did not talk about their intentions quite so much. They just went ahead and established what they knew the African needed—good, barefoot English public schools. Because some of these schools were very good in their way, and because African institutions were condemned mostly by implication and the cold shoulder, the message escaped many Africans who were able to go on being African while also playing cricket, singing 'Land of Hope and Glory', chanting Latin declensions, and reciting *Paradise Lost*. They were not compelled by the system to submit their names for the ballot and take out club membership. The French system encouraged a more overt discarding of African values as a qualification for the French club card. Therefore the French subjects felt the need to burn their cards in public when they found themselves compromised by their membership.

This leads to the second reason why Soyinka could afford to be himself in the fifties and sixties. It is simply that by that time the repudiation had taken place—by Senghor and Césaire and others in France in the thirties and forties. But, to repeat—in so far as the aim of negritude was to use the African experience meaningfully in art, the movement could have found no better exponent than Soyinka. This is not to say that there is no difference between his work and, for example, Senghor's.

Perhaps the essential difference is in the amount of reverence with which the two use the African heritage. There is in the negritude writers a kind of worship of Mother Africa which is absent in Soyinka's work. For him the 'ancients' were no better than the 'moderns' even though the former built great empires. Our ancestors were people of the same mould as ourselves with the same capacity for greatness as well as for appalling stupidity and selfishness; they were, like ourselves, a mixture of honest men and rogues, each perhaps a mixture of each. For Soyinka, the gods were and still are often guilty of either callousness or caprice in their dealings with men, so that one is forced to bring them too to judgment. Both men and gods are under arraignment in *A Dance of the Forests*. Of both the present and the past, of both men and gods, Soyinka is apt to raise the most embarrassing questions. This is where his greatest value lies—and his greatest personal danger; he is an irritant to complacency and a wet blanket to romance.

Soyinka's ideas matured early. The seeds of his essential ideas are seen in his earliest work, and he has remained consistent throughout. They can be seen in works of small compass and light tone, as well as in longer and more sombre works. 'The Other Immigrant', an early poem, portrays one false solution to the complexities of life—an attempt to turn away from the struggle and insulate oneself

'Into the lining of a three piece suit'.[1]

This is no solution; it is an escape from one. Similarly the companion poem 'The Immigrant' portrays a futile attempt at revenge in which the rejected dancer seeks to bolster his deflated ego by a process which only humiliates him further:

> He makes his choice at random
> Haggles somewhat at the price,
> Then follows her, to pass
> The night
> In reciprocal humiliation.[2]

Throughout his works Soyinka is rejecting false solutions and in as late a work as *The Interpreters* he is still engaged in showing how one set of people avoid the struggle by holding on to old beliefs and avoiding conflict, while others try to face the complexities of life. In works early and late he is concerned with the individual's struggle with his environment. In this struggle he has first to try to know himself, body and soul, and then to face the world with the help of other men if this is forthcoming, in spite of other men when this is necessary; with the help of the gods when this is available, and in desperation without even this. It is in this sense that his interpreters in the novel of that name are truly on their own, battling their way against themselves and the world.

In all this, as has been said earlier, Soyinka starts with the local environment. In *The Swamp Dwellers*, the scene is a Nigerian village, but the tensions treated are fundamental and hence universal. All aspects of life under the sun are portrayed in this short play—the struggle with the physical environment, the struggle with other men, the struggle with the gods. The result is a powerful play.

Igwezu's efforts in the basic and necessary struggle to make the land yield him a living are a total failure. He comes back from failure in the city to fall back on the land (land is ironically and characteristically represented by the riverine, flood-prone swamps) and he finds total devastation:

> Not a grain was saved, not one tuber in the soil. . . . And what the flood left behind was poisoned by the oil in swamp water. . . . It is hard for him, coming back for a harvest that isn't there.[3]

The tragedy of failure is a double one because Igwezu had also failed in the harsh city. The city is commonly contrasted in many literatures with the country; the city is harsh and unpitying, but the country is soft and indulgent. (Ekwensi's novels typify this tradition in the African novel.) Igwezu had hoped for success in the city but had not *expected* it; when it did not come, he returned to the comfort and security of the country:

> When I met with harshness in the city, I did not complain. When I felt the nakedness of its hostility, I accepted it. When I saw its knife sever the ties and the love of kinship, and turn brother against brother. . . .[4]

He took all this philosophically, confident that the land was still there:

> It was never in my mind . . . the thought that the farm could betray me so totally, that it could drive the final wedge into this growing loss of touch.[5]

In the city, Igwezu's failure had been made total by the final humiliation of having his wife taken by his own twin brother. So another fundamental relationship—'the ties and the love of kin hip'—had been broken. But the land was supposed to be reliable—particularly if one observed the rites of the gods and paid one's dues to their priest. So the gods too had failed Igwezu through their representative on earth. Was there any point in the sacrifices and rites? As Igwezu asks the priest—for once under his power as he held the razor over him—

> If I slew the fatted calf, Kadiye, do you think the land might breathe again? If I slew all the cattle in the land and sacrificed every measure of goodness, would it make any difference to our lives, Kadiye? Would it make any difference to our fates?[6]

The implied answer is no. Indeed it is made explicit later:

> I know the floods can come again. That the swamp will continue to laugh at our endeavours.[7]

What then? Is there no hope in man, in God or the land? Neither here nor in any other work does Soyinka hold out easy solutions, though he never (which would have been equally unrealistic) closes the door totally to hope. But hope is always equivocal. In *A Dance of the Forests* the hope of mankind is represented by a child; but a half-child whose future is made even more uncertain by his being the stake in a game of chance. In the seemingly hopeless situation in *The Swamp Dwellers* there is also hope; there is someone to whom Igwezu can leave the farm; someone who has faith enough to say:

The swallows find their nest again when the cold is over. Even the
bats desert dark holes in the trees and flap wet leaves with wings of
leather.

.   .   .

I shall be here to give account.[8]

Words of faith yet, ironically, spoken by a blind beggar. Ironic, but
not cynical, since after all the beggar did work his way down from
the north. He may after all find a path where sighted men can find
none in spite of their eyes. The blind beggar is a broken reed, but he is
the one thing to hold on to; he provides a link in the chain of hope,
albeit a weak one.

Irony has always been a part of Soyinka's art. In both early and
late works, the end is never quite the expected one, and the characters
are often different from what they seem. The lady in 'Telephone
Conversation' is not a vicious barbarian. These lines indicate her
urbanity:

> Silenced transmission of
> Pressurised good-breeding. Voice when it came,
> Lipstick-coated, long gold-rolled
> Cigarette-holder pipped.[9]

But of such is the kingdom of racial prejudice.

There is irony too in *The Lion and the Jewel*, a play which is so easily
(and erroneously) interpreted as a clash between progress and reaction,
with the play coming down surprisingly in favour of reaction. The
real clash is not between old and new, or between real progress and
reaction. It is a clash between the genuine and the false; between
the well-done and the half-baked. Lakunle the school teacher would
have been a poor symbol of any desirable kind of progress. (He is in
total contrast for example with Eman of *The Strong Breed*.) He is a man
of totally confused values, who would plunge head first into a mess of
breakable plates, high-heeled shoes, kisses, and Victor Sylvester. The
Bale is more cautious as he explains to Sidi:

> I do not hate progress, only its nature
> Which makes all roofs and faces look the same.
> And the wish of an old man is
> That here and there,
> Among the bridges and the murderous roads,
> Below the humming birds which
> Smoke the face of Sango, dispenser of

> The snake-tongue lightning, between this moment
> And the reckless broom that will be wielded
> In these years to come, we must leave
> Virgin plots of lives, rich decay
> And the tang of vapour rising from
> Forgotten heaps of compost, lying
> Undisturbed. . . . But the skin of progress
> Masks, unknown, the spotted wolf of sameness. . . .
> Does sameness not revolt your being,
> My daughter?[10]

On balance the Bale's caution is to be preferred to the equation of progress with

> High-heeled shoes for the lady, red paint
> On her lips.[11]

The Bale, if he is worth anything, is so because of the traditional values of which he is so confident and in which he so completely out-manœuvres Lakunle who really has no values at all. The Bale at least seems to be looking in the right direction.

An even more enigmatical figure is the Professor in *The Road*, one of Soyinka's later works. The Professor has been driven for blasphemy from the church where 'the Word' is expected to be found. He now seems sceptical that the word was ever there at all:

> I stood often behind the bronze wings of the eagle; on the broad span of the eagle's outstretched wings rested the Word—oh what a blasphemy it all was but I did not know it.[12]

It is not surprising that with Soyinka 'the Word' should not be found where everyone thought it was. The Professor is still dedicated to the search for the Word, but how can one hope for anything from a figure such as the Professor? Appearances certainly are against him:

> a tall figure in Victorian outfit—tails, top-hat etc; all thread-bare and shiny at the lapels from much ironing. He carries four enormous bundles of newspaper and a fifth of paper odds and ends impaled on a metal rod struck in a wooden rest.[13]

It is in this mass of useless paper—nothing can be less fruitful than an out-of-date football pools coupon—that the Professor searches for the Word which he had so obviously failed to find in the book on the brass lectern still visible through the open window of the church. Indeed, he still wants to keep the bronze eagle in view, 'for his brazen image bore on its back the first illusion of the word'.

Soyinka deliberately avoids making the Professor a martyr; a victim of reactionary members of the church hierarchy. His comparison in a Sunday school class of God's purpose in creating the rainbow with his purpose in creating the palm trees seems to have brought doctrinal matters to a head, but even apart from his unorthodoxy he was not an honest minister as he himself confesses:

It is likely that I left the church coffers much depleted. . . .[14]

The Professor is hardly likely to lead men to the true word whatever it is. And yet in his half-mystical, half-nonsensical words seems concealed some urge to find something. He only finds it in death where there is the only finality, and where the Word is apparently to be finally found. It is not without meaning that the Professor's haunts on earth are next to the shadows of death: the road which as ever is always famished and continually swallows its victims, and the grave yard:

A gravestone turns slow on the hinge; angels trapped by day in illusions of concrete rise in night's parole.[15]

In so far as anyone has the secret of 'the Word' it is Murano, who is dumb and cannot reveal it: 'Murano, crawling out of the darkness from the last suck of the throat of death. . . .' So perhaps 'the Word' can only be looked for in life; the search may lead from the respectable brass lectern to the drivers' shack, but it can only be found in death.

There is no one among Soyinka's characters who has found 'the Word', and so can afford to rest. The greatest virtue apparently is to keep looking, and the greatest vice is the pretence that one has found the final answer and therefore can abandon the search.

Just as there is no final answer in our time, so, the author seems to suggest, there never has been. Soyinka's look into Africa's glorious past in *A Dance of the Forests* is as disillusioning as his look at the present and the future. There is no false resting-place there either. The almost disdainful way in which Aroni refers to the glorious past is itself a sign that we are not going to see demi-gods in the African past. To Forest Head's request: 'Remind me, how far back are we?' the reply is

About eight centuries. Possibly more. One of their great empires. I forget which.[16]

Hardly a way to introduce a glorious epoch! What Adenebi the Council Orator was expecting was quite different: 'Mali. Songhai. Perhaps a descendant of the great Lisabi Zimbabwe. May be the legendary Prester John himself. . . . I was thinking of heroes like they.' (This inventory slyly suggests historical confusion in Adenebi's mind.) The court of Mata Kharibu provides an anti-climax to Adenebi's expectations. It contains all too familiar characters. Soyinka heightens the comparison with our imperfect present by making the human characters in the play double as both contemporary and historical characters, thus making the point that the more men change, the more they remain the same. The specific guise or garb may change but the basic human characters remain fundamentally unaltered.

Rola in our time works on the philosophy that everyone must look after himself, and if one is outdone by cleverer folk, that is just too bad. To Adenebi's accusation that she has ruined countless men, both young and old, she replies:

> What is it to me? When your business men ruin the lesser ones, do you go crying to them? I also have no pity for the one who invested foolishly. Investors, that is all they ever were—to me.[17]

Rola has no heart. Neither had her counterpart in the court of Mata Kharibu, Madame Tortoise. She sent men to their death with no compunction. While she is sending yet another man to possible death in pursuit of her pet canary she casually confirms the death of a previous emissary:

> *Court Poet:* Did not a soldier fall to his death from the roof two days ago, my lady?
> *Madame Tortoise:* That is so. I heard a disturbance, and I called the guard to find the cause. I thought it came from the roof and I directed him there. He was too eager and he fell.[18]

Of another who, rejected after earlier encouragement, jumped to his death she again callously reports:

> He could not understand that I took him, just as I select a new pin every day. He came back again and could not understand why the door was barred to him. He was such a fool.[19]

Adenebi, the twentieth-century rhetorician, had been equally facile in the Court of Mata Kharibu in the character of the Court Historian; he had put into learned language just what the great dictator had wanted to hear. Mata Kharibu (he has no modern counterpart in *A Dance of the Forests*, but Kongi of *Kongi's Harvest* is an excellent modern parallel from Soyinka's pen) was determined to go to war for what

120

amounts to no reason at all: he had stolen the wife of a neighbouring ruler, and now wished to fight him for her dowry! The objections of the Captain (the dead man in the modern parallel) who had fought in worthier causes were overwhelmed by the rhetoric of the Court Historian—an advocate of pure war or war without cause.

> War is the only consistency that past ages afford us. It is the legacy which new nations seek to perpetuate. Patriots are grateful for wars. Soldiers have never questioned bloodshed. The cause is always the accident, your Majesty, and war is the Destiny. This man is a traitor. He must be in the enemy's pay.[20]

When Soyinka writes like this, his audience is not a local one; it is a universal one. Indeed at this point in the play he widens his immediate range of reference by making the Court Historian invoke the precedent of the Trojan war:

> I have here the whole history of Troy. If you were not the swillage of pigs and could read the writings of wiser men, I would show you the magnificence of the destruction of a beautiful city. I would reveal to you the attainments of men which lifted mankind to the ranks of gods and demi-gods. And who was the inspiration of this divine carnage? Helen of Troy, a woman whose honour became as rare a conception as her beauty. Would Troy, if it were standing today lay claim to preservation in the annals of history if a thousand valiant Greeks had not been slaughtered before its gates, and a hundred thousand Trojans within her walls? Do you, a mere cog in the wheel of Destiny, cover your face and whine like a thing that is unfit to lick a soldier's boots, you, a captain?[21]

Against such rhetoric and learning mere common sense cannot prevail, and the Captain's real courage in resisting causeless war is accounted both cowardice and treachery. His warning to the Physician falls on deaf ears:

> Unborn generations will be cannibals most worshipful Physician. Unborn generations will, as we have done, eat up one another.[22]

Thus Soyinka speaks out of the court of a fictitious African dictator of eight centuries ago to the world on the subject of war. The setting is local but the audience is universal.

A similar anti-war theme, namely that it is impossible to contain war, and that men had best be wary of resorting to it even when they think they have good cause, is given poetic expression in the long poem *Idanre*. This poem is another excellent example of how Soyinka uses the Yoruba background of myth and legend to present universal truths. Men inviie Ogun, the Yoruba God of War, to supper at their peril. In one particularly spirited passage the poet portrays the God who has been called down by men to fight on their behalf, indiscriminately slaughtering friend and foe alike, heedless of the cries of women.

> There are falling ears of corn
> And ripe melons tumble from the heads
> Of noisy women, crying
> > Lust-blind god, gore-drunk Hunter
> > Monster deity, you destroy your men!
> He strides sweat encrusted
> Bristles on risen tendons
> Porcupine and barbed. Again he turns
> Into his men, a butcher's axe
> Rises and sinks
> > Behind it, a guest no one
> > Can recall.
> Where do we seek him, they asked?
> Where conflict rages, where sweat
> Is torrents of rain, where clear springs
> Of blood fill one with longing
> As the rush of wine
> > So there they sought
> > And there they find him
> And youth that came to teeth on the encounter?
> What greater boon for the fledgeling! The wings
> Of a god enclose him wholly, there is
> No room for air
> > Smothered in wind-deafness
> > Blinded in light-paths of suns
> There are air-beams unfelt by human breath
> Unseen by sight, intangible. Whose throat
> Draws breath in a god's preserve
> Breathes the heart of fire
> > Murderer, stay your iron hand
> > Your men lie slain—Cannibal!
> Ay, ring summons on the deafened god
> His fingers sow red earth. His being incarnate
> Bathes in carnage, anoints godhead
> In carnage

To bring a god to supper is devout, yet
A wise host keeps his distance till
The Spirit One has dined his fill. What mortal
Brands a platter with an awesome name,
Or feeds him morsels choice without
Gauntlets of iron. A human feast
Is indifferent morsel to a god.[23]

The message is to all men whether they fight with swords or with nuclear weapons. It is the warning of the Court Historian of the Court of Mata Kharibu re-enacted. Soyinka's own note to this poem, written some time afterwards, significantly shows how close the myth is to reality. He writes:

> *Idanre* lost its mystification early enough. As events gathered pace and unreason around me I recognised it as part of a pattern of awareness which began when I wrote *A Dance of the Forests*. In detail, in the human context of my society, *Idanre* has made much sense. (The town of Idanre itself was the first to cut its bridge, its only link with the rest of the region during the uprising of October 1965.) And since then, the bloody origin of Ogun's pilgrimage has been, in true cyclic manner most bloodily re-enacted.[24]

To return to ideas in *A Dance of the Forests*, the Court Historian is a secular version of the false prophet, a figure which is constantly appearing in various disguises in Soyinka's work. In one of his earlier works the subject had been playfully, almost affectionately treated in *The Trials of Brother Jero*. Subsequent treatments have been increasingly grimmer. Soyinka had flirted with Jero in the way Shakespeare had flirted with Falstaff and Autolycus, and Ben Jonson with Face. Yet even so Brother Jero emerged, not as a hero, but as a successful rogue; a threat to society which society itself nurtures.

Kadiye in *The Swamp Dwellers* is a more sinister figure, because unlike Brother Jero he does not admit even to himself that he is a rogue. Brother Jero (*The Trials*) bares his bosom to the audience in a frank soliloquy:

> I am glad I got here before my customers—I mean worshippers—well, customers if you like. I always get that feeling every morning that I am a shop-keeper waiting for customers. The regular ones come at definite times. Strange, dissatisfied people. I know they are dissatisfied because I keep them dissatisfied. Once they are full, they won't come again. . . . Everything, in fact, is planned.[25]

E

Here, if one can use such a phrase, is an 'honest' rogue. But Kadiye never once admits that he is a false prophet; he goes on blandly promising plenty and demanding more goats for sacrifice. Soyinka brings him closest to a bloody account when Igwezu, razor in hand, subjects him to a forced catechism. He demands where all the sacrifices have gone:

> And so that the Serpent might not vomit at the wrong season and drown the land, so that He might not swallow at the wrong moment and gulp down the unwary traveller, did I not offer my goats to the priest?[26]

He also wants to know what has happened to all the glib promises:

> And when the Kadiye blessed my marriage, and tied the heaven-made knot, did he not promise a long life? Did he not promise children? Did he not promise happiness?[27]

Then in the silence which ensues Igwezu brings out the crucial question which implies all the answers:

> 'Why are you so fat, Kadiye?'[28]

Kadiye is another charlatan feeding on the trust of the people and giving them nothing but words in return. The Court Historian (*A Dance of the Forests*), Chief Winsala, Sir Derinola, Professor Iguazor (and others in *The Interpreters*), the Elders in *The Strong Breed*, are all similarly false prophets; leaders lay and religious who do not really show the way.

In Soyinka's portrayals, these figures are resisted only at great risk of social or religious excommunication. This treatment runs through Soyinka's work and is tied to the theme of sacrifice, another pervasive theme, but we shall take them one at a time.

Chume in *The Trials of Brother Jero* at last discovers that his master is a fraud:

> That one no fool me any more. 'E no be man of God.[29]

This of course is a threat to the prophet's career and so Chume has to be got rid of. The ease with which Brother Jero disposes of his gull is itself a telling comment on justice in the society:

> I have already sent for the police. It is a pity about Chume. But he has given me a fright, and no prophet likes to be frightened. With

the influence of that nincompoop I should succeed in getting him certified with ease. A year in the lunatic asylum would do him good anyway.[30]

Thus the naïve Chume is sacrificed so that the smart charlatan may live. Such is society, the play seems to say; the bad and powerful are resisted only at the resister's peril.

Igwezu's audacity (*The Swamp Dwellers*) in questioning the sincerity of the Kadiye will not go unpunished. The Kadiye's threat, once he is free, 'You will pay, I swear it. . . . You will pay', is not an empty one. Igwezu's father knows their import, so his son must go back into exile in the hostile city:

I must go after him or he'll stir up the village against us. This is your home, Igwezu, and I would not drive you from it for all the world. But it might be best for you if you went back to the city until this is forgotten.[31]

The priest is untouchable.

In *Kongi's Harvest* nearly everyone knuckles under to the President of Isma. The Carpenters Brigade, quite pardonably perhaps—they know no better—mindlessly mouth his slogans; but the Reformed Aweri are only a corporate manifestation of the earlier Court Historian of *A Dance of the Forests* who put into fine language what the master wished to hear. The traditional ruler, Oba Danlola, resists the dictator's power and is detained until he agrees to hand over his traditional authority by presenting the new yam to the dictator. In *The Interpreters* the five young protagonists find themselves constantly coming into collision, often only to their own damage, with the established figures of society. They indeed become in various ways the sacrifices to their own ideas.

The theme of sacrifice, as has been hinted, pervades Soyinka's work. In their own way, Chume, Igwezu, the Captain in *A Dance of the Forests*, the five interpreters, Oba Danlola, and of course Eman in *The Strong Breed*. The whole of Soyinka's work, like the road which he so often uses as a symbol of both sides of the coin of progress, is strewn with the debris of sacrifice. This theme appears so often and in so many different ways that it needs a special mention.

The Road as an insatiable receiver of victims is one of Soyinka's most common images. No doubt the Lagos–Ibadan road on which the author must have made innumerable hazardous journeys, and which is strewn with the wreckage of uncountable crashes, must have burned this particular form of sacrifice into his brain. One of his poems,

'Death at Dawn', is a direct result of an actual occurrence, and in this poem the image of sacrifice is the dominant one. The involuntary sacrifice of the white cock which should have appeased the road, the folk augury, and the fruitless prayer, all suggestive of attempts to appease the gods, are found in these lines:

> On this
> Counterpane, it was—
> Sudden winter at the death
> Of dawn's lone trumpeter, cascades
> Of white feather-flakes, but it proved
> A futile rite. Propitiation sped
> Grimly on, before.
>   The right foot for joy, the left, dread
>   And the mother prayed, Child
>   May you never walk
>   When the road waits famished.[32]

The sacrifice, like the augury and the prayer were all vain. The famished road demanded human sacrifice. The Traveller was

> Silenced in the startled hug of [his] invention.[33]

Other personal experiences contributed to Soyinka's near obsession with death (particularly instantaneous death) on the roads. The death of Segun Awolowo in a road accident was another such instance when the road became personified in Soyinka's writing:

> The road, the aged road
> Retched on this fresh plunder
> Of my youth
>
> An error of the sun
> A mirage upon earth's
> Apostate face.[34]

Not for nothing is death called 'The Scrap iron dealer'. The prayer 'May you never walk when the road waits famished' occurs in one form or another in 'Death at Dawn', in *The Road*,[35] and elsewhere in Soyinka's work.

In *A Dance of the Forests* the theme of death on the roads is combined with that of municipal corruption when the smoky truck nicknamed 'Chimney of Breko' becomes a funeral pyre for sixty-five of the seventy-five luckless souls who trusted themselves to its overloaded body. In *The Interpreters*, Sekoni loses his life in a road accident (the language is reminiscent of 'Death at Dawn'):

> Too late he saw the insanity of a lorry parked right in his path, a swerve turned into a skid and cruel arabesques of tyres. A futile heap of metal, and Sekoni's body lay surprised across the open door, showers of laminated glass around him, his beard one fastness of blood and wet earth.[36]

All these deaths on the roads may be called involuntary sacrifices to progress. (One here recalls the Bale of Baroka's reservations on progress and his reference to 'the murderous roads'.) The victim of the road as unwilling victim is only one facet of Soyinka's treatment of the theme of sacrifice. Throughout his work there are voluntary sacrifices when the victim walks to an avoidable fate with his eyes open, urged on by a compelling inner prompting which makes a fatal end almost inevitable. Such is the sacrifice of Eman in *The Strong Breed*, the most obvious example of this theme in Soyinka's work.

Eman is a martyr to society. He offers his life to an ungrateful society when, by just doing nothing, or obeying the voice of an easy prudence (represented by Sunma) he could have gone on living. Time after time Sunma tries to drag him away:

> You are wasting your life on people
> Who really want you out of their way.[37]

The tooting lorry signals his last chance of going away with Sunma, but he cannot help himself. In his own words, 'Renouncing one's self is not so easy'.[38] And again, stressing the loneliness of the martyr:

> Those who have much to give fulfil themselves only in total loneliness.[39]

Eman, being only human (in spite of his heroism), had once sought to avoid his fate in his own village, but his father had warned:

> Your own blood will betray you, son, because you cannot hold it back. If you make it do less than this, it will rush to your head and burst it open.[40]

When the actual ordeal comes Eman's body flinches, but in the end, having offered himself in Ifada's place, he is sacrificed. Eman is represented in the play as a Christ-figure; the parallels are obvious: he is willing to die for a thankless people, at the end he flinches at the physical ordeal, and he dies lifted high on a tree. It would have been uncharacteristic for Soyinka to prolong the play in order to show a people totally repentant and converted as a result of witnessing Eman's sacrifice. Yet he does give a faint glimmer of hope. According to tradition, the villagers were supposed to cast their evils on their selected victim by cursing him. They would have done this cheerfully to the idiot Ifada, an unwilling victim. But at the sight of a willing victim, one who had done only good to the village,

> One and all they looked up at the man and words died in their throats. . . . Not one could raise a curse.[41]

They sulk away from their leaders who have to have strangers for victims and dare not sacrifice themselves. Eman's death had at least sown doubt. Perhaps what he could not achieve by his life he could begin to achieve with his death. Eman made the ultimate sacrifice which not everyone is called on to make, but there are lesser sacrifices to society's demands throughout Soyinka's work.

In his poem 'The Dreamer' there is another Christ-figure whose sacrifice seems to have a glimmer of hope. The poem starts with the figure (one of three) mounted higher than trees, an obvious reference to the Crucifixion, and ends with the bitter flowering of seeds sown by the act of sacrifice:

> Higher than trees a cryptic crown
> Lord of the rebel three
> Thorns lay on a sleep of down
> And myrrh; a mesh
> Of nails, of flesh
> And words that flowered free.
> A cleft between the birches
> Next year is reaping time
> The fruit will fall to searchers
> Cleansed of mould
> Chronicles of gold
> Mourn a fruit in prime.
> The burden bowed the boughs to earth.
> A girdle for the see
> And bitter pods gave voice birth
> A ring of stones
> And throes and thrones
> And incense on the sea.[42]

We are reminded of Tertullian's words, 'the blood of martyrs is the seed of the church'. Like the church, society's flower too seems to need stronger nourishment than water. It often demands blood. We seek for life in death.

In a poem which reminds us of Soyinka's earlier humour (he still has humour, only time has made it grimmer) he looks at this theme literally, as he pictures the pathologist exploring the corpse of the dead man to increase the fund of knowledge; but the tone is also mocking of the limitation of the pathologist's knowledge:

> his head was hollowed and his brain
> on scales—was this a trick to prove
> fore-knowledge after death?
>
> his flesh confesses what has stilled
> h's tongue; masked fingers think from him
> to learn, how not to die.[43]

There is hope, but no certainty. The masked fingers are still groping for knowledge; man is still engaged in the unending task of getting to know himself better and trying to conquer his own limitations: learning 'how not to die'.

Most of the themes which appear in Soyinka's work find room for expansion in his only novel to date, *The Interpreters*. The five principal young men, Sagoe, Bandale, Egbo, Kola and Sekoni, represent a new generation equipped with new skills, striving to get to grips with themselves and their environment. With them may be coupled other characters in the novel trying to battle their way into a personal understanding of themselves and the world, while still trying to live in it. Monica Faseyi, for example, an English girl thrown into a new environment, yoked with an incompatible partner, also has to make sense of her situation; this she tries to do. Dehinwa, a young Nigerian girl in a situation which is comparatively new in her society, that of a career girl living alone in the big city and yet trying to keep on her feet in the swirl, is yet another representative of her generation. So is the female university student who surrenders herself to nature and Egbo, finds herself pregnant and goes away not in a mood of despair but of decision. Her decision is stunning even to Egbo and Bandele:

> Now she's going to keep the baby she said, and continue here as a student.[44]

As far as her relations with Egbo are concerned, there is no pressure from her side:

When you are sure what you want to do you are to tell me and I will pass it on. And I am supposed to make you understand that you are under no obligation.[45]

This is no light decision but the girl had been helped to arrive at it by the very nastiness of 'respectable' people like Dr Lumoye. This unnamed girl is as much a symbol for the new generation as the male interpreters whose role is more obvious.

The strong vein of social criticism and comment which is found in Soyinka's work appears in full flower in *The Interpreters*. There are roughly two sorts of characters in the society that the novel portrays; the establishment figures, and the mavericks who do not accept without question the rules which in fact only govern surface appearances. This is indeed the crux of the matter. To a large extent, the mavericks are what they seem, while the establishment figures, on close examination, merely present a façade that does not represent their real selves. Since the mavericks so openly reject the insincerity of the establishment, and the establishment so thoroughly rejects the irreverence of the mavericks, the two groups are irreconcilable.

The case of Professor Oguazor's daughter neatly exemplifies the double standards of the establishment:

... Professor Oguazor had three sons and one five-year-old daughter only and the daughter gave him much sorrow and pain because he could not publicly acknowledge her since he had her by the housemaid and the poor girl was tucked away in a private school in Islington and in fact was Oguazor's favourite child and the plastic apple of his eye.[46]

Whatever sympathy Oguazor's inner anguish may have otherwise elicited is, even in this passage, undermined by the adjective 'plastic'. The Professor's natural feelings which would have elicited sympathy have been replaced by a plastic substitute—an artificial exterior. Indeed, all the flowers and fruit which form the main motif in the décor of his house are plastic, symbolizing the fact that the whole façade of his 'meral' (the pronunciation is his) exterior has nothing to do with his real life. This is what revolts Sagoe and makes him almost involuntarily start throwing Professor Oguazor's plastic treasures out of the window, a sign of his rejection of Oguazor's values:

In his hand was another of the apples and his hand was pulled back to send it after its brother. Vaguely he recalled that his hand had gone through a similar motion within the past . . . but time was now diffused for him—he could not recall the actual start to the ejection act.[47]

What the novel implicitly rejects is not so much the fact that Oguazor has a daughter by his housemaid, but the insincerity which makes him totally suppress that fact, a process which makes him totally uncompassionate when he discovers that a young student at the university is pregnant. When he decrees punishment for the young man responsible, his 'meral' tone is uncompromising:

> Well, see that he is expelled, of course. He deserves nothing less.
>
> . . .
>
> The college cannot afford to herve its name dragged down by the meral torpitude of irresponsible young men. The younger generation is too merally corrupt.[48]

It is this blatant hypocrisy and its accompanying total lack of compassion that the novel seeks to expose in figures like Professor Oguazor.

Professor Oguazor is only one example; Sir Derinola, the judge is another. His public image is that of the incorruptible judge, an image which he himself jealously nurtures:

> He, not a judge of character? What had he acquired from years at the bench if not this one ability, this wizardry to tell a man apart from his clothes, from his assumed humility or contrition? What was he if not the Oracle Divine who pierced the hearts of men and bared their hidden dreads and passions. For he was unimpeachable. For he was the last word but God.[49]

But this is only the façade—all the more monstrous because the insincerity verges on blasphemy. Sir Derin is however stripped of his façade, first in fantasy when in Sagoe's hangover vision he appears out of the brash, cheap wardrobe; a most appropriate setting for the cheap man he really is:

> . . . the wardrobe door pressed outwards, very slowly, and the good knight himself, came out, naked except for a pair of Dehinwa's brassières over his chest.[50]

(Why the brassière? To pin his medals on, of course!) Thus in fantasy Soyinka starts the stripping of Sir Derin. But there is also one scene from real life when Sir Derinola, tired of waiting outside Sagoe's hotel for the outcome of Chief Winsala's negotiations with Sagoe for a bribe, tiptoes in gingerly to investigate the cause of the delay, and stands revealed for what he really is:

. . . Sir Derinola was truly paralysed at the confrontation of a future image, and could not move to help. Now he saw Sagoe move forward, and tried to shrink back behind the palm. They gazed into each other, all subterfuge pointless. It was Sagoe who took his eyes away.[51]

This is Soyinka's technique of demolition. The values of the pillars of society are shown to be unreal. The interpreters on the other hand are engaged in finding a life which would be consistent—from which the pretences would be stripped. This so far society will not tolerate. This is the confrontation which *The Interpreters* presents. It is not an 'African' problem. Events all over the world have shown in the new generation a similar dissatisfaction with what to them is a façade concealing a rotten structure. Thus Soyinka, using a Nigerian setting, has portrayed a universal problem. This is what makes both this novel and the whole corpus of Soyinka's work universally valid. Through the particular and the local he sees through to the basic universal human problems.

Soyinka's ideas matured early. What has developed through his writing career is technique. This maturing of technique can be seen even in his use of the Nigerian background. As early as *The Lion and the Jewel* he was using Nigerian song, dance and mime, and using them meaningfully as part of the exposition and revelation process. The flashback to the photographer's first visit to Ilujinle is portrayed through drumming, dancing, and miming, as is the flashback to the visit of the white surveyor in the same play. This certainly enhances the spectacle of the play; but compared to the integration of Nigerian forms in *A Dance of the Forests* and *Kongi's Harvest*, this earlier use is just embellishment.[52] In *Idanre* too, the mythology is not just added on; the mythology is the poem. There is now total integration of theme and background.

There is a similar maturing in his other poetry. The wit is there, but it is now far more controlled; it has indeed become almost sombre. One can begin to see the Wole Soyinka of the 'three white hairs'.[53] Indeed the mature writer seems to be looking over his output and deciding what he would wish to be remembered by. *Idanre and Other Poems* excludes those early sparkling satirical portraits which for many readers still remain the essential Soyinka—'The Immigrant', 'The Other Immigrant', 'Telephone Conversation'. It even excludes the more serious 'Requiem'. If Soyinka has his way, his first play will now never be printed. He does not even want it referred to. If these early works are buried for ever, one part of Soyinka would be lost, but not the essential Soyinka. For all the ideas which appeared so early in his work reappear in more mature forms, and are presented with even greater technical skill, in the later works.

Notes

1 *An African Treasury*, Gollancz, 1961, p. 196.
2 Ibid., p. 196.
3 *Five Plays*, Oxford University Press, 1964, pp. 172-3.
4 Ibid., p. 196.
5 Ibid., p. 188.
6 Ibid., p. 195.
7 Ibid.
8 Ibid., pp. 197-8.
9 *Reflections*, African Universities Press, 1965, p. 62.
10 *Five Plays*, op. cit., p. 144.
11 Ibid., p. 101.
12 *The Road*, Oxford University Press, 1965, p. 68.
13 Ibid., p. 8.
14 Ibid., p. 69.
15 Ibid., p. 40.
16 *Five Plays*, op. cit., p. 51.
17 Ibid., p. 24.
18 Ibid., p. 53.
19 Ibid., p. 64.
20 Ibid., p. 57.
21 Ibid., pp. 57-8.
22 Ibid., p. 55.
23 *Idanre and Other Poems*, Methuen, 1967, pp. 75-6.
24 Ibid., pp. 57-8.
25 *Five Plays*, op. cit., p. 211.
26 Ibid., p. 193.
27 Ibid., p. 194.
28 Ibid.
29 Ibid., p. 231.
30 Ibid., p. 233.
31 Ibid., p. 196.
32 *Idanre and Other Poems*, op. cit., pp. 10-11.
33 Ibid., p. 11.

34 Ibid., p. 14.

35 *The Road*, op. cit., p. 60.

36 *The Interpreters*, André Deutsch, 1965, p. 155.

37 *Five Plays*, op. cit., p. 244.

38 Ibid., p. 246.

39 Ibid., p. 250.

40 Ibid., p. 261.

41 Ibid., p. 275.

42 *Idanre and Other Poems*, op. cit., p. 17.

43 Ibid., p. 31.

44 *The Interpreters*, op. cit., p. 242.

45 Ibid., p. 242.

46 Ibid., p. 149.

47 Ibid.

48 Ibid., p. 250.

49 Ibid., p. 80.

50 Ibid., p. 64.

51 Ibid., p. 92.

52 (According to Professor Jones's sources, *The Lion and the Jewel* was produced in Ibadan in 1959 and in London before then, whereas *A Dance of the Forests* was commissioned for Nigeria's independence later. *Editor.*)

53 *Idanre and Other Poems*, op. cit. See poem, 'To my first White Hairs', p. 30.

Christopher Okigbo

by Paul Theroux

There is no question about it: Okigbo is an obscure poet, possibly the most difficult poet in Africa. There are two ways of approaching him; one is to look at his poems, the other is to listen to his music.

By 'looking' I mean examining each word he uses, each echo from another poet (for there are many echoes; he was an extremely well-read person). To do this one would have to make a long list which would include such strange words as *kepkanly, anagnorisis, Yunice, Upandru, enki, Flannagan* and perhaps a hundred others. The meaning of these words would have to be found, and then it would be necessary to fit this meaning into the line, ignoring the word for the time being.

I tried this once and I was fortunate in having Okigbo a few feet away to correct my mistakes in interpretation. I was especially disturbed by 'Flannagan'; I could not find a reference to it. I asked Okigbo to tell me what it meant.

'Flannagan,' said Okigbo, 'was a priest that used to teach me in Primary School. He ran the Mission near my village.'

This can be deduced from the context I think, for the lines run:

> And to the cross in the void
>   came pilgrims,
> Came floating with burnt-out tapers:
> Past the village orchard
>   where FLANNAGAN
> Preached the Pope's message. . . .[1]

The capital letters, so huge in a poem, can be rather frightening. But the explanation is unnecessary: if someone preaches 'the Pope's message' he must be either a Catholic priest or an ardent parishioner. One other example will show how looking may yield an approach. In the poem *Heavensgate*, these lines occur:

> etru bo pi alo a she[2]

and these sound like a mysterious vernacular, very obscure. Their meaning is

little Bo-Peep has lost her sheep

and they are from a poem celebrating past experiences, events in youth. But I needed Okigbo to tell me this personally.

Many people have criticized Okigbo for writing as he did, and some of this criticism is well-founded. How can the average reader know that Flannagan is a priest and that those odd words quoted above are really a children's nursery rhyme? The other words mentioned above are equally obscure, and there are many others in Okigbo's poems that baffle and anger readers. Is it fair for a writer to use words that his readers don't understand? Fair or not, many writers do it. Obscurity itself is not the sign of a talented writer. Very often, deliberate obscurity signals that the writer does not know what he is talking about, or may mean that the writer does not know how to say what he wants. A poet may present us with a mysterious little poem and teachers and critics may make a name for themselves by unravelling the mystery and showing us what exactly the poet meant to say or what he was getting at. It is possible that, in this exercise of interpretation, the critic may find more in the poem than the writer put in. This happens all the time, and it happens with Okigbo's critics more than others because there is often a smokescreen of obscurity thrown up which hides the meaning of the poem.

With Okigbo this must be accepted. There is not much use in saying that he is not obscure, because he certainly is, but once this has been accepted an approach to the poem can be made.

The approach can be made through the second method. That is, by listening. Looking is confusion: what we see in the poem may be an impenetrable mystery, and there are words and phrases in Okigbo's poetry that are nearly impossible to figure out. Listening is simpler and more rewarding; there is music in this poetry, and if we listen closely we hear three separate melodies: the music of youth, the clamour of passage (that is, growing up) and lastly, the sounds of thunder.

Often, the themes are mixed, the youthful music is overshadowed by sounds that suggest movement and growth. In 1962, in a little note to *Silences*, Okigbo wrote:

The author wishes to acknowledge his debt to those composers whose themes he has used or varied in certain parts of the present work. The *Introit* is a variation on a theme in Raja Ratnam's *At Eight-fifteen in the Morning:* the first three passages of the first movement are variants on a theme by Malcolm Cowley; 'Sandbanks sprinkled with memories' in the 4th passage of the same movement is a variation on Stéphane Mallarmé's 'au bosquet arrosé d'accords' in his *L'Après-midi d'un Faune*; the 6th passage of the same movement . . . etc.[3]

Besides showing how widely influenced Okigbo was, this also shows how he combined the elements of many different themes into one, by making it musical; he used an American and a Bengali theme and mingled these separate voices together with his own.

In the youthful music, therefore, there is also the portent of growing and danger. In *Heavensgate* (i) he says:

> On far side a rainbow
> arched like a boa bent to kill
> foreshadows the rain that is dreamed of.[4]

This contains a kind of warning; the lovely rainbow is snakelike, 'arched like a boa'. Then he goes on. The next lines are:

> Me to the orangery
> solitude invites,
> a wagtail, to tell
> the tangled-wood-tale;
> a sunbird, to mourn
> a mother on a spray.[5]

This is clear. Solitude invites him to tell his story; he is a bird, first a wagtail, then a sunbird (later he will take on other forms). At the end of this significant section he says first:

> Rain and sun in single combat[6]

which, in the Heavens, seems to describe storm feuding with sun. This is going on high above the bird, and the bird is, for the moment, uninvolved. He is

> on one leg standing
> in silence at the passage
> the young bird at the passage.[7]

Here, in all these lines, we have a wonderful picture of youth, one set in the open with sun and rain, the twittering of birds, a rainbow and beneath it all—but able to fly above it all—the bird. Perhaps, the

137

'sunbird' represents the poet, or maybe it represents the poetic spirit
or it could be that the sunbird is a kind of conscience singing warnings
and delivering visions. Whatever it is, it appears again and again, not
only in *Heavensgate* but also in other poems where it is a significant
feature, one that we recognize and hang on to, for its familiarity
reassures us when we are faced with obscurity. The obscurity ceases to
matter, for Okigbo is able to create his own personal comprehensible
myth and to offer us a number of images that constantly recur. In
Limits the sunbird appears again:

> The Sunbird sings again
> From the LIMITS of the dream,
> The Sunbird sings again
> Where the caress does not reach,
> of Guernica,
> On whose canvas of blood,
> The newsprint-slits of his tongue
> cling to glue. . . .[8]

This is a more frightening vision than that of a simple snake. The
'Guernica' mentioned in the second stanza is the painting by Pablo
Picasso of a bombing in Spain during the Civil War; the texture of the
painting is described minutely. This also illustrates the point of the two
themes, the two kinds of music we sometimes find in Okigbo. The
consistent use of imagery in these poems indicates that Okigbo knew
what he was doing. The bird imagery is the most constant in these
poems of youth, for *Limits* begins:

> SUDDENLY becoming talkative
> like weaverbird
> Summoned at offside of
> dream remembered. . . .[9]

And along with these vivid images of fluttering birds is the figure of the
poet himself, for these poems *Heavensgate* and *Limits* are two long poems
of youth and the process of maturing (which sometimes Okigbo calls
'purification' or 'cleansing'). The birds remain present, sometimes in
the speaker, sometimes representing the speaker, sometimes outside
the speaker:

> And when we were great boys
> hiding at the smithies
> we sang words after the bird—
> .   .   .   .   .   .

> still sings the sunbird
> under the lamp. . . .[10]

While this is going on the presence of the boy is felt; attention shifts from this person who appears in all the poems (we can call him 'The Poet', or 'The Voice' or even Okigbo) to what is happening around him. First he stands ceremoniously

> Before you, mother Idoto,
> naked I stand,
> before your watery presence,
> a prodigal. . . .[11]

This figure wanders through the poems and is referred to, in *Heavensgate*, as 'the prodigal', for his return is a return to innocence. The striking section of *Heavensgate*, one which is often quoted as a separate poem, is the one in which the 'prodigal' passes by the landscape he knew well. But this is the same person or 'identity' that is seen in all the other poems; and when this following section is taken into consideration with all that is said later (in the poems *Limits*, *Silences* and *Distances*) it takes on a larger significance, for the 'newcomer' is just beginning to experience the feelings and sensations of his surroundings:

> In the chill breath
> of the day's waking
>
> comes the newcomer
> when the draper of May
> has sold out fine green
> garments, and the hillsides
> have made up their faces,
> and the gardens,
> on their faces
> a painted smile:
>
> such synthetic welcome
>
> at the cock's third siren
> when from behind bulrushes
> waking
> in the teeth of the chill Maymorn
>
> comes the newcomer.[12]

With growth come pain and disappointment; the 'synthetic welcome' the newcomer gets here is nothing compared to the disillusionment he realizes later on (the vision of Guernica, for example). The image changes in *Limits*; the 'newcomer' is simply 'He'. But his passage is never comfortable; he is always reaching upwards, seeking the sky, like the bird that guides him:

> FOR HE WAS a shrub among the poplars
> Needing more roots
> More sap to grow to sunlight
> Thirsting for sunlight[13]

And later in the same poem:

> HE STOOD in the midst of them all
> and appeared in true form,
> He found them drunken, he found none
> thirsty among them.[14]

He needs sunlight; he tries to grow. The image of the 'shrub among the poplars' changes to that of a prodigal when he sees, with disappointment, that there is no one to help, no one to hear him. But he offers, with this difficulty of growing, a solution and it is the same as was seen earlier, in the first stanzas of *Heavensgate*. It is to become bird-like, if one is unique and one can sing; recognizing that he is a stranger, he suggests in *Limits*:

> Then we must sing
> Tongue-tied without name or audience,
> Making harmony among the branches.[15]

If *Heavensgate* and *Limits* are concerned with youth and growth, then *Silences* and *Distances*, two other long poems, are concerned with emptiness and disappointment at having arrived. Before I proceed I should make one point clear: all these long poems appear to me to be about the same person. As I said above, this person could be Okigbo, or 'The Poet' (or The Creative Personality) or simply a man. For the sake of simplicity I think we should call the subject of these poems 'Okigbo', for there are too many similarities between Chris Okigbo and the 'He' of the poems for us to ignore this fact.

Silences is a meditation on emptiness. The first stanza of this poem is significant, for two reasons: it has a religious quality (it even begins with an 'Introit') that is not found in any of the other poems, and it has a note of quiet futility that appears in most of the other poems; these two qualities, one new, one familiar, are quite characteristic of Okigbo. He does not introduce something new in a poem without blending it with something familiar, either an image, or a favourite word or sound. The first line of the poem sets the mood:

> So one dips one's pen in the ocean,
>   and begins
> to write on the mushroom of the sky. . . .[16]

This vivid image of a vast task is only the beginning, but it comes after the turbulence of growth. As this is a meditation, Okigbo puts himself into perspective: the image is both 'literary' and about a writer. The next incident in the poem shows futility:

> And there was a continual going to the well,
>   until they smashed their calabashes. . . .[17]

To reinforce this, Okigbo introduces a 'Chorus' which begins chanting in verses which call to mind T. S. Eliot; the echo is so strong that we may usefully question the skill of lines such as these:

> We are the dumb bells
> We are the dumb bells
> Outside the gates
> In hollow landscapes. . . .[18]

When Eliot in his poem 'The Hollow Men' begins:

> We are the hollow men
> We are the stuffed men
> Leaning together
> Headpiece filled with straw. Alas![19]

And Eliot's first stanza ends:

> In our dry cellar.

Obviously Okigbo was trying to say something; unfortunately, what he was trying to say, and the way he was trying to say it, is rather too close to the way Eliot is making and thinking his poem. If we are sure that Okigbo means no parody of Eliot, then these lines are not really to Okigbo's credit; they're too close for comfort. When form *and* meaning are being copied, then we can't use the word *influence*. It is more like imitation.

But this is not as serious as it sounds, for Okigbo's intention is to extend the lines that he composed earlier in *Limits*:

> They cast him in mould of iron,
> And asked him to do a rock-drill:
>   Man out of innocence—
> He drilled with dumb bells around him.[20]

This is the sort of repetitive image ('dumb bells') that Okigbo uses. He was talking about newly lost innocence then; now, in *Silences*, he is brooding over the effects of this lost innocence: *Silences* is important for this, for it contains lines which are central to an understanding of Okigbo the poet, and Okigbo the person, moving through the poems. He says:

> In our worlds that flourish
> Our worlds that have failed.
>   This song is our swan song
>   This song is the stillness of our breath.
> No song is your swan song
> Let every voice keep its own breath.
>   This song is our swan song
>   This song is our senses' silence.
>
>   .   .   .   .   .
>
> Each song is the sigh of your spirits:
> Unseen shadows, like long-fingered
> Winds, are plucking from your strings the—
> This song is the—music of the firmament.[21]

This sounds confusing and contradictory, but if it is remembered that the poem is called *Silences* then it should not be hard to grasp the meaning. I think we can take the line:

> No song is your swan song

to mean that the end is met in silence ('No song') and without music there can be no statement. It is a plea for maintaining the music that is in all his poems and it is an affirmation of the meditative individual ('Each song is the sigh of your spirits'). So 'No song is your swan song' and 'This song is our senses' silence'. There is silence without music; and music creates its own silence (the 'senses' silence'). Besides being musical itself, the passage is a calm reflection, very peaceful, at the centre of an unbelievably turbulent cycle of poems. He ends *Silences* with the lovely lines:

> One dips one's tongue into the ocean;
> Camps with the choir of inconstant
> Dolphins, by shallow sand banks

> Sprinkled with memories;
> Extends one's branches of coral,
> The branches extend in the senses'
> Silence; this silence distils
> In yellow melodies.[22]

It is safe to say that very few poems achieve the music and harmony that *Silences* does, and the poem can be read aloud simply for the pleasure of hearing beautiful syllables like these sliding against each other.

Distances, the next poem in the cycle, is painful. It was written by Okigbo while in hospital undergoing an operation, and all the pain of surgery is present in the poem. The epigraph to the poem is:

> When you have finished,
> and done up my stitches,
> Wake me near the altar,
> *& this poem will be finished.*[23]

So we have an echo of the pain we first heard in *Limits* (iv), again repeated in this poem of a later passage. *Distances* seems to be the last poem in the series concerned with what I called 'the clamour of passage'. There are shocking images in *Distances* and, while we may have been lulled or calmed by the words in the cycle until now, we have never been shocked. The language in this poem is at times violent and seems to be a forewarning of 'the sounds of thunder' that we will hear later. The opening is stark:

> From flesh into phantom,
> On the horizontal stone:
> I was the sole witness to my homecoming. . . .[24]

The 'horizontal stone' is of course a slab in a morgue which holds a corpse, the imagined corpse of Okigbo, transforming into a spirit. But this also seems to indicate understanding; the line 'I was the sole witness to my homecoming' means that something has been achieved, the long-sought-after maturity has been reached; but it has been reached at such a distant point that Okigbo is alone in his reverie of understanding. He understands only himself. This line is repeated throughout the poem. The death is described:

> Death lay in ambush,
> that evening in that island;
> and the voice sought its echo,

> that evening in that island.
> And the eye lost its light,
> and the light lost its shadow. . . .[25]

Again, we have the compulsive repetition of images, but this time it is Okigbo's own voice, not the borrowed phrases of Eliot. It is worth printing the whole following section of the poem to show just how horrific the images of death are. And when one considers how Okigbo died in 1967, these lines take on an even grislier significance. It might be worth while mentioning the fact that Okigbo often wrote his poems to the accompaniment of drums, or imagined drumbeats with his poems, highlighting the imagery. While reading these following lines, one can imagine the steady beat of an ominous drum, thudding *doom, doom, doom*:

> And it was an evening without flesh or skeleton;
> an evening with no silver bells to its tale;
> without lanterns; without buntings;
> and it was an evening without age or memory—
> for we are talking of such commonplace things,
> and on the brink of such great events—
> and in the freezing tuberoses of the white
> chamber, eyes that had lost their animal
> colour—havoc of incandescent rays—
> pinned me, cold, to the marble stretcher,
>   until my eyes lost their blood,
>   and the blood lost its odour;
> and the everlasting fire from the oblong window
> forgot the taste of ash in the air's marrow . . .
> Anguish and solitude . . .
> Smothered my scattered
> cry, the dancers,
> lost among their own
> snares; the faces,
> the hands, held captive;
> the interspaces
> reddening with blood . . .
> And behind them all,
> in smock of white cotton,
> Death herself,
> the chief celebrant,
> in a cloud of incense,
> paring her fingernails . . .
> At her feet roll their heads like cut fruits;

about her fall
their severed members, numerous as locusts.
Like split wood left to dry,
the dismembered joints
of the ministrants pile high.[26]

That is the end of the second section of *Distances*. There are six sections in the complete poem, all tracing the agony of suffering through death's narrow passage. But it is clear that Okigbo here has passed through death to another form; he has traced his death in the poem and equates death not with silence but rather with the ultimate purification. And at the end of this poem, this segment of poetry which is part of his whole poem, familiar images are seen and heard, even the titles of the separate poems are given at one point:

lo, it is the same blood that flows . . .
Shadows distances labyrinths violences,
skeletal oblong of my sentient being. . . .[27]

'Shadows', 'Distances', and 'Violences' are all poems that Okigbo either wrote or planned to write as part of his large body of work which was to be published under the title *Labyrinths*. So here is the link, and again here:

and in the orangery of immense corridors,
I wash my feet
in your pure head, O maid,
and walk along your feverish,
solitary shores,
seeking . . .
I have fed out of the drum
I have drunk out of the cymbal
I have entered your bridal
chamber; and lo,
I am the sole witness to my homecoming.[28]

The 'orangery' mentioned above is the same as that in *Heavensgate*:

Me to the orangery
solitude invites . . .[29]

and the 'Maid' mentioned is the 'Watermaid' of *Heavensgate*. He has woven all these images into this last, triumphant sequence of dying and rebirth. The loneliness of the lines 'I am the sole witness' is intentional.

145

He was trying earlier on to preach, to carry others along with him; he failed and is now, in a state of precious purification, alone.

This all seems clear when the significant passages are removed from the body of the various parts of the long poem. But in the poems, all through them, along with the familiar images we have come to recognize and understand, are still obscurities, impenetrable images and difficult words. It is best to ignore these for the time being; understanding may come. There is not space enough in this little essay to explain them all. Okigbo was a careful craftsman; when he wanted someone to understand, when he considered something important enough to be made absolutely clear, he took pains to write with the utmost clarity. One could make too much of the obscurities, but as the poems stand—*Heavensgate, Limits, Silences, Distances*—there is plenty to digest without complicating the essential point: a man in search of purification, beset by visions and delays, fighting his way toward death.

Okigbo's last poems, written from December 1965 to January 1966, are entitled 'Path of Thunder'.[30] They were hailed as 'poems prophesying war' but they are more than this; they are poems announcing Okigbo's involvement in the war as well, and all through them the ravages of war and death are described. It is clear from them which side Okigbo had chosen to support, but these are anything but partisan poems. They are an attempt to link all the earlier poems to the events in Nigeria in 1965-6. In all the poems that precede these it is sometimes hard to tell where they are set; they are certainly set in the open, in jungles or holy forests, but the symbols are universal, with the exception of some small obscure details that must be Nigerian. But 'Path of Thunder' is different. The concern is Nigerian; the voice is definitely Okigbo's (these are the only poems in which he used his own name) and they are about politics and war. He was well aware of the risks he was taking in speaking so bluntly:

> If I don't learn to shut my mouth I'll soon go to hell,
> I, Okigbo, town-crier, together with my iron bell.[31]

In *Heavensgate*, there were the lines:

> And he said to the ram:
> disarm.[32]

This image of a ram appears again, as forceful as before. If there were ever any doubts as to whether Okigbo was making one large poem out of all these cantos, it should be clear reading 'Path of Thunder' that he not only maintained the earlier poetic impulses but also fused these

146

into a statement about military politics which is both a lament and a
call to action:

> O mother mother Earth, unbind me; let this be
>   my last testament; let this be
> The ram's hidden wish to the sword the sword's
>   secret prayer to the scabbard—
>
> .   .   .   .   .   .
>
> THE GLIMPSE of a dream lies smouldering in a cave,
>   together with the mortally wounded birds.
> Earth, unbind me; let me be the prodigal; let this be
>   the ram's ultimate prayer to the tether.[33]

'Path of Thunder' is divided into six sections. In the first, 'Thunder
Can Break' there is 'Fanfare of drums, wooden bells: iron chapter' and
an incident is retold in circling language, which at times is brutal,
celebrating a savage ritual, at other times gently ironic:

> Iron has made, alas, masterpieces—
> Statuettes of legendary heroes—iron birds
>   Held—fruit of flight—tight;
>
> For barricaded in iron handiwork a miracle caged.
>
> Bring them out we say, bring them out
> Faces and hands and feet,
> The stories behind the myth, the plot
> Which the ritual enacts.[34]

In the next poem, 'Elegy of the wind', Okigbo meditates, as in *Silences*.
The effect is particularly unsettled, for it combines peaceful reflection
with the sounds of thunder in the background. At one moment he
considers the earlier image, 'he was a sapling among the poplars'
(*Limits*, IV):

> For I have lived the sapling sprung from the bed
>   of the old vegetation;
> Have shouldered my way through a mass of ancient
>   nights to chlorophyll. . . .[35]

In the next moment, the emotion shifts to fear, with lines of terrible
beauty, the quaking man, the poet unfaltering:

> The child in me trembles before the high shelf
>   on the wall,

> The man in me shrinks before the narrow neck of
> a calabash;
>
> And the chant, already all wings, follows
> In its ivory circuit behind the thunder clouds,
> The slick route of the feathered serpent. . . .[36]

The poet is urging himself out of his solitude and requiring a summoning of masculine powers. Emerging, the landscape (again 'The hollow landscapes' of *Silences*) appears in all its horrible aspect; war is coming and Okigbo sees it, describes it, witnesses it. It is a homecoming, and we might even say that he was the 'sole witness' to it, but here there is a greater involvement, for all the fury of the lines indicates that he is not alone:

> The smell of blood already floats in the lavender-mist of the after-
> noon.
> The death sentence lies in ambush along the corridors of power;
> And a great fearful thing already tugs at the cables of the open air,
> A nebula immense and immeasurable, a night of deep waters—
> An iron dream unnamed and unprintable, a path of stone.
>
> The drowsy heads of the pods in barren farmlands witness it,
> The homesteads abandoned in this century's brush fire witness it:
> The myriad eyes of deserted corn cobs in burning barns witness it;
> Magic birds with the miracle of lightning flash on their
> feathers. . . .[37]

The simple phrase, 'An iron dream unnamed and unprintable' surely must be one of the best descriptions of war's horrors ever written. But he does not stop there. He goes on in 'Elegy for slit drum', with war symbols juxtaposed with the definite. First the forest tyranny:

> the panther has delivered a hare
> the hare is beginning to leap
> the panther has delivered a hare
> the panther is about to pounce.[38]

Then, the refrain with variations is repeated through this Elegy, 'Condolences already in flight under the burden of this century' he goes on:

> parliament has gone on leave
> the members are now on bail
> parliament is now on sale
> the voters are lying in wait.[39]

The two stanzas quoted above are characteristic of the mingling of the obscure and the familiar: the strange symbolism of panther and hare, and then the sarcasm of parliament and voters, not waiting to vote, but 'lying in wait'. One of the final stanzas of this elegy sharply depicts war's madness. Throughout 'Path of Thunder' is the recurring image of an elephant, large, obdurate, powerful, towering among lesser animals:

> the elephant ravages the jungle
> the jungle is peopled with snakes
> the snake says to the squirrel
> I will swallow you
> the mongoose says to the snake
> I will mangle you
> the elephant says to the mongoose
> I will strangle you. . . .[40]

Here is the aggression; it is aggression that is unexpected, but predictable. There were beasts in all the earlier parts of the long cycle, but they sang; these beasts are killers. In *Heavensgate* and *Limits* there were birds: the wagtail, the sunbird and others. These small birds do not appear in this last poem. The bird that is most constant in 'Path of Thunder' is the Eagle:

> THE EAGLES have come again,
> the eagles rain down on us
>
> .   .   .   .   .   .
>
> THE EAGLES have chosen their game,
> Taken our concubines—[41]

This is the last section of the poem, and may be considered to be the final word of Okigbo. It is 'Elegy for alto', a staccato lament, riddled with alternating images of robbers, eagles and politicians. It is poetic without being the least bit obscure:

> POLITICIANS are back in the giant hidden steps of howitzers, of
>   detonators—
> THE EAGLES descend on us,
> Bayonets and cannons—
> THE ROBBERS descend on us to strip us of our laughter, of our
>   thunder—
> THE EAGLES have chosen their game,
> Taken our concubines—
> POLITICIANS are here in this iron dance of mortars, of generators. . . .[42]

This is how the cycle of poems heads towards an untimely end. Okigbo died in batttle in 1967, near Nsukka. It seems clear that he was trying to control his material, all the factors that influenced his loyalties, trying to make these images fit the larger structure of his imagined poem, *Labyrinths*. And I think all of it does fit, for he conceived the poem so that it would embody all experience, and however unpoetic war is, he managed to combine this as well.

Many biographies of Africans have been written, detailing the early rural life, the amazement at discovering education and political independence, the confusions and complexes wrought by urban life; and later the coups, the disappointment, the corrupt politics. In a much shorter space Okigbo has done all this; he has composed, in verse, an African autobiography, with all its pain and beauty, terror and mystery. At times it seems unfathomable, but the moment passes, and soon we are in familiar territory, the obscurity is like a cloud passing, it is brief but leaves an impression on us that we do not forget. Later, we may be able to piece this obscurity with something known and the result is often enlightenment.

'Path of Thunder' is a war poem; it is about the war that killed Okigbo himself. It is perhaps a testimony to his skill that even in this poem describing war's horrors, there is beauty. The end of this poem is also the end of the cycle of poems that began with *Heavensgate*. The last four lines describe what Okigbo stood for, constantly hoping that against chaos there could be beauty and order:

> AN OLD STAR departs, leaves us here on the shore
> Gazing heavenward for a new star approaching;
> The new star appears, foreshadows its going
> Before a going and coming that goes on forever.[43]

Notes

1 *Limits*, Christopher Okigbo, Ibadan, 1964, Part VII (pages not numbered).

2 *Heavensgate*, Christopher Okigbo, Ibadan, 1962, p. 9.

3 'Silences', *Transition Magazine*, No. 8, Kampala, 1963, pp. 13-16.

4 *Heavensgate*, op. cit., p. 8.

5 Ibid.

6 Ibid.

7 Ibid.

8 *Limits*, op. cit., Part X.

9 Ibid., Part I.

10 *Heavensgate*, op. cit., p. 9.

11 Ibid., p. 5.

12 Ibid., p. 37.

13 *Limits*, op. cit., Part II.

14 Ibid., Part VI.

15 Ibid., Part III.

16 'Silences', *Transition*, No. 8, p. 14.

17 Ibid.

18 Ibid.

19 T. S. Eliot, *Selected Poems of T. S. Eliot*, Faber, London, 1954, p. 72.

20 *Limits*, op. cit., Part VI.

21 'Silences', op. cit., p. 14.

22 Ibid., p. 16.

23 *Limits*, op. cit., Part IV.

24 'Distances', Christopher Okigbo, *Transition*, No. 16, Kampala, 1964, pp. 9-13.

25 Ibid., p. 10.

26 Ibid.

27 Ibid., p. 13.

28 Ibid.

29 *Heavensgate*, op. cit., p. 8.

30 'Path of Thunder', Christopher Okigbo, *Black Orpheus*, Vol. 2, Vol 1, 1968, pp. 5-11.

31 Ibid., p. 8.

32 *Heavensgate*, op. cit., p. 19.

33 'Path of Thunder', op. cit., p. 11.

34 Ibid., p. 5.

35 Ibid., p. 6.

36 Ibid., pp. 6-7.

37 Ibid., p. 7.

38 Ibid., p. 8.

39 Ibid.

40 Ibid., p. 9.

41 Ibid., p. 10.

42 Ibid.

43 Ibid., p. 11.

The Poetry and Drama of John Pepper Clark

by Dan Izevbaye

For the student of Nigerian literature J. P. Clark is interesting not only for the quality of his poetry but for his historical importance as one of the first poets to begin writing the type of verse that should eventually lead to the foundation of a national tradition of Nigerian poetry. He first showed promise of this as founder of the now defunct student magazine, *The Horn*.[1] The work of student contributors to this magazine, together with verse by a few others like Soyinka and Okara, first indicated a new trend in Nigerian poetry. About the time of the début of these poets, Ulli Beier, one of the first critics to appreciate the value of this new direction, noticed that these writers were handicapped by the absence of appropriate literary models.[2] The only existing poets were the pioneers of the forties and fifties; but no serious young writer would have chosen these poets for his literary mentors, and nobody now reads pioneer verse except political historians interested in West African nationalism. And although the new poets showed, like the pioneers, an occasional tendency to lean on conventional English poetic models because of the absence of a clearly defined written tradition in English, they represented not merely a more fundamental approach but an altogether new direction. Clark's verse was an example of this new fundamental approach, and Ulli Beier was quick to recognize this quality and to pick out Clark as one of the few who captured the spirit of the local setting in verse. Clark's success was due not only to this gift for re-creating the local environment but also his genuine interest in the oral traditions which formed the only extant tradition. Clark was to complain later that Nigerians did not know as much about their oral traditions as they did about European mythologies.[3]

Apart from the absence of a written tradition which made the creation of a genuine national verse tradition a difficulty, the Nigerian poet also had to contend with the prejudice that the writer in a developing country is free from those sophisticated inhibitions which stifle the creative mind. Apparently he had only to look in his heart and write. Because of the spontaneous nature of his own verse Clark has had to contend with this prejudice in a greater measure than other writers. That is why he has objected to the biographical note which informs the reader that Clark has facial marks 'as is the custom of his tribe'.[4] That is why too there is a similar incident in the report of his American experience in which Clark attempts to convince a medical man at a party that the marks on his face are not 'tribal marks' but inoculation scars.[5]

Clark's protest at these two varieties of the image of the noble savage has wider implications than the implied primitivism which it attacks. The critic who approaches the poetry from such a standpoint might tend to suggest, even inadvertently, that craftsmanship is not an important concern of the African poet. Therefore if the following comment on Clark's poetry seems to highlight an important quality of his poetry it does not really represent the literary goal at which Clark was striving:

> I imagine him writing in a kind of explosion, under the extreme pressure of experience, writing only if cornered by life, as it were, and then having got the thing off his chest losing interest and turning to the next thing.[6]

There is evidence that Clark sought to discipline this Romantic type of creative spontaneity. That he does not lose interest in his poems once they are written may be evident in the slight, occasional changes which occur in poems republished in his second poetry volume, *A Reed in the Tide*.

The collection falls almost neatly into two halves. The first part ends with the two segments from 'Ivbie', nineteen poems, all re-collected from the 1960 Mbari publication; and the second part contains the new poems, sixteen in all, mainly those written during Clark's visit to America as a Parvin scholar. Some of the poems do not of course fall strictly into this neat grouping. Thematically speaking, 'Emergency Commission', 'His Excellency the Masquerader' and 'Child Asleep' do not belong to the second part.

Between these two broad divisions there may be discerned a continuity of attitude. There is, however, a falling off in literary performance in some of the latter poems. The first two poems, 'For Granny (from Hospital)' and 'Night Rain', are poems about early childhood and innocence in a setting in which the poet feels perfectly at ease. Later there is 'Agbor Dancer', in which the poet expresses a sense of alienation from the native culture which should have sired his poetic creations. And appropriately, although the subject of 'Agbor Dancer' is indigenous, its literary model is 'scribal' in origin, for, apart from the Wordsworthian note on which it closes, its theme and even the alliterative pattern point to 'Kubla Khan'.

> Could I, early sequester'd from my tribe,
> Free a lead-tether'd scribe
> I should answer her communal call
> Lose myself in her warm caress
> Intervolving earth, sky and flesh.

It is clear from 'Agbor Dancer' that for all its expressed alienation from the mother culture, the poet's attitude to his subject is sensual and involved.

Just before the end of the first half of the collection, in 'Horoscope', the poet argues that the means of acquiring knowledge of the physical world has no more validity than the knowledge arrived at through a mystical probing of the spiritual. Here the poet's sympathies are with that communal lore which belongs to a different world from that of technology. As yet his attitude is not directly hostile to technological civilization, although it does indicate a slight shift from the 'detribalized' stance of 'Agbor Dancer'.

The last poems in this section of the collection are the two segments from 'Ivbie'. Published in its entirety in the Mbari collection, 'Ivbie' is a lament dealing with the infiltration of the white man into the household of the African because the gods who should be guarding the gates have been taken unaware. So the poet sounds the alarm in a threnodic note. In the two segments republished in *A Reed in the Tide*, the poet dissociates himself from the world of Western technology. He is no longer part of it as he suggested he was a part of the allied 'scribal tradition' in 'Agbor Dancer':

> Pass on in mad headlong flight
> So winding up your kaleidoscope
> Leave behind unhaunted
> An innocent in sleep of the ages.

The poet's self-identification with the innocence of his 'antediluvian' upbringing is clearly reflected in the primordial metaphors which he employs in the second half of *A Reed in the Tide*. Here the poet is no longer of that complex civilization of which the scribal tradition is but a symptom. Rather, there is an increasing rejection of the 'missile-hurled' civilization which once induced the smugness of 'Agbor Dancer'. Even the mechanical wonders which stimulated the gusto of 'Service' are played down by the closing comparison with the equivalent, but non-technological, wonders performed by Moses, the Hebrew law-giver:

> A dime
> in the slot,

And anything
from coke to coffee
Spews down your throat,
from crackers to candy
Breaks against the enamel
wear of your teeth . . .

Now, old Moses
for whom, they say,
Manna fell in the desert,
did he push a button as this,
and who knows at what price?

It is obvious, so far, that there is a development in the poet's attitude throughout *A Reed in the Tide*. There appears to be a search for a literary tradition that is not only national but also personal, and there is an increasing movement away from the borrowed tradition in spite of the continued use of its linguistic and technical apparatus. That is, the latter poems show less reliance on English poetic models, and pastiches like 'Ibadan Dawn' are few. But in spite of the gain by way of a more individual, more flexible idiom, the general effect of this section is less satisfying than that of the first. This is possibly because the sense of significance is absent in many of the latter poems. This has nothing to do with the content of the poems, for there is in fact frequent use of the epic device for conveying a sense of consequence by ranging over great space and time in verse. There is, for example, the bridging of the historical gap between a Boeing flight and a mythical flight:

Now, Sinbad
The Sailor, they say, got caught
Between the beak of Roc, and though dangling
Asleep, under unfailing spell,
Was whisked among the several
Wonders of this world.

Still in the same epoch, perhaps, the poet descends spatially into the sea bed in the world of fable:

the whale that shuns
Stars and sun, in a manner
Not really unlike ours, delivered
Jonah early enough to keep
Date with a certain destiny.

F

155

Thus the latter poems carry the impression of space and time, and this impression is strengthened by the allusions to world mythology, just as the local allusions lend vigour to the earlier poems.

But not many poems carry a strong sense of significance. 'Flight across Africa' is one of the few. In this aerial picture, railway tracks and train coaches are reconstructed in the metaphor of a religious sacrifice which occurred in the poet's youth:

> Earth, from miles up, lies
> Slaughtered, the splintered green of plantain
> About her. Still the coaches and trucks
> Pummel the body, their tracks
> Of scars, sharp lines against the skies,
> Horizontal spits and stakes that pin
> Down the calf.

The contrast which develops between the mechanical construction and the sacrifice at the shrine emphasizes the purposeless waste created by man's technological ravage of nature. To the poet, the sacrificial rites of his youth were purposeful—they effected a ritual cleansing for the tribe:

> We stripped entrails, wet and warm, wide
> Open in the streams. And the tide
> Whichever way it came, took
> Care of the mess and shook
> Us all free.

The pastoral reaction against industrialization is common to various traditions of poetry from nineteenth-century England to modern negritude, although it is not always a purposeful attack.

Although 'Flight across Africa' shares the theme of many of the poems in the second part of the book it is purposeful in its attack on modern technology. This purposefulness is not shared by poems like 'Cave Call' and 'Boeing Crossing'. 'Flight across Africa' is similar to the earlier poems in its use of traditional matter. But it is not merely for this that it is satisfying. Although the content is important because it forms an essential ingredient in the making of an indigenous tradition of written Nigerian poetry, the co-existence of what critics have often described as the 'traditional' and the 'borrowed' elements in the poems is of little intrinsic worth except that for the reader they provide light for understanding the poem, and for the poet they are a means of achieving a new element, the completed poem:

156

As the off-shoot of such a union, a man
not only fuses elements of both sides but he
also constitutes a new independent whole.[7]

Therefore for the modern Nigerian poet writing in English, as for any other poet, a spontaneous outburst of emotion is inadequate, for the poet must not merely translate emotions or ideas from the life of one culture into the language of another, he must create a product that is a new whole in itself. He must not merely write as if so 'hard pressed' that 'he is writing in a kind of explosion, under the extreme pressure of experience', but he must also ensure the quality of the expression. Mere reproduction of the experience could easily become sociological. So Clark attempts to escape from this through technique, first by experimenting with the techniques of other poets, then moving away from this pastiche making. Such an approach will not always yield successes at first, although the results themselves could be interesting. This is why Paul Theroux finds the failures among Clark's poems the most interesting ones for critical comment.[8] The failures may be measured in terms of technique, since technique is the vehicle for achieving the necessary synthesis which accomplishes the successful poem.

In two poems, 'The Imprisonment of Obatala' and 'The Return of the Fishermen', the poet demonstrates his concern not so much with 'accuracy' of content as with formal excellence. In these, as in many of the poems, the meaning of the poems grows from the union of technique and content—more from the effect of technique on content. The mythological poem, 'The Imprisonment of Obatala', is not anthropologically accurate in its use of the details of the original Yoruba myth, but it is nevertheless authentic in its own way since it has adapted the original myth to re-create a new poetic myth:

> . . . that mischievous stir, late sown or split
> On the way between homestead and stream,
> Wells up in pots long stagnant on stilt. . . .

As Clark explains in his notes, the story told is about the ritual imprisonment of Obatala, the Yoruba creator god, and the point of the story is the scourge and expiation which follows upon the imprisonment. The poem itself is not a strict reproduction of the myth. As in most of Clark's poems, 'Obatala' starts off with inspiration from a concrete object, in this case, Suzanne Wenger's fascinating painting of the myth. And it is to the peculiar forms of Wenger's figures that Clark owes the peculiarity of phrasing:

> Those stick-insect figures! They rock the dance

Of snakes, dart after him daddy-long arms,
Tangle their loping strides to mangrove stance.

The first stanza remains faithful to the concrete source that inspired it—emphasis throughout is on visual effect, especially on movement—the fluidity of the dance, the speed of the chase and the feeling of impotence which the long, dangling arms convey. The line 'they rock the dance / Of snakes' describes the centre of Wenger's painting. The figures here are formed around interlocking snakes which close in the sun that forms the centre-piece, so that they seem to dance ('rock') round a drum. But the dance describes only the movement, not the mood, of the poem. The verbal picture in this stanza presents a forbidding scene: the dry stick-insect, the snakes and the dark mangrove roots anticipate 'alarms' which form the dominant mood of the poem.

The next set of images suggests the sowing of mischief—the fermenting pots of charms, the angry ancestors, the raging waves unmindful of the fate of caterpillars. Furthermore, the images are mainly those of involvement. Although the main impression created in the description of the dance of snakes is that of grace and suppleness, there is also a slight suggestion of a death embrace in the 'daddy-long arms' (an obvious pun on 'daddy-long legs') from which there is no escape. This meaning is intensified by 'Tangle', by the idea of the chase in 'mangrove stance' and of the cornered prey in 'roped' and 'tight'ning pit'. While carrying on the idea of exhaustion from the pursuit, 'Dangles' recalls its sound equivalent, 'Tangle', which occurs two lines earlier. But the last line, 'Invincible limbs cramp'd by love of their strength', heightens the macabre drama by the paradox of the Strong One rendered impotent by a full awareness of his strength.

The obscurity of the poem comes partly from the absence of a continuous narrative thread which the first stanza leads us to expect by its use of two distinct narrative forms of the myth—the visual story of Wenger's batik and the oral tradition. Since both are essentially variations of the same myth, the use of both versions necessarily involves compression. But a forward movement is achieved by the sweep of the description of set scenes in stanza one, through the story of cause and consequence in the other two stanzas. Superimposed upon this description is the less localized interpretation which sees the myth as a universal ritual drama of wrong, wrath and reparation. This has been anticipated in the first stanzas by the use of the phrase 'stick-insect' which, in addition to being an apt verbal representation of Wenger's forms, is also an appropriately ominous symbol because of the nature of the emotions to which it gives rise, as well as its significance as an ominous symbol for the Ijaw people.

158

The third stanza which deals with the actual cause and course of the chaos also particularizes the myth in one respect at least, for the lines

> . . . the cry of a child at which it knows not
> Evokes trebly there the droop, mud-crack and clot

are an essential part of Clark's own world-view. The lines recall 'Cry of Birth' in which there is a similar echo of childhood disturbed in its innocence by an oppressive universe it does not understand.

Thus the elements which contribute to the artistic wholeness of 'Obatala' include, first, the use of the original myth for continuous narrative and Wenger's batik for phrasing and suggestion; secondly, images drawn from the poet's own riverain home and finally, the artistic form which largely determines the meaning. For example, 'the charcoal-coloured ass' is really a horse in the original myth, but 'horse' does not rhyme with 'grass'. It would of course be too simple to argue that the poet is influenced solely by rhyme and poetic form rather than by originally-intended meaning. But here the poet seems to be as much concerned with poetic form as with what he sets out to say.

'The Return of the Fishermen' is a good example of this argument. Apparently it says what the poet set out to say, if we go by his explanatory notes. So it is permissible to extract a prose 'meaning' from it. It deals with the return home in the evening of exhausted fishermen listening for omens in the cries of the kingfisher. The omen is a happy one, for the shore is filled with villagers waiting to welcome home the fishermen. But the poem does not readily yield a prose meaning, and it is a poem which a reader might justifiably admire without first fully understanding.[9] Its attraction for the reader lies in its rhythm, its sound-effects and its neat form, though these cannot of course be considered apart from the theme of the poem. The strength of the poem is primarily onomatopoeic:

> Pins and needles effervescent up heel,
> Dabble, dabble, dip paddle blades,
> And silent you furrow up from sea.

This sound-meaning collaboration is reinforced by the usual play of tones that is an important part of Clark's verse.

Perhaps more interesting still is the neatness of form. The poem uses two rhymes occurring alternatively as first and last lines. It is part of the formal pattern that the second stanza is an inversion of the first, both rhyme-wise and meaning-wise. The last line of stanza 2, 'And low is the squirming down keel', seems an inversion of the first line of stanza 1, 'Pins and needles effervescent up heel'. Similarly the first line of stanza 2, 'O, quick now goes the sun to sea', somehow suggests an inversion of the last line of stanza 1, 'And silent you furrow up from sea'. In between both stanzas is the unrhymed, onomatopoeic line, 'Dabble, dabble, dip paddle blades' (stanza 1), and 'Tick-twit, squirrels stow their seeds' (stanza 2).

But it is not to sound and form alone that the early poems owe their charm. There is also the poet's power to suggest a complexity of meaning by the use of image or metaphor, as in 'The Imprisonment of Obatala'. In another poem, 'For Granny (from Hospital)',

> the raucous voice
> Of yesterday's rain
> Tumbling down banks of reed
> To feed a needless stream

does more than merely describe the physical scene; it is charged with a suggestion of

> the loud note of quarrels
> And endless nights of intrigue
> In Father's house of many wives.

Granny's 'recognition' of the note of quarrels in the raucous voice of the rain is clearly linked with 'the needless stream' and 'the house of many wives'.

In the popular poem, 'Night Rain', the pictures are more than just realistic. The images carry uneasy suggestions from which only the innocence of the young ones helps to set them free. There is the suggestion of death in the metaphor of the doped fish, and an eeriness in the 'silent cocks', of terror in the storm that slit open the roofs through which the rain comes falling like fruits, while the metaphor of the spell cast by drunkenness suggests a witch that might be flying that night, for the birds referred to are those traditionally associated with witches, as the iroko tree on which they stand is also usually regarded as spirit-infested. But there is child-like empathy in spite of the atmosphere of terror. The spell-binding wetness of the rain evokes the children's sympathy for the birds so soaked to the skin, 'that wet of wings may not fly':

> Bedraggled up on the iroko, they stand
> Emptied of hearts, and
> Therefore will not stir, no, not
> Even at dawn for then
> They must scurry in to hide.

Is it any wonder then that Clark should insist on reinstating the words 'and free', which anthologists Moore and Beier eliminate presumably on account of the possible effect of sentimentality at the end of the poem?[10]

> So let us roll over on our back
> And again roll to the beat
> Of drumming all over the land
> And under its ample soothing hand
> Joined to that of the sea
> We will settle to our sleep of the innocent and free.

The last words are proper, for the night horrors of the children's imagination are alleviated only by the anchorage of innocence and freedom; the dark and the storm which bring terror and unrest are also the night and the rain which provide rhythm and quiet as sources of refuge and peace.

The picture of the world as a vale of tears is a common one in Clark's poems, especially in the early poems. Childhood cries and 'noise of babel' are not infrequent. For consolation the poet seems to seek refuge in the dark peace of the womb or the warmth of the maternal breast. Thus the poems about early childhood, like 'For Granny (from Hospital)' and 'Night Rain', form what may be regarded as a traumatic unit in Clark's poetry. It is in them that we may look for the source of the yearnings for comfort and escape from what is referred to, in 'New Year', as 'world blight'. The fact that the figure of the mother is so prominent in some of the poems, while that of the father is almost completely absent, encourages such a reading. Furthermore, poems like 'Obatala' and 'For Granny (from Hospital)' contain images of cosmic chaos, while others like 'Two Seedings', 'New Year' and 'Tide Wash' contain images of loss of bearing and of separation, sometimes physical, often spiritual. But this attitude exists only as a darker undercurrent in Clark's poetry. More immediately felt is the strong thirst for animal life that is evident in many of the poems, notably 'Agbor Dancer' and 'The Year's First Rain'.

> Rain comes,
> Hot breathing, alert . . .
> And earth all the while waiting, waiting inert . . .
> Now with more than tongue can tell
> Thrusts, he strokes her, swamps her,
> Enters all of him beyond her fell,
> Till in the calm and cool after

> All alone, earth yawns, limbers her stay,
> Swollen already with the life to break at day.

While illustrating the joy of living often expressed in many of Clark's liveliest poems, 'The Year's First Rain' remains statement without comment. This is not always so in Clark's verse. Quite often there is the tendency to be reflective, though concreteness remains the chief quality of the poetry. Consequently the poems, which generally start off with a picture or an action, usually end with a meditation or a philosophical tag. This can often be a weakness. In the earlier version of 'Fulani Cattle' the poet implores the cattle to

> vouchsafe to me,
> As true the long knife must prevail
> The patience of even your tail.[11]

Later, he replaces 'vouchsafe' with 'reveal'.[12] Still the attitude is hardly reassuring and these concluding lines just avoid being an anti-climax to the poem.

As in 'Night Rain', however, the attitude becomes less absurd if regarded in the context of Clark's attitude as a whole. There is in Clark's works a sympathy or admiration for the uncomplaining, bound victim. This is present even in his prose writings. An essay on African verse takes a South African poet to task for not enduring patiently like the trussed-up ram.[13] And in one or two poems he extols the stoic virtues of silence and endurance. This respect for the silent, fettered prisoner dictates the form of 'The Leader' which, apart from 'The Imprisonment of Obatala', is his most important poem on this theme.

'The Leader' is the last poem in *A Reed in the Tide*, but though it belongs to the second half in its use of animal images, it recalls the reaching for the timeless and universal that is typical of the first part. 'The Leader' belongs to the group of 'political' poems concerned with power struggle and consequent disaster. 'Emergency Commission' and 'His Excellency The Masquerader' are the other poems in this group. An earlier poem, 'Hands over Head', is the first of these poems, but 'Emergency Commission', which is closer to 'The Leader' in treatment, has as its theme an actual political upheaval which it describes metaphorically as a storm in a wood. The image of the uprooted tree which is used as metaphor for the great fallen man recalls the more widely known symbol of the falling star. In 'The Leader', as in 'Emergency Commission', the power struggle is transformed into the more fundamental form of a physical contest.

'The Leader' tells the tale of a fight for supremacy culminating in betrayal and defeat. The action takes place in the Ijaw swamps, now familiar as the early home of the child in 'Night Rain' and 'For Granny (from Hospital)'. Here it is also an appropriate setting for treachery. The animal images function as metaphors for describing the main manœuvres in the conflict: iguana and alligator to indicate the influence and power involved, and 'laggard dogs' to describe the ease with which treachery finds allies in fawning lackeys.

The form disciplines the content as effectively as the sonnet form which it mimics. The metaphors are organic to the theme, and help unify the poem. For example, the protracted conflict is not merely physical. The 'decade of tongues' metaphor indicates this, and this is followed by the image of the 'locked jaw' which closes the poem as well as the contest.

Most of the other poems in the second section of *A Reed in the Tide* are less satisfying, although they show greater flexibility of idiom and fewer clichés than the earlier ones. Their failure to satisfy stems partly from the nature of the subject, for Clark is here for the first time experimenting with poetry about a complex modern civilization, the American, not about the largely traditional communal culture which he had been dealing with. Sometimes he handles this new subject with some competence, as in 'Times Square'. The main problem with most of his poems, however, is the inability to fuse the two halves of his experience. Clark has rightly pointed out his debt to the two cultures to which he owes his education. But as he himself says in the passages quoted earlier, it is not enough for a man to be part of two cultures. The important thing is the degree to which he unites his twin inheritance rather than his ability to preserve the two elements as separate entities.

An example of such a synthesis appears in 'Who Bade the Waves'. Here a phrase reminiscent of King Canute's command to the waves is used as metaphor for the Bornu horsemen of the colourful northern Nigerian Durbar, who charge towards the honoured royal guest to stop short of the pavilion with upraised fist as acknowledgement of the omnipotence of royalty:

> Who bade the waves, like horsemen of Bornu, stop
> A foot short
> Of swamping the stands, rode
> Them breast-breaking to sea and
> Back, dry-shod.

This dramatic picture is merged with the American image of the bronco-buster, and then used as a simile for the omnipotence and tyranny which the poet defies, in the equestrian metaphor 'will

163

not / Ride me rodeo one step'. The stance is one now made popular by Henley's 'bloody but unbowed head'. As in many of the poems, the statement here is an extended metaphor. It is effective here in the first part, but there is loss of control in the second half.

In the poems about America, however, the statement often falls into two separate halves. The poet starts off by rejecting the other half of his cultural experience, through a too-easy escape into primitivism:

> . . . a return
> To bed, my brothers
> In the wild of America!

This use of primordial images begins as early as 'Las Palmas', a purely descriptive imagist piece which attempts to repeat the success of 'Ibadan'.

In 'Boeing Crossing' the poet is not impressed by the achievements of modern air travel, which is made to suffer in comparison with earlier modes of travel. The V.I.P.s of the modern world have nothing on the earlier voyagers, Sinbad and Jonah, who took Roc and Whale to their destinations, and were delivered

> early enough to keep
> Date with a certain destiny.

Then apparently for no reason Clark adopts the cynical stance of the outsider in his remark that the destiny which Jonah sought is still denied the tribe. There is thus some inconsistency here. The more primitive resources of travel have been brought in specifically as a foil against the idea of modern air transport. So when we get to the mockery implied in

> O you
> Who have faith in the fable of fowl
> And fish,

it is obvious that the reader's sympathy has not been given direction. The reason is that the poet is more strongly attracted by the possibilities of language. So that ironically he resorts to these same rejected fables and converts them into metaphors and uses them to play word pranks:

> pray,
> That we who today prowl
> The skies and bowels of the sea,
> And so successfully play

> Pranks with both distance and
> Dawn, twisting Time's own tail
> Right back into its jaws,
> That old dragon does seem to pause
> In its path. . . .

In this, as in the other 'American' poems, especially 'Cave Call', Clark takes refuge in metaphors drawn from primitive life forms. These poems reveal a reliance on such metaphors and on those drawn from communal life for their sustenance. They do not as yet have the finished quality of the earlier poems, probably because the images are alien to the theme, for in the earlier poems the images are an organic part of their subject, they deal with experiences that are fundamental to mankind. That is why the emphasis is on the mythical and timeless in both the poems and the plays.

Clark's *Casualties* (1970) is mainly a collection of poems on the Nigerian crisis, although it contains some occasional poems. The poems are presented more or less in a chronological order except for the first two which set the mood by their theme of friendship and loss. The poems are less to be considered individually than as a group of related responses to the crisis, since they are an individual's psychological history of the war. For example, the title poem, 'The Casualties', is the poet's attempt to interpret dishonest peace activities in terms of the tragedies of war.

One of the most interesting poems in the collection, 'The Cockerel in the Tale', deals with the most controversial of the coup-makers who, in his haste at what was considered a job well done,

> proclaimed
> The break of day uncertain then
> Where the sun should rise.

The notes inform the reader that the cockerel is Major Nzegwu, and later, in 'The Leader of the Hunt', Clark attempts to correct the popular belief that Nzegwu rather than Ifeajuna is the leader of the coup. Here, as elsewhere in the book, the accompanying notes provide more information than is necessary for an understanding of the poems, and are obviously a prose analysis of the crisis. What is of real interest to the reader is not this attempt to put the records straight but the development of the myth-making technique which first appeared in the second half of *A Reed in the Tide*. In 'The Cockerel in the Tale', the actual geographical area of the coup is transformed into fictional terms through the substitution of a more generalized geographical equivalent:

> At the desert end of a great road
> To the sea

is a generalized description of Kaduna where Nzegwu carried out his assignment. Furthermore most of the actors in the drama are animals rather than humans, as in the folktale: a hint of one way in which history develops into legend and myth.

Folktale and folksong provide the form for some of the poems, as in the tale of the vulture in 'Vulture's Choice', or the cantor-chorus pattern of 'Seasons of Omens' in which the refrain about the five hunters illustrates the traditionally heroic role of the hunter. In the traditional tale the hunter is often the village guard who also hastens to the community's aid in moments of crisis. The change of form in the second section suggests the chaos which follows when the hunters pursue individual ideals of action. 'The Rat in the Hole' opens with a form in which traditional wisdom often finds expression, i.e. the *saw*—a timeless truth arrived at through observation or direct experience and illustrated from animal life:

> A couchant leopard in its cage
> Is a coil of steel with the catch
> In a cage . . .

It is this maxim that guides the poet's reaction in the second part. The final part, on the face of it a reference to an imminent thunderstorm at sunrise, is in fact also a symbolic image of the actual situation, with the East as the location, the Sun as the dictator of future action, and thunder as the holocaust to follow.

Generally, the affected language of Clark's early verse is absent in this volume, as are the frequent derivations. The alliterative patterns persist, but not obtrusively; in 'July Wake', for instance, one hears 'jungle-geared jeeps roar, Glint of SMG', and 'The gang in green got him then/By legs in loosening pyjama'. The most important gain in this collection, however, is the fact that the basis of form and image in the collection is the folktale. This is probably why the language is essentially prosaic, and primarily colloquial. It is on the whole a more flexible idiom, and often well handled as in 'Seasons of Omens' where he manages to invest the banal and commonplace with some life. One occasionally misses the type of poetry found in 'Abiku' and 'The Leader', but still it is something good that Clark is beginning to turn from English models to traditional African forms in his more recent poetry and drama.

Like the poems, the plays deal with themes which persist from communal societies to contemporary times. The problem is the attempt to adapt traditional ideas to the modern stage. This is at the root of the difficulty encountered by critics of his plays, especially by those unsympathetic to dramatic experiment. In one extreme case, a critic places Ene Henshaw in a more favourable light than Clark because

Henshaw writes straight plays which present no serious linguistic or dramatic problems.[14] But to compare Clark and Henshaw is to view Clark through the wrong perspective. Clark belongs to a different tradition—one which draws its themes and metaphors from traditional life and lore. Because this is the most virile tradition today, it would be misleading to exalt the simpler dramatic form at the expense of the new tradition of synthesis.

It is clear that Clark's problem as a dramatist arises mainly from his lack of interest in, or experience of, the stage. An example from *Song of a Goat* will illustrate how this problem of adaptation sometimes sticks out in his plays. Martin Banham reports that at one of its earliest performances, the producer had to substitute a symbolic gesture for the ritual exposure of Tonye's adulterous betrayal of his elder brother.[15] Yet the means of exposure devised by Zifa is more than just a means, and such a substitution does not do justice to its organic relationship to the overall meaning of the play. The bleating goat which disturbs the drunken dreams of Orukorere, the Cassandra-like old woman, points to the affair between Ebiere and strong-man Tonye, who may be likened to a leopard:

> I must find him, the leopard
> That will devour my goat.

Earlier, Orukorere had seen visions of fire consuming their house, and the image of the harmattan fire in the Masseur's speech clearly refers to the burning of lust:

> Don't you see the entire grass is gone
> Overlush, and with the harmattan may
> Catch fire though you spread over it
> Your cloak of dew?

Apart from suggesting Ebiere's plight in the play, the goat also represents the sacrifice offered as propitiation after the forbidden deed. It heads the list of sacrificial objects ('Blood of a goat . . . kola-nut') prescribed by the Masseur. That is why the scene of exposure should appear too charged with meaning for the woman to bear, and that is why she betrays herself by fainting.

If actors fail to put this significance across to the audience, then the play becomes no more than a mere adulterous tale. Clark's problem here is how to preserve the weight which the story would have in its traditional context, given the situation—a fertile woman, an impotent husband, and a virile younger brother in a society which expects procreation from every wife, while placing strong taboos on adultery.

167

The play begins appropriately at a point which defines the atmosphere
for the audience—at the arresting moment when the Masseur, with
hand on Ebiere's bare belly, sounds the keynote by emphasizing the
fertility which the society expects of every young wife:

> Your womb
> Is open and warm as a room;
> It ought to accommodate many.

The background is clear. The idle hands and hungry mouths of modern
civilization find no place in this society where there is no turning aside
the stranger at the gates. That is why in this society birth control is not
only unheard-of, but inability to have children often has the consequence of sin. The play does not succeed because of the failure to
communicate this tense situation. Its highly metaphorical and evasive
language which states by analogy is obviously meant to approach the
situation obliquely because of the delicacy of the problem, but it is a
drag on the action.

The second play, *The Masquerade*, is related to the first in that the
hero is the son of Ebiere in *Song of a Goat*. It is more successful in its
use of traditional material. It dramatizes a well-known African folktale
about a girl who rejects all local suitors until she falls victim to the
borrowed charms of the stranger who turns out to be a demon. As
Obumselu points out about this type of tale: 'In the traditional society
the story must have warned the young generally to beware of strangers,
the young women in particular to submit to the wise counsel of their
parents.'[16] The particular source from which Clark adapts his story,
The Palm-Wine Drinkard, specifically heads a section of the tale with
the caution,

> *Do not follow unknown man's beauty*

Knowledge of Clark's source leads one to expect that Clark's interest
is in the sinister shadow beneath the surface glitter, and its danger to
those bewitched by it. In the original tale the devout suitor of the girl,
usually a hunter, saves her from the danger when the stranger-suitor
turns out either a fiend, as in Tutuola's tale, or a python seeking to
devour the bride:

> The transformation
> Was into a python later shot down
> By one who had loved her all her virgin
> Life.[17]

Clark's interest is not in the moral lesson, however. As in the poem

'His Excellency The Masquerader', Clark is fascinated by the gusty interior which lies behind such showiness:

> The masks!
> O take off the mask! And behind?
> What wind! What straw!

There is nothing really sinister about Clark's stranger, and Clark's sympathy is obviously with Titi, 'the poor innocent girl' who has been taken for a ride by 'a scarecrow capped with a vacant skull'. The tragic centre of the play is obviously meant to be Titi's determined but futile attempt to keep her romance with her 'sun figure'.

The third play in the collection presents the tale of four raftsmen drifting towards destruction. *The Raft* does not rely on traditional material for its theme as much as the first two plays. It is rather an expression of the same tragic view of life which we find in some of his poems. In *The Raft* life is one long nightmare. In the midst of this murk the raftsmen attempt to buoy up their spirits with sardonic humour. The journey is thus a series of anecdotes and local gossip loosely strung together, and the style is digressive. *The Raft* suffers from the fragmentary nature of Clark's vision. The figures of speech occasionally create a particularized satire which runs counter to the main intention of the playwright:

> Man, it is
> We ordinary grass and shrubs who get crushed,
> As the mahoganies fall.

Such passages, along with those scenes which deal with famine on the raft, the breaking up of a section of the raft with its lost 'captain', and the hostile European ship, have obviously been taken as symbolizing the plight of the country.[18] But the writer's intention does not appear to be prophetic or satiric; rather it seems to present in more universal terms the general plight of man. First the blackout,

> Fog has stuffed its soot and
> Smoke in our eyes, has shut up the world
> Like a bat its wings. Don't you see?
> All is blindness and scales.

Then the end:

> Aren't you afraid to be left alone
> In this world, aren't you?

.   .   .   .   .

> Shout, shout, Ibobo, let's shout
> To the world—we woodsmen lost in the bush.

Ozidi is an epic celebration of the engendering of evil and its purgation. The process begins with a community which requires purification. But envy and malice prevent the purification and give birth to wrong and revenge. Revenge proves a sterile approach, for it contains the germs of its own destruction since it sets in motion a terrible cycle of violence which cannot be arrested until natural forces set in to restore order after a ritual cleansing.

The wrong of the community gradually becomes the burden of an individual who is used as a scourge against the community and who eventually undergoes scourge and purification himself. When the State Council of Orua meets, the councillors decide to select a new king, although it is no time for king-making. Six kings have followed one another in rapid succession to the Orua graveyard. Oracles have specified the origin of the short reigns:

> We have enslaved too many,
> Ravished too many lands.

Instead of acts of repentance and expiation, however, there are political intrigues. The house of Ozidi is much feared and envied for its success in war and acts of valour, so Temugedege the idiot brother is put on the throne to spite his successful warrior-brother, Ozidi, whom they finally slay for demanding the customary tributes for his brother.

That the wronged house of Ozidi might not pass unavenged, Oreame the witch brings up her grandson to be a machine for revenge. The planned revenge itself appears at first to have divine sanction, for Ozidi is

> a son who Oyin Almighty
> Herself is sending forth to put right
> This terrible wrong done his father.

But having accomplished his immediate mission he cannot halt his career of blood, and his witch grandmother encourages him to spread ruin all over the land. But violence recoils upon itself and, blinded by the magic herb with which his grandmother renewed his strength in a battle, Ozidi cuts her down. That is the first act of reparation, but it also leaves Ozidi vulnerable. With the removal of the instrument of evil, Ozidi is attacked by smallpox. But before the usual ritual despatch can be effected, what is left of the house of Ozidi is brought to acknowledge its need for purification, just as this need was first brought to the notice of the community by wise counsel:

Orea, it's a thorough purification ceremony
You of this house require.

Salvation comes from Orea's humble acceptance of this advice. A simple woman, she goes about the process of prayer, repentance and cleansing in the simplest manner. First she disclaims responsibility for the evil done. Next her purification objects are the simplest and most elementary. It is significant that they include no blood sacrifice: 'Here's common water then, here's common soap.' Finally, she refuses to acknowledge the imminence of (the ritual despatch through) smallpox:

> I need nothing more before I scrub dry a mere riot of yaws
> Broken over my son. When a guest
> Comes on a visit, he goes home after.

And the 'guest' does return home. Insulted at being mistaken for common yaws, the Small Pox King with his retinue of symptoms releases Ozidi with a disdainful vow never to return to the land anymore. The House of Ozidi is purified at last, as well as the land.

Notes

1 Some of the verse from this poetry magazine has been collected and published as *Nigerian Student Verse 1959*, by Martin Banham. It contains no poem by Clark, however.

2 Ulli Beier, 'Some Nigerian Poets', *Présence Africaine*, Vol. 4/5, Nos. 32/33, pp. 61-63.

3 Clark, 'The Communication Line between Poet and Public', *African Forum*, Vol. 3, No. 1, 1967, pp. 51-2.

4 Clark, 'Poetry in Africa Today', *Transition*, No. 18, 1965, p. 26.

5 Clark, *America, Their America*, André Deutsch, London, 1964, p. 58.

6 Ulli Beier, 'Three Mbari Poets', *Black Orpheus*, No. 12 n.d., p. 48.

7 'A Personal Note', in *A Reed in the Tide*, Longmans, London, 1965, p. vii.

8 Paul Theroux, 'Six Poets', *Introduction to African Literature*, ed. Ulli Beier, Longmans, London, 1967, pp. 100, 120-5.

9 Gerald Moore, 'The Language of Poetry', *African Literature and the Universities*, ed. Gerald Moore, 1965, p. 100.

10 Moore and Beier (ed.), *Modern Poetry from Africa*, Penguin, London, 1963, p. 87.

11 Clark, *Poems* 1960, p. 6.

12 *A Reed in the Tide*, op. cit., p. 4.

13 'Poetry in Africa Today', op. cit., p. 23.

14 Peter Kennard, 'Recent African Drama', *Bulletin of the Association for African Literature in English*, No. 2, 1965, pp. 11-17.

15 Martin Banham, review in *Journal of Commonwealth Literature*, No. 7, July 1969, pp. 132-3.

16 Ben Obumselu, 'Background of Modern African Literature', *Ibadan*, No. 22, June 1966, p. 56.

17 *Three Plays*, O.U.P., London, 1964, p. 62.

18 See Eldred Jones, 'African Literature 1966-1967', in *African Forum*, Vol. 3, No. 1, 1967, p. 5.

Form and Style

by Abiodun Adetugbo

Nigeria has a literature written in English rich and intricate enough to merit evaluation by the critical standards that have sustained good literature elsewhere in the world. Cultural differences notwithstanding, the experience that good literature affords can be appreciated anywhere. An understanding of the cultural background from which a work springs may help both reader and critic in appreciating more fully a particular work, but any great literary work must have an appeal beyond the culture in which it is rooted. This probably partially accounts for the choice of English as the medium of expression by many Nigerian writers.

The choice of the English language which guarantees a wider readership as against a native Nigerian language, say, the primary language of the writer, imposes in theory and often in practice some limitation on the style of these writers. As a foreign language does not have a one-to-one correspondence with the writer's native language, how much translation may the writer do from his native language into English without doing violence to the grammar of the English language? Tutuola, and Okara in *The Voice*, come to mind here. And assuming that the writer's mastery of the English language comes close to the English native speaker's (and this is the case with Clark, Soyinka and others), how far can he transfer wholesale his non-English experience into the English language's mode of thought and expression? And how much can he conform to conventions of form and style in English literature without falsifying the native experience he is relating?

These questions are raised here only to bring out some critical problems raised by Nigerian literature of English expression. The way the writers themselves react to these problems may provide the unique characteristics of Nigerian literature.

Prose

We may examine form and style in Nigerian literature within the various literary genres. Nigeria has produced significant works in all the genres, but it is probably in the novel that the achievement has

173

been greatest. The novel, too, seems the most foreign of all the genres to Nigerians if we understand that the closest to it in traditional oral literature is the folktale. The development of the novel in Nigeria can hardly be traced to these folktales. A discussion of the works of both Fagunwa and Tutuola will bear this out.

Fagunwa is, to my mind, the only Nigerian who has attempted a novel-type work in a Nigerian vernacular language. Fagunwa writes in Yoruba, his native language. His works include *Ogboju Ode Ninu Igbo Olodumare, Ireke Onibudo* and *Àdììtú Olódùmarè*. For these works, Fagunwa has two sources: fiction of the author's creation and fiction culled from the folktales which his community shares. The blend of materials from these two sources is one of Fagunwa's achievements in his long stories. But his works fail as novels because each work is highly episodic. His plots ramble along with very little organization. Fagunwa fails in another sense as a novelist. The human interest in his work rarely exceeds the opportunity to moralize. It is true that his heroes and heroines are human beings; they are, however, not developed in any way to make them come to life. Fagunwa's plot is usually a folktale cast in the picaresque tradition.

Yet Fagunwa's works are well received in Nigeria and he remains the best known writer to the Yoruba people. This achievement lies in part in Fagunwa's story-telling technique and in his language. Here Fagunwa draws very largely on the techniques of oral story-telling among the Yoruba people. Folk stories are communally shared by the people. A good story-teller's achievement therefore lies in his linguistic techniques and not in his invention. He is one who must be versed in Yoruba rhetoric, loading every rift of his narration with plays on words, nuances, sayings and proverbs. Fagunwa achieves this. His language is heightened, and highly decorative. His descriptions are often apt and palpable, picturesque and visual. Even more than this, he has enriched the Yoruba language by his use of non-standard idioms taken from his own dialect. He uses and invents proverbs and he is a master of rhetoric. This is Ulli Beier's translation of Esu Kekere Ode's questioning of Olowo-Aiye:

> Who are you? What are you? What are you worth? What are you up to? What will you become? What are you seeking? What do you want? What are you looking at? What are you seeing? What are you thinking? . . . Answer me, child of man, answer me in one word?[1]

The piling up of one question after the other is one of the rhetorical devices in traditional story-telling. Again quoting from Beier's translation, one may visualize Fagunwa's use of personification. The potency of Olowo-Aiye's father as a doctor is described thus:

And my father punished smallpox and attacked rheumatism and turned stomach pain into a pauper; and headache becomes a helpless child and backache was speechless; cough went into hiding and pneumonia fled . . . dysentery bent its head, the sore wept and the stomach ulcer was disgusted; the rash wrinkled its brow and the cold cried for help.[2]

One of the features then that Fagunwa and subsequently other Nigerian writers share from traditional oral literature is a predilection for language in itself.

From Fagunwa to Tutuola, the first Nigerian 'novelist' of English expression, the line of development is not a direct one. While Fagunwa is interested in narrating his story in the vernacular, using every rhetorical device available to him through the medium of traditional story-telling and seizing every available opportunity to moralize, Tutuola *translates* his experience into the medium of English, and uses less traditional rhetoric. Though occasionally his style of narration becomes long-winded and slow in pace, he often achieves a directness of narration and simplicity of style.

Tutuola's works are concerned with man alone rather than man in society. He places his hero or heroine on the road, on a quest. The Palm-Wine Drinkard sets out to find his tapster who has long died. The whole tale is about the Drinkard's experiences in subhuman and inhuman abodes. The work is a prose epic rich in episodes most of which are culled from the folktales of Tutuola's tribe. Tutuola's specific achievements are in the directness and simplicity of his narration through which he has been able to impose a unity of tone upon what would have been unrelated episodes. The Drinkard directly opens his story with:

I was a palm-wine drinkard since I was a boy of ten years of age. I had no other work more than to drink palm-wine in my life. In those days we did not know other money, except COWRIES, so that everything was very cheap, and my father was the richest man in our town.[3]

In this opening autobiographical sketch, the ringing voice of the Drinkard can be heard. The speech rhythms, and the naïve directness of the narration which results in a dislocation of a logical sequence in reasoning (everything being cheap cannot result directly from the type of currency in use), are part of the oral quality that Tutuola strives to preserve in his writing but which is often lost because of the distance of his audience, the reader of the printed page.

Tutuola obviously enjoys story-telling, and each new work of his shows a further development in narrative skill over the previous one. In his later works he makes use of 'stage directions', rarely used in the earlier works. Again in the later works, his narrative moves at a faster pace than in the earlier works; dialogue is also used to heighten the dramatic interest. In *Simbi and Satyr of the Dark Jungle*, for instance, we have Simbi saying:

'Of course, my wish before I left our village was to seek for the 'Poverty' and 'Punishment' but I have regretted it since when Dogo had just kidnapped me and sold me,' *Simbi explained coldly.* 'But before you will regret your wish will be when you return to our village,' *Bako replied and then she asked sharply from the rest* 'or is it not so?' 'Yes, it is so!' *the rest confirmed loudly.*[4]

Tutuola is praised in Europe and condemned at home for the wrong reasons. For Europeans, Tutuola has provided a work of anthropological interest: some of his mythological figures have been identified in Europe with personages in European myths. Tutuola's development of the Drinkard's quest also follows the West European pattern of departure, initiation and return. Thus to his European readers he has provided a new story within a familiar mythic framework. This is true, but his achievement lies somewhere else. At home Tutuola is rejected because the few readers he has here cannot see anything unique in his writings except his imperfect use of English which, it is feared, might be regarded by others as typically Nigerian.

Tutuola's language is undeniably a dialect of Nigerian English upon which he imposes his own idiosyncracies of style. But this uniqueness arises from his lack of mastery of the grammatical structures of English. As mentioned earlier, he translates his experience directly from Yoruba into English not realizing that there is not a one-to-one correspondence between the systems of the two languages. Two examples will suffice: 'When I entered the room, I *met* a bed.'[5] The Yoruba word *ba* which Tutuola translates as *met* has a wider semantic field than the English *to meet*. It also means *to overtake, to discover*, etc. Tutuola also translates *ilu-orun-ayuibo* (i.e. town-heaven-unreturnable), which means 'a heavenly town to which whoever goes never returns', as 'unreturnable Heaven's town',[6] giving a one-to-one English equivalent to the non-parallel Yoruba structure.

Tutuola's tales follow the same pattern as Yoruba folktales. His success in imposing some unity upon the different episodes in each work and his naïve simplicity and directness of narration are to me his significant achievements.

Chinua Achebe's achievement is probably the most significant of all Nigerian novelists. This achievement rests squarely in Achebe's acceptance of the novel in the great English tradition. His use of structure, plot and characterization is within English conventions of fiction; in these directions Achebe seldom experiments. Except for the setting of his novels and the Ibo flavour of his written idioms any of Achebe's works could read like any modern English novel.

To date, Achebe has published four novels: *Things Fall Apart*, *No Longer at Ease*, *Arrow of God* and *A Man of the People*. In *Things Fall Apart* and *Arrow of God* Achebe looks back towards the disintegration of some Ibo society and shows that this disintegration was only hastened, not caused, by colonial intervention. In the other two novels, *No Longer at Ease* and *A Man of the People*, he studies contemporary Nigerian society and shows that whatever the faults of past colonial governments, Nigerians themselves must accept the greater blame for the cynicism and corruption of their own society.

Achebe's plots have a rigid structural coherence. Each episode is neatly fitted within the overall structural pattern of the work and precipitates another; the ultimate resolution of each work can be anticipated. But this tightly-knit artistic order takes its toll on Achebe's characterization. Were the structure of the plots less monolithic, Achebe perhaps would have been able to develop his characters more fully, make them round, and not flat as they are, and give them some greater psychological depth. Achebe does not allow his readers much insight into the inner conflicts and choices that beset his characters; he presents an almost one-dimensional figure for each. In fact, the conflicts the heroes face are all too often external; Okonkwo in *Things Fall Apart* wants to live down the image of his 'loafer' father, and is therefore always on the side of courage: 'And so Okonkwo was ruled by one passion—to hate everything that his father Unoka had loved. One of these things was gentleness and another was idleness.'[7] 'To show affection was a sign of weakness, the only thing worth *demonstrating was strength*.'[8] Even though Okonkwo's is a psychological case, a man with a perverted sense of fear, little is made to dramatize his inner consciousness.

The lack of depth in depicting the character of Chief Nanga in *A Man of the People* might have been deliberate. It might be a means to demonstrate what a shallow perception the self-seeking and gain-pursuing politician might have. Not so for Odili, whom the author is unsuccessful in portraying as a likeable figure. He is passive and unimpressive. Perhaps, too, Odili is not meant to be likeable.

Achebe's style is very simple and sometimes irritatingly so, especially when it becomes formalized and studied. This is the impression one gains from his dialogues where, except for the occasional use of pidgin English, informal colloquial language is rarely used. This is not to imply that his characters do not have distinguishing speech features.

The diction in his dialogues reflects most often the tone appropriate to his characters. Ezeulu in *Arrow of God* never opens his mouth except to use images, proverbs and saws. He is full of such speeches as 'The world is a mask dancing. If you want to see it well, you do not stand in the same place' or 'The death that will kill a man begins as an appetite' or 'He is a fool who treats his brother worse than a stranger'.

Achebe's descriptions often call up an Ibo atmosphere in which superstitions and folk beliefs abound, as in:

> The night was very quiet. It was always quiet except on moonlight nights. Darkness held a vague terror for these people, even the bravest among them. Children were warned not to whistle at night for fear of evil spirits. Dangerous animals became even more sinister and uncanning in the dark. A snake was never called by its name at night because it would hear. It was called a string.[9]

Almost all his images are drawn from his cultural background. So Okonkwo's popularity in *Things Fall Apart* has grown 'like a bush fire in the harmattan'. In *Arrow of God*, the white man is compared to 'a hot soup' which must be taken 'slowly from the edges of the bowl'.

One weakness of Achebe is his use of repetition. Perhaps he intends that the symbols of the *nza* bird wrestling with its *chi* and that of the python (signifying the conflict between the traditional Ibo society and the new society ushered in by the missionaries) be seen as central to his theme and as underlying all his historical novels. Otherwise why should both occur several times in each work? A few examples of this repetition are:

> The little bird *nza* who after a big meal so far forgot himself as to challenge his *chi* to single combat.[10]

> the little bird *nza* who so forgot himself after a heavy meal that he challenged his *chi*.[11]

> like the little bird *nza* who ate and drank and challenged his personal god to single combat.[12]

In fact, the set of images he uses recurs in almost every novel of his and this gets in the way of the pace of each work. Also there are similarities in characterization from one novel to the other; Winterbottom in *Arrow of God* parallels the District Officer in *Things Fall Apart*.

Achebe nevertheless remains possibly the best Nigerian novelist. He uses all the techniques within the great tradition of the novel and it is against this background that his work must be set to be appreciated.

He uses the novelist as observer in both *Things Fall Apart* and *Arrow of God*, the flash-back technique in *No Longer at Ease* and autobiographical narrative in *A Man of the People* for some variation in his point of view. He has to some extent compelled the English language to conform to his mode of experience by seeking the appropriate diction that will portray the type of experience he is describing.

Nigeria has many other novelists, among these Ekwensi, Aluko, Okara and Soyinka. To the extent that Achebe's works stand up significantly among Nigerian novels, Achebe may be used as the standard of comparison in discussing the achievements of these other novelists.

Ekwensi shares the same cultural background with Achebe, but this is little reflected in his novels. In his first novel, *People of the City*, Ekwensi writes a novel which is more like a journalist's commentary on city life. Most of the characters do not come to life and the author loses control of the plot half-way through the work. Characterization is facile. The women whom Amusa Sango meets are all portrayed as beautiful. Aina is an 'ebony black girl with an easy smile'; 'everything about her [Beatrice the third woman] was *petite*, delicate'. Amusa Sango himself lacks depth of character. In both *People of the City* and *Jagua Nana*, Ekwenski's most popular work, the author does not make his plots convincing or likely. Thus in the latter work, Jagua Nana, a woman who has been immersed in city life and whose trade—harlotry—can only be profitably carried on in the city, retires finally to her native village. Resolution by escape is used in *People of the City* when Sango leaves the city for a different country.

Ekwensi's use of English is that of a journalist. He can evoke a physical picture with the use of accurate descriptions especially of city life and he dwells very much on details. His use of pidgin English makes some of his dialogues come to life. But again, like Achebe, his style lacks the easy grace and pace of colloquial speech. It is indeed sometimes too formal and stilted.

Only Soyinka's *The Interpreters* and Okara's *The Voice* come close to Achebe's handling of the plot and structure of the novel. *The Interpreters* is unique among Nigerian novels for many reasons. It is, like Okara's *The Voice*, an experiment, but Soyinka's experiment is more wide-ranging. Soyinka brings together a circle of close friends from different professions—engineer, artist, journalist, intellectuals—and through first the author's point of view and later through the consciousness of one of the characters, the novel traces the experiences of these characters objectively. The author believes that at this stage in the development of the African novel its task should be to interpret man and life. He tries this through a series of episodes strung together only by the constant questionings of the characters of themselves and

179

of society. The shifts in focus are quick and sudden. Flashbacks into the past, flashbacks within flashbacks, close-ups into the psyche of some of the characters, condensed narratives, all help to achieve a feeling of the bubbling life which the characters live. Various themes are introduced and not fully developed and each pulls in a different direction. The symbols in the novel are too involved. Kola's pantheon is to be interpreted as an artist's interpretation of some of the interpreters, as a creation myth, and also as Sekoni's *dome of continuity*!

Such a novel attempting to interpret life in its different aspects should have offered Soyinka an opportunity for psychological depth in the delineating of his characters, but, as with Achebe's characters, we only are shown a glimpse, an occasional peep beyond the surface.

Okara's *The Voice* is an experimentation with language only. In this novel, Okara tries to translate the speech rhythms of his native language into English. Even though he sometimes achieves a satisfying play on the nuances of words and the rhythms of the spoken language, his pace is heavy, the work *plods* along, ironshod, and before long the reader is bored. Okara should have realized the experiment was doomed to fail, for all we have is a transposition of grammatical categories like 'we are the elders be', 'she with all her inside spoke'. This is neither English nor Ijaw syntax. It is a strained and artificial language. By contrast, Soyinka's language in *The Interpreters* is 'fluent writing'. The diction in the opening section is too heightened to be sustained through such a huge work. The imagery is often beautiful; but the general impression the reader has is that Soyinka's style is too self-conscious. Even though one is occasionally carried back to earth by the use of colloquialisms in the dialogues, most of the supposedly Nigerian expressions in these dialogues are stilted and unrealistic.

In general, Nigerian novels are concerned with outer reality: that is with conflicts that are socially significant. Hence characterization is often of types rather than individuals and the types are meant to have large ranges of public experience summed up in them. Soyinka tries in *The Interpreters* to portray some characters with an inner reality of their own and psychological interest; to do this he uses interior monologues that present the movements of the consciousness of their characters directly through either their feelings or their moods. But there is only a little of this. The style of the Nigerian novels is often studied and artificial. Only occasionally do we have a feeling of spontaneity in the dialogues.

Poetry

The works of J. P. Clark, Christopher Okigbo and Wole Soyinka have dwarfed earlier attempts at versification, say by Imoukhuede and

Osadebay, to the extent that Nigerian poetry is now thought of only in terms of the works of these new practitioners. The elderly attempts at poetry in English by Osadebay and Imoukhuede are not of such depth as, say, Okigbo's, yet they are relevant to the development of modern Nigerian poetry.

To be sure, Osadebay is a poet only if all versification is poetic. In most of his attempts, he lacks emotional depth both in symbolism and idea. Each work is an attempted restatement of some communally shared sentiment and the restatement lacks any intense personal feeling. In spite of this Osadebay is closer to oral poetry in at least one respect than any other Nigerian poet writing in English: his direct statements, though often shallow, guarantee that his sentiments can be publicly shared:

> Don't preserve my customs
> As some fine curios
> To suit some white historian's tastes.
> There's nothing artificial
> That beats the natural way,
> In culture and ideals of life.[13]

This is impersonal. It is also prosaic though the author strives at some poetic effect through versification and grammatical transposition in lines 5 and 6. It is also too shallow and vague. What for instance are 'the natural way' and 'ideals of life'?

Imoukhuede's verses offered us a new attempt at a poetic medium—pidgin English. The sheer force of the novelty in this experiment, coupled with the then newly discovered potential of the medium for intense though generalized emotion, guaranteed some success. 'One Man One Wife' reproduces for us both the diction and the tempo of actual speech pattern:

> Suppose, self, say na so so woman your wife dey born
> Suppose your wife sabe book, no sabe make chop;
> Den, how you go tell man make 'e no' go out
> Sake of dis divorce? Bo, dis culture na waya o![14]

But again the naïveté of the statement and its being geared towards a limited audience narrow the scope of the achievement.

Christopher Okigbo stands out among the modern Nigerian poets of English expression. Here is a poet who, though somewhat obscure, is conscious of his art. With him, statement becomes loaded, imagery and symbolism are deep and eclectic, diction is highly personal though often too self-conscious, feeling is intense, and we have the satisfaction that comes from the fusion of message and medium.

Okigbo is an intensely personal poet who is interested in objectifying his inner quest through religion and myth for a new mode of perception. He constantly dramatizes his inner conflict between an acceptance of what is and its rejection for a higher, more personal mode of perception. It is, I think, this motif that pervades his cycle of poems even though it is played upon with some variations. It is also this underlying theme that lends a unity to all his works and which allows for his creation of a personal yet understandable myth with the recurrence of the same images from one work to the other. Each work starts with the evocation of a mood. In *Heavensgate*, the poet is first seen standing naked before the shrine of a pagan goddess to whom he is a devotee:

> Before you, mother Idoto,
> naked I stand,
> before your watery presence
> a prodigal, . . .[15]

In *Limits* the poet is

> Summoned at offside of
> dream remembered
> Between sleep and waking.[16]

The poet then develops his theme through the incongruous use of eclectic images, some pagan, some Christian, some traditionally Igbo, while others are culled from Western literature. The image of the bird is one that constantly recurs and through which the poet is able to ensure an underlying unity for his work:

> The Sunbird sings again
> From the LIMITS of the dream
> The Sunbird sings again
> Where the caress does not reach. . . .[17]

Okigbo's poetry is deeply rooted in personal experience, hence his imagery and diction are sometimes too private, too subjective and too impressionistic. His attempt to blend incongruous images of different origins and associations has been previously mentioned. Yet the concreteness of Okigbo's symbols, the piling up of images one after the other, the juxtaposition of symbols of different sensual planes as 'your silences suffused in fragrance' 'long fingered winds', 'painted harmonies' invest his poetry with a delicacy of perception. Or see Okigbo's twist to Christian thought where he presents John the Baptist coming

> with bowl of salt water
> preaching the gambit
> life without sin, without
> life[18]

Okigbo's private diction gets in the way of the readers sharing to the full the poet's experiences. Obtrusive Ibo idioms are used with no glosses offered:

> *ebili malo; ebili com com, ebili te que liquandem.*

Other obscure forms such as *kepkanly, enki, upanduru* and *kratosbiate* occur without glosses.

The most satisfying aspect of Okigbo's work is his music. Okigbo is a highly meditative poet and this shows in his lyricism. All his work is a cycle of music. There is, for instance, the music of youth in *Heavensgate*:

> Me to the orangery
> solitude invites
> a wagtail, to tell
> the tangle-wood-tale;
> a sunbird, to mourn
> a mother on a spray.[19]

where the second of each pair of lines reads like a chorus to the first. We may also note his use of choruses in his poems. Okigbo's music derives not only from the measured cadence of his lines but also from assonance, alliteration, the timbre of his vowels and consonants. See his use of sibilants in these lines, for instance:

> Each song is the sigh of your spirits
>
> No song is your swansong
>
> This song is our sense's silence.

The works of J. P. Clark do not have a thematic unity like Okigbo's, and Clark avoids much of the obscurity and the telegraphic mode of Okigbo's writing. Clark is more concerned with finding a simple message and medium synthesis: the difference between his good poems and the others which are less successful lies mainly in the achievement of this synthesis. In the good works, Clark's idiom is simple, his metrics unobtrusive, and the personality of the poet is submerged below the beauty of the language and a satisfying fusion of thought and expression.

'Streamside Exchange' is an example. Here Clark presents us with a dramatic lyric which breaks into the middle of the incident:

> *Child:* River bird, river bird,
> Sitting all day long
> On hook over grass,
> River bird, river bird,
> Sing me a song
> Of all that pass
> And say,
> Will mother come back today?
> *Bird:* You cannot know
> And should not bother;
> Tide and market come and go
> And so has your mother.[20]

The little setting here is part of the drama. The statements are given with all simplicity. The rhyme pattern and the rhythm emphasize the naïveté of the dialogue. Yet Clark's theme in this poem and the impression it makes on the reader cannot be said to be simple. Wherever Clark casts aside his simplicity of diction and wherever he becomes too self-conscious with his metrics (and there are many instances of this in his works, as for example 'Tree' and 'Easter') his medium of expression becomes obtrusive to the appreciation of his poems.

In his description of landscape Clark can be a poet of the eye, as his often cited poem 'Ibadan' shows:

> Ibadan
> running splash of rust
> and gold—flung and scattered
> among seven hills like broken
> china in the sun.[21]

or his 'Olumo Rock':

> Stone reared on the crest of Olumo
> And far-out-flung by lightning-hand.[22]

Clark's images are always direct and unelaborated. In 'Night Rain' we have:

> She moves her bins, bags and vats
> Out of the rain water
> That like ants filing out of the wood
> Will scatter and gain possession
> Of the floor.[23]

Clark also uses the devices of alliteration and onomatopoeia for musical effects as in 'The Return of the Fishermen':

> Pins and needles effervescent up heel
> Dabble, dabble, dip paddle blades
> And silent you furrow up from sea.
> O, quick now goes the sun to sea
> Tick-twit, squirrels stow their seeds
> And low is the squirming down keel.[24]

Clark has published two collections of poems—*Poems* (Mbari Publications) and *A Reed in the Tide*. (The latter includes many poems from the former.) Each volume shows Clark as a derivative poet owing much of his metric style to both Hopkins and Eliot: the run-on stressed line, the stylized repetition, the rhetorical excess all derive from these masters. But Clark has been able in many instances to absorb these in such a way as to evolve his own personal style. Where he has been unable to evolve a personal idiom, his versification shows through as artifice and his language becomes affected as in:

> Give me your water whole
> And slake slake my soul
> The irresistible blight
> Spiriting in the night[25]

where *whole* is used only to sustain the rhyme pattern, where *slake* is repeated to patch up the metre.

Wole Soyinka established himself as one of the major Nigerian poets with the publication of *Idanre and Other Poems*. In this collection, Soyinka achieved a personal idiom in the use of elevated language and a deliberate weightiness. There is an intricate pattern of organization in each poem. The recurrent mood, except in a few poems, is brooding. In the title poem 'Idanre', Soyinka uses a highly rhetorical style to reinterpret the creative myth of the Yoruba and to show its relevance to modern life. Here, he overreaches himself in the wealth of images taken from Yoruba lore and in the inexplicable multidimensional symbolism. If the reader fails to understand the meaning of the multi-layered symbol of 'The wine-girl, dazed from divine dallying',[26] explained by the author as 'Also Oya, wife of Ogun, latterly of Sango. Also a dead girl, killed in a motor accident', the poet is to blame. While Oya symbolizes the fusion of the two essences Ogun and Sango, is the wine-girl to be taken as a reincarnation of Oya and also that of the girl killed in a motor accident? The reader is often at a loss in interpreting many of Soyinka's symbols.

Soyinka's images are also complex even when the myth from which they are drawn is simple:

> Rather, may we celebrate the stray electron, defiant
> Of patterns, celebrate the splitting of the gods
> Cannonisation of the strong hand of a slave who set
> The rock in revolution—and the Boulder cannot
> Up the hill in times unwind.[27]

Apart from his 'Telephone Conversation', a humorous lampoon on prejudice, most of Soyinka's poems show the serious side of his personality. In 'Death at Dawn' we have:

> Traveller, you must set out
> At dawn. And wipe your feet upon
> The dog-nose wetness of earth . . .
> This soft kindling, soft receding breeds
> Racing joys and apprehensions for
> A naked day, burdened hulks retract
> Stoop to the mist in faceless throng
> To make the silent markets—swift, mute
> Processions on grey byways. . . .[28]

Here we have the tempo of spoken language. The poem starts with a dramatic tone, then stops for a painting of the setting. Soyinka then adds material from traditional belief:

> The right foot for joy, the left, dread
> And the mother prays, child
> May you never walk
> When the road waits, famished.

The killing of the white cock, however accidental, should have been enough sacrifice to the famished road, nevertheless a human being is 'Silenced in the startled hug of his invention.' The cock's death then presages the death of a human being that is to come. The subdued tone of the narrative, the tempo and rhythm of spoken language, the blend of materials from both traditional belief and the present, the introspective brooding:

> is this mocked grimace
> This closed contortion—I?

all are essential qualities of Soyinka's work.

Drama

Wole Soyinka and J. P. Clark have also made significant contributions to drama in Nigeria. Of the two, Soyinka's achievements in play-writing are more impressive.

Soyinka believes in 'a people's theatre' for which the themes of his plays are drawn from the culture and experience of his audience. To this end, he tries to break away from the restrictions of conventional European theatre by fusing dramatic techniques from the Yoruba traditional dance-drama with those of the European stage. Thus he incorporates into his plays a lot of spectacle in the form of dance, mime and masks; he also makes use of music and song. The dramatic situations in his plays usually arise from conventional situations of mis-understanding, human fears and ambitions and conflicts in personality; with these he works up his plot through myth, proverbs, allusions and dance.

Soyinka's impact on the Nigerian theatre has been immense. He has already published seven plays; in each play, he has used the theatre as a medium of social comment. In *A Dance of the Forests*, the playwright draws largely on Yoruba mythology in his bid to show that the past can illuminate the present. If there is any pervading theme among the many introduced in this play, it is probably that which debunks the negri-tudist's glorification of his past and his ancestors. This play is a puzzling one, perhaps Soyinka's most difficult to understand. The plot is loose, the cast too large, the language almost inscrutable. Yet the dramatic situations of the play, made up of surprises most of the time, are very effective.

The Lion and the Jewel is a tightly constructed comedy satirizing Lakunle the school-teacher's superficial concept of civilization. Even though the theme is a serious one, modernity versus tradition, it is treated with sly humour. In its resolution, Soyinka shows that progress and tradition are not mutually exclusive, for Baroka does not hate progress but 'its nature / which makes all roofs and faces look the same'.[29] Soyinka constructs this play using the Greek unities of time, place and action. He divides the action into three movements of Morning, Noon and Night. His use of dance and mime in this play must be mentioned. Mime is first introduced with the flashback technique showing the press photographer's entry into Ilujinle. This technique is highly effective in his play while the dance that follows is not merely decorative but expresses the characters and comments on them. Both dance and music are well integrated with the plot.

Two major plays, *The Road* and *Kongi's Harvest*, are satires on aspects of social and political life of West Africa respectively. In *The Road* the action is divided into two parts; in *Kongi's Harvest* it is divided into

Hemlock, First Part, Second Part and Hangover as if the conventional division of action into Acts would not do. *The Road* makes use of the mask-idiom of Agemo. Characterization in this play is richly done: Say Tokyo Kid and Particulars Joe are done with depth, even though they are types within the social background of the play. The symbolism is also complex; one may, however, enjoy the play without the symbol getting in one's way. *Kongi's Harvest* is an ambitious play: a study and ridicule of dictatorship. It is a tightly constructed play with the conflict in the personalities of Kongi and Oba Danlola all pervading. But one wonders how Segi the courtesan furthers the development of both theme and plot.

Soyinka varies his dramatic dialogue. He can shift from highly formalized free verse to down-to-earth colloquialism, from impeccable standard English idiom to Americanism, pidgin English or to Yoruba. In fact, Yoruba idiom and songs are major features in some of these plays. Soyinka's attitude to language in these plays is in keeping with his idea of 'a people's theatre' in which the language has to be evocative to call up the experience, beliefs and emotions of the audience. The language is rich in allusions to folklore and custom. In *The Lion and the Jewel*, we have:

> *Sidi:* If the tortoise cannot tumble
> It does not mean that he can stand
> *Baroka:* When the child is full of riddles, the mother
> Has one water-pot the less.[30]

Soyinka's language, whether verse or prose, works through image and allusion.

Soyinka brings together in his plays many technical devices and it is a measure of his genius that he can integrate all these devices: his dance, while sometimes decorative, is most often introduced to express comment upon characters and events; his music has a place in the drama for, apart from its providing some relief, the drums talk to the actors and audience[31]; his mime is most often used within the flashback technique to illuminate the present, though it is sometimes overdone. Soyinka remains the best poet-dramatist in Africa.

Ozidi is Clark's most ambitious play and probably his best. Here, Clark to some extent forgoes his Greek classical model for a relatively romantic one featuring dance and music. The themes—universal human fortunes and reverses, human will, revenge, etc.—are treated on an epic scale. The play is a cycle based, according to the playwright, 'on the Ijaw saga of Ozidi, told in seven days to dance, music and mime'.

Ozidi is a well-constructed play meshing together both the fairy-tale legend and references to contemporary society:

Men that yesterday were only teachers
Depending on schoolboy collections and firewood . . .
Are today ministers of state riding in cars as big as ships.[32]

There is a deliberate attempt to individualize Ozidi, the hero, and his characterization is in some depth. He is perhaps one of Clark's most satisfying stage characters, yet he still looks like a 'type'.

Clark's dialogue in *Ozidi* is in the medium of the free verse. The poetic medium is the playwright's device to give his play a dimension of universality and timelessness even though the setting is drawn from Clark's local culture. The poetry is moving and evocative and there is an attempt to capture the rhythm of speech:

. . . So for several days
They buffeted each other without stop: they fought with swords
They fought with sticks, they fought with stones, and tiring of
    weapons
They grappled with hands: wrestling, rolling times out
Of number from one end of the field to the other.[33]

A noticeable weakness of the play is its complexity in scene shifting. Act I has nine scenes, Act II, seven, Act III, eight, while Act V has 'a twin scene' played on 'two parallel planes'. Moreover, the cast of the play is a very large one. To produce this play will tax all the resources of both the stage and a seasoned play director.

Clark's earlier plays, *Song of a Goat*, *The Masquerade* and *The Raft*, may be considered together even though the thematic connection between the three is loose and thin. *The Masquerade* is a sequel to *Song of a Goat*, for we have Diribi say of Tufa

. . . Did he tell you also his father
Usurped the bed of his elder brother . . .
. . . and for shame
Of it after hanged himself in broad daylight
While her unfortunate abused husband
Walked of his own will into the sea?[34]

This is a summary of *Song of a Goat*.

For these three plays, Clark chooses Greek tragedy as a model. The defects of the model are also carried over. In the first place, characterization yields precedence to thematic development with the result that the characters do not come to life. This is noticeably so in *The Raft* where the four lumbermen are so generalized that their individual traits from their different backgrounds are not made much of. Could

this be deliberate? Is the playwright showing that the common plight
of these men in their journey to perdition conditions their common
reactions? Were this so, it would not account for the lack of convincing
character delineation of Zifa or Tonye in *Song of a Goat*. Secondly the
convention of such a model warrants the use of stylized free verse
which in Clark's treatment outrages dialogue conventions in the
medium of English: the characters speak out of character. In *Song of
a Goat*, for instance, one can shift the speeches around among some of
the characters without much loss. Another point here is that because
of the formal nature of the verse used, the dialogues are far removed
from everyday speech. Many other seeming defects in Clark's plays
may be mentioned, but they are in a different category from the ones
already cited: for thinness of characterization and formalized language
are weaknesses not of Clark as a playwright but of the model he has
chosen. The other defects are these: are the themes in *Song of a Goat* and
The Masquerade treated convincingly as the subject of epic tragedies?
I still have some doubt in my mind about this, for unless one accepts
the plot through a knowledge of the culture that Clark is portraying,
one would find it difficult to believe that late impotence would
culminate in the death of the two brothers in *Song of a Goat*. For,
according to the Masseur, Zifa should have considered that his brother
'Take over the tilling of the fertile / Soil . . .'[35] a thing their 'fathers did
not forbid even in days / Of old'. Of course, the curse, the element of
the supernatural, is the only agent for the final tragedy.

Clark is more of a poet than a playwright and the weight and the
movement of his plays are carried by the sheer brilliance of his lines.

> Not a rustle of leaves
> Not a cry of bird, nor the sudden charge
> Of sheep or goats between wake and sleep
> The moon takes a surprise interception; only
> The leaden drop of dew in monotone
> Down cheeks and limbs of the plaintain
> To where the bahama creeps.[36]

This is the description of night solitude by Women of the House in
The Masquerade.

The direction towards which Nigerian literature is moving is the
establishment of its own unique characteristics. While in its beginnings
it was a mere appendage to West European literature whose style and
format it aped, significant and worthwhile experiments are being made;
in these experiments may lie the characteristics of this type of literature.
In the novel, for instance, Soyinka, in spite of all the influence of the
techniques of post-Joycean novels, may be said to have attained some

uniqueness in characterization and idiom. Nigerian plays have something enriching to offer the theatre in their utilization of dance and music. And whatever one may object to in the type of the English idiom employed by Nigerian writers, this idiom will continue to be a differentiating feature setting this literature apart from other literatures written in English.

Notes

1 Ulli Beier, *Introduction to African Literature*, Longmans, London, 1967, p. 190.

2 Ibid.

3 Amos Tutuola, *The Palm-Wine Drinkard*, Faber, London, 1962, p. 7.

4 Amos Tutuola, *Simbi and the Satyr of the Dark Jungle*, Faber, London, 1955, p. 49.

5 Amos Tutuola, *The Palm-Wine Drinkard*, op. cit., p. 13.

6 Ibid., p. 57.

7 Chinua Achebe, *Things Fall Apart*, Heinemann, London, 1958, p. 11.

8 Ibid., p. 24.

9 Ibid., p. 7.

10 Chinua Achebe, *No Longer at Ease*, Heinemann, London, 1960, p. 163.

11 Chinua Achebe, *Things Fall Apart*, op. cit., p. 26.

12 Chinua Achebe, *Arrow of God*, Heinemann, London, 1964, p. 17.

13 Dennis Osadebay, 'Young Africa's Plea', in *Anthology of Wes African Verse*, ed. O. Bassir, p. 57.

14 Aig Imoukhuede, *Modern Poetry from Africa*, ed. Gerald Moore and Ulli Beier, Penguin, London, pp. 100-101.

15 Christopher Okigbo, 'Overture', *Heavensgate*, Ibadan, 1962.

16 Christopher Okigbo, *Limits* (1) Ibadan, 1964.

17 Ibid., (X).

18 Christopher Okigbo, 'Initiation', *Heavensgate*, op. cit.

19 Ibid., 'Passage' (1).

20 J. P. Clark, *A Reed in the Tide*, Longmans, 1965, p. 16.

21 Ibid., p. 12.

22 J. P. Clark, *Poems*, p. 7.

23 J. P. Clark, *A Reed in the Tide*, op. cit., p. 2.

24 Ibid., p. 15.

25 J. P. Clark, 'The Watermaid', in *Poems*, p. 23.

26 Wole Soyinka, *Idanre and Other Poems*, Methuen, London, 1967, p. 62 and Note II, p. 86.

27 Ibid., p. 82.

28 Ibid., pp. 10-11.

29 Wole Soyinka, *The Lion and the Jewel*, O.U.P., London, 1963, p. 52.

30 Ibid., p. 42.

31 A feature of the 'talking drum' (tension drum) is that its manipulator can use it to imitate the tonal patterns of some saws in the Yoruba language. Hence, actors usually react appropriately to the intentions of the lead drummer.

32 J. P. Clark, *Ozidi*, O.U.P., London, 1960, p. 4.

33 Ibid., p. 112.

34 J. P. Clark, *Three Plays*, O.U.P., London, p. 68.

35 Ibid., p. 11.

36 Ibid., p. 77.

Nigeria, Africa and the Caribbean: A Bird's Eye View

by Clive Wake

Concepts like negritude and Pan-Africanism, with their emphasis on 'African culture' and 'African political unity', tend to give both the creative writer in Africa and his readers the impression that there is a single, uniform 'African Literature', a notion which is easily extended to take in the Caribbean as well. This kind of attitude to the creative writing in modern European languages in the black world has in fact tended to colour the view of a great many people. Certainly, the European critic, brought up to an awareness of the tremendous national diversities within the notion of 'Western civilization', be it its English, French, Italian or American manifestations, has rather paradoxically been inclined to talk of African literature as if it were a uniform whole. This attitude is perhaps to some extent excusable, since a modern African literature has only come into being since the Second World War, and not enough has been produced in single African countries to make it possible to talk about Senegalese literature, Ghanaian literature, or even, perhaps, Nigerian literature, in spite of the fact that the latter is the one African country that has produced a great flowering of creative writing.

This difficulty has been compounded by the fact that throughout the black world the main preoccupation of the creative writers has, quite naturally, been the conflict between white colonialism and the black man's aspiration towards control of his own destiny. It is to be expected as well, at this stage, that the culture of the relevant colonial power should have a strong influence on the creative writing in its former colonies. This factor has both delayed the emergence of distinctive national literatures, as well as, of course, providing inevitably part of the basis upon which they will be constructed. There is an underlying tension in the black world itself, chiefly in West Africa, between the notion of Pan-African unity and national identity. The former tended to dominate African politics mainly in the pre-independence period, and was a very powerful rallying cry that enabled the individual colonies to give one another mutual support, even if it was primarily moral, within the framework of a common political aim. Since independence, however, individual states, preoccupied inevitably with the internal problems of independence, have tended to go their own way, and this is beginning to lead to an almost unconscious stressing of national characteristics. I think it is true to say that, in a general way, writing before independence tended to have a Pan-African orientation—one could give Senghor as a typical example. But if one looks at Nigerian writing since independence, one realizes that it is more and more set in a Nigerian context. It is difficult to be very categorical about this, since Nigeria is the only West African country to have produced a sufficiently large body of writing covering all the main literary *genres*. For this reason it may be possible to begin talking about a Nigerian literature and to see something like the emergence of a distinctive type of writing with an aura of its own. Already the general reader is becoming aware of certain typically Nigerian features, mainly a kind of vitality and ebullience which is very Nigerian and which one senses in the people themselves on arriving in Lagos from Dakar or Accra. The nearest comparison one can make in West Africa is with the novelists of the French-speaking Cameroon. Here too we find a kind of bubbling over with life, especially in Ferdinand Oyono and Mongo Beti, although it is equally true, in a more restrained way, of a new Cameroonian writer, Francis Bebey. Yet there is a big difference between the Nigerian enjoyment of community life, be it that of the city or the country, and the more Rabelaisian bawdy and satirical humour of the Cameroonians.

One has to remember, in making comparisons between the writing of the different regions of the black world, that, although the common general theme is the conflict between white colonialism and its influence, and the black man's desire to be independent, the nature and circumstances of this conflict vary from region to region and even from country to country. Within West Africa alone there is the almost radical difference between the influence of French and English culture. It is undoubtedly true that French culture has had a more marked impact on the creative writing of the former French territories. The philosophy of negritude, which is most strongly associated with French-speaking Africa, is as much a product of French culture, with its love of literary schools and literary manifestoes, as it is a reaction against it. French Africans of Senghor's generation were as obsessed with the primacy of culture as the French themselves, with their *mission civilisatrice*. This French influence has tended to impose a certain uniformity on the creative writing of French-speaking Africa which has no parallel in English-speaking Africa. As different as individual talents like those of Senghor, Beti and Camara Laye may be, there is nevertheless a striking similarity between them, coming possibly from the way they accept with little variation the strict requirements of the French language and style. Already in Nigerian writing, almost imperceptibly, a new style of English is emerging which will eventually distinguish Nigerian literature not only from English literature but also from other African writing. This is probably due to the fact that the imposition of English political thinking on the former English colonies was not accompanied by the rigorous application of English literary culture. This has given the Nigerian writer a much more immediate access to his own culture, which he is not afraid to make use of, as well as a freer choice of English literary influences. The Nigerian writer has no need or urge, therefore, to resort to a literary philosophy before he puts pen to paper. Perhaps the greatest weakness of negritude in the long term is the fact that it is really an intellectual return to Africa, and therefore unlikely to take root. This argument could be countered, however, by pointing out that in France in the sixteenth century, in very similar cultural circumstances, a conscious literary movement, the Pléiade, had a lasting influence on French literature, in spite of the subsequent reaction against it.

A further distinction between French- and English-speaking writing is to be found in the reaction to the presence of the white man's culture. In Nigerian literature at least there is an acceptance of the fact of the presence of the white man's culture, without the arguing about it that occurs in the French-speaking countries. Achebe, for instance, is primarily concerned with the conflicts within Nigerian society. In *Things Fall Apart*, the arrival of the white missionaries merely precipitates a drama already under way, and in the two novels dealing with contemporary Nigerian politics and society, *No Longer at Ease* and *A Man of the People*, he is concerned more with the way his characters react to an already existing situation than with criticism of the white man for having created that situation. If we take his first novel, *Things Fall Apart*, as an initial statement of his approach, it is clear that in Achebe's view, African society had begun to fall apart before the advent of the white man; the latter's arrival merely leads to the creation of a more complex situation with which to cope. This is probably true also of *The Arrow of God*, since it is really a dissension within the African society itself which, as in the earlier novel, is precipitated by the interference of the white man. In other words, the white man has created the political framework in which men like Chief Nanga function, not as men corrupted by the white man, but as men, and perhaps, in particular, Nigerian men. As Achebe's idealistic hero discovers, in a land of poor people it is taken for granted that those who manage to gain access to the good things of life should enjoy them to the full. Similarly Nzekwu, in *Wand of Noble Wood*, deals with the conflict between traditional customs and the new society in a way which shows that he accepts that the situation is what it is; he is not concerned with apportioning blame. Achebe, it seems to me, in so far as he passes judgment in his novels, is condemning the dishonesty of individuals, and not the more abstract colonialism. If one were to compare this approach with that of almost any novelist from French-speaking Africa, one would discover, I think, that the latter is more inclined to see things literally in terms of conflict between black and white with, frequently, the kind of generalizations which are bound to result from this kind of approach. The Nigerian writer is as torn in his cultural loyalties as any black writer from any part of the world, but he does seem capable of recognizing the realities of his situation and of trying to cope with them. There is, moreover, a kind of spontaneous enjoyment of life in the big city, the creation of the white man. One finds it in Achebe, perhaps in Soyinka's *The Interpreters*, but chiefly in the work of that great student of the city, Cyprian Ekwensi.

Nevertheless, the cultural predicament of the modern African is seen in the Nigerian novel with a dramatic clarity and directness which is very different from the more nuanced approach of West Indian writers. This is because the Caribbean situation is very different from that of Africa. The Caribbean writers express the predicament of a people who are dispossessed. This applies as much to the French-speaking as to the English-speaking Caribbean writer, although one has to make the same kind of distinction between them as in West Africa. Caribbean society is made up of indigenous people, the descendants of African slaves and Indian indented labourers, as well as the descendants of mixed liaisons. The majority of West Indians have no natural culture to which to turn; they can only aspire, if this is what they want, to the European culture of their former masters. This aspiration, as their writers tell us (one thinks of G. Lamming's *Of Age and Innocence* and John Hearne's *Stranger at the Gate*[1]), tends to create a class structure based on colour which is much more complex than anything to be found in colonial Africa (except Southern Africa). There is in West Indian writing as a whole a longing for cultural roots which the emulation of the white man or the transplanting of Indian social patterns does not seem to satisfy.[2] This has led writers like Wilson Harris and Edgar Mittelholzer to delve into a poetico-mythical or historical past in an attempt to find some kind of synthesis.[3] English-medium writing in the Caribbean, of all the literature of the black world, seems least concerned with the white man himself. As in Nigerian writing, the impact of the white man is, on the whole, taken for granted, but unlike the Nigerian writer, who analyses a conflict between the old and the new, the Caribbean novelist analyzes a single, highly complex situation containing little in the way of solid foundations or clear choices, and yet which leaves him with very little room for manœuvre.

It is this absence of polemic or protest which, on the whole, distinguishes the writing of the English-speaking black world from that of the French. This is perhaps why E. Braithwaite's long poem, *Rights of Passage*,[4] seems to stand out. In tone and theme it resembles Césaire's *Cahier d'un Retour au Pays Natal*.[5] The conflict theme in French black writing very often takes the form of an angry attack on the white man for his destructive impact on African society. There tends, therefore, to be a much stronger racial awareness in their writing which, with the best will in the world, cannot always be prevented from showing in its negative aspect. A major poet like Césaire, in his *Cahier*,[6] is able to give his anger a poetical, as well as a political, validity through his mastery of his language and his medium. A poet as sensitive as Senghor, deeply in love with French culture, is almost always able to keep his praise of the black world just this side of racial expression, and he has admitted that at first it was indeed racialist.[7] This delicate balance which he has had to maintain partly explains why many people still regard negritude as a form of racialism. It would be absurd to expect otherwise; the situation is indeed a racial one, and if writers choose to base their work on the conflict between white and black, it is extremely difficult to avoid some kind of racial expression. Major poets and novelists like Césaire, Senghor, Camara Laye and Mongo Beti have, because of their greater insight and ability, managed to avoid this kind of failure, but where the talent is not so great, this kind of protest does have a weakening effect on the literary work if it becomes more important then the concrete expression of experience. It is, indeed, chiefly because the *Cahier* relates a personal return home and because Senghor's poetic account of black-white relations is seen in terms of personal experience, that these works transcend their potential weakness on the literary level. Polemic or protest, whether it takes the form of an attack on the white man or its corollary, praise of the black man and Africa, often prevents a poem from having any inner vitality because it tends to exaggerate and to have little relation to real experience. This is even true of the masters of French-speaking protest poetry, poets like Damas and David Diop. In their case, in spite of their ability, their poetry eventually becomes monotonous because it is too repetitive in its basic, unsubtle themes and in its forms. A reader can obtain a good idea of what I mean by reading the contributions published in the *New Sum of Poetry from the Negro World* by Présence Africaine.[8] Excluded from this volume are the major poets of the older generation, except David Diop, possibly because he died so young and still seems to belong to the younger generation. The comparison between the poetry written in French and the poetry written in English is very revealing. Nearly all the poetry in French belongs to the polemical type—poems attacking the white man, poems in praise of Africa, poems extolling the black man's suffering. The preoccupation with the theme takes precedence over any sense of form, and the result is a kind of repetitive doggerel almost entirely lacking in inspiration (with the exception of poems by Tchicaya U Tam'si, David Diop and Francis Bebey). In a sense, the trouble with these poets is that they are standing at the door hurling insults at the unwanted guest after he has departed, instead of going inside to tidy up the mess. There is room, of course, for a new kind of protest poetry which will be able to express the continuing racialism of white men that is so clearly a major feature of our post-colonial world.

Contrasted with this approach, the Nigerian representatives in the anthology, Okigbo, Soyinka and J. P. Clark, and to some extent Lenrie Peters and George Awoonor Williams from Sierra Leone and Ghana, and Derek Walcott from the Caribbean, make a much stronger impression. This is partly because they have a true sense of the poetic use of language, they have a real sense of form and of what is relevant, and above all, their poetry starts from personal experience. Wole Soyinka's *Telephone Conversation* (not included in the Présence Africaine anthology) and David Rubadiri's poem *A Liverpool Docker* are telling indictments of the white man's failure, but they are successful as poems because they are based on concrete situations and, in a tradition of poetry often out of favour now in Europe, they do so with considerable beauty of language, form and insight.

It is the combined sense of the concrete, of form and of poetic insight which gives contemporary Nigerian poetry its vital quality. This is as true of Okigbo as of any other significant Nigerian poet, such as Soyinka or J. P. Clark, in spite of Professor Ali Mazrui's claim that Okigbo is abstract and therefore not a good African poet.[9] He may be difficult, which is probably what Mazrui really means, but there is nothing abstract either about the experience evoked by the poet or the language and imagery used. The fact is that the English-medium black poets writing at the moment have been able to root their poetry in personal experience. In this they resemble Senghor and Césaire, but whereas the latter expressed themselves in voices which went from the private to the public experience, the Nigerian poet is much more concerned about the private experience itself, because he expresses the universal experience in terms of personal experience: this is true, I think, both of Okigbo's search for a poetic language and, in the Caribbean, of Derek Walcott's sense of being a castaway.[10]

My point can best be illustrated, however, by drawing a comparison, or rather a contrast, between the drama of Césaire and that of Soyinka. Césaire's two plays, *Le Roi Christophe* and *Une Saison au Congo*,[11] portray the black man's situation vis-à-vis the white man. Césaire's plays work like mediaeval morality plays, with their large numbers of characters and the emphasis on ideas rather than characters; with so many characters, in fact, there is no time to use them in any other way than as emblems. Their form has very likely been inspired by the drama of Bertolt Brecht, who has in recent years enjoyed great popularity in France. Yet these plays have plenty of vitality and movement, plenty of potential for the imaginative producer, and it is this perhaps which gives them their quality. Soyinka, on the other hand, is more interested in human situations at the level of the individual, and he is more interested in the human problems created by certain typical situations. He therefore sets his plays in a Nigerian village or a Nigerian town or bases them on Nigerian activity, and he uses the age-old dramatic situations of misunderstanding, personality conflicts, ordinary human fears and ambitions. It is obvious, then, that Césaire and Soyinka are poles apart in their approach to drama, and it seems to me that this difference of approach is dictated as much, if not more, by their different cultural backgrounds as by their individual talents.

A similar contrast could be drawn between the verse dramas of the Malagasy playwright, Jacques Rabémananjara, and J. P. Clark. Both of them are interested in features of their respective countries' traditional culture. But whereas, in *Les Boutriers de l'Aurore*,[12] Rabémananjara is using a legendary account of the way Madagascar was first settled by the Polynesian people who constitute its chief racial element, in order to glorify the national past, Clark, like Soyinka, is concerned with the portrayal in dramatic terms of eternal and universal human situations, for which he draws on their Nigerian expression, either in village life or through legend. In this sense, both Soyinka and Clark differ also from playwrights from other parts of West Africa, who tend still to create their drama out of the conflict between the old and the new in Africa. Soyinka seems to do this in *The Lion and the Jewel*, but one leaves the play with the impression that he has enjoyed the dramatic quality of the situation rather than tried to expound his view on a social problem. Some readers may understand better what I mean if I recall, by way of comparison, the eternal argument as to whether Molière, the French seventeenth-century playwright, was chiefly interested in writing good drama or in satirizing social follies.

A situation which is essentially one of conflict does not lend itself easily to what one might call a comic view of life, taking comic in its older sense of order; a view, that is, in which conflict is resolved and this resolution is taken for granted. There is of course plenty of humour, but this is frequently of the essentially uncomic satirical kind, especially in the writing of novelists like Oyono and Beti. Soyinka, in *The Lion and the Jewel*, portrays what is, in fact, a comic vision, but he has not continued this approach in his later drama. Almost all of Tutuola's novels are comic: his is a world in which the heroes encounter all kinds of difficulties and dangers, but, as in a nightmare, somehow it all comes right in the end and the dead hero always returns to life. Camara Laye's novel, *The Radiance of the King*,[13] is also a comic novel, not only for its humour but chiefly because of the way the hero, the white man Clarence, in the end finds salvation. Yet Clarence's pilgrimage is not unlike the wanderings of Tutuola's heroes, even though the worlds in which they function are, on the one hand, the world of legend and fantasy and, on the other, the world of realism and mysticism. A comparison between these two writers along these lines could indicate perhaps the tremendous potential of Tutuola's medium. There is little or nothing of the comic vision in either the French-speaking or the English-speaking Caribbean. One can easily understand this, since the predicament of the Caribbean is so much more tragic in essence than that of the African, who has something positive to turn to in the form of his traditional way of life and the oral literature of the past. The Caribbean predicament seems so hopeless that many Caribbean writers have left their native West Indies to settle in Britain. The satirical comedy of Naipaul, a good deal more subtle and complex than that of Oyono or Beti, is still, in the final analysis, not truly comic, for it reveals a deeply sad and hopeless vision of Caribbean society. A striving towards the comic state is contained in the epic nature of Wilson Harris's world. The only West Indian writer I can think of who has a vision which could be called comic is Michael Anthony,[14] whose characters move and act in a world which they do not question; significantly it is the prelapsarian world of the child, who has not yet attained the age of awareness which eventually destroys his comic vision. French-medium writers, influenced by negritude, seek to establish the lost paradise of the African way of life—Senghor refers to it as Paradise,[15] but this idyllic world is not truly comic because it is so manifestly a vision seen through rose-tinted spectacles; it does not exist, it is a dream. An example of what I mean is to be found in Senghor's poem, *The Return of the Prodigal Son*,[16] where he evokes the pastoral way of life he knew as a child. At least in Senghor's poetry, this poem included, this idyllicism does have a poetic or dramatic function quite distinct from its ideological intent: it enables the poet to dramatize his situation more effectively by contrasting absolutes—the perfect past and the present. There is, however, a tendency among some French-medium writers to idyllicize the rural way of life for its own sake, as for example, Camara Laye in *The African Child*,[17] and especially in his latest novel, *Dramouss*,[18] where the glorification of Guinea is almost embarrassing in a writer of such achievement. There is plenty to compensate for this approach in the novels of Mongo Beti, but it is something which I do not think is to be found very much in the writing of Nigerian authors. I must, however, mention in this connection the Caribbean writer, Jacques Roumain, in whose novel, *Gouverneurs de la Rosée*,[19] the idyllic presentation of the peasants of Haiti nevertheless attains a kind of artistic perfection through its very simplicity. It is a book which ought to be better known.

Along with most other West African writers, Nigerians have on the whole tended to prefer the novel as their medium in prose. The short story is not very common, although in a sense Tutuola's novels are a series of short stories strung together. There is, however, that strange phenomenon peculiar to Nigeria, the Onitsha market literature, where the short story is in its element. Achebe's *The Sacrificial Egg and other stories* was published in Onitsha by a local publisher.[20] The Onitsha market literature must surely be a unique phenomenon in the black world and is a striking indication of the Nigerian *rage de l'expression* which has made this country one of the most prolific in creative writing in either Africa or the Caribbean. In contrast, however, to the general trend in Nigeria and elsewhere, the one region which definitely does favour the short story is South Africa. There could be many explanations for this: the appeal of the magazine short story, much encouraged by *Drum*, as well as the personal insecurity, and the sense of living from day to day, that is the constant way of life for so many talented Africans in South Africa, if not for every African in the country. It is a short story which specializes mainly in illustrating the way racialism and apartheid affect the lives of ordinary Africans in South Africa, and emphasizes the human suffering involved. One thinks of writers like Richard Rive, Denis Brutus and Ezekiel Mphahlele, to mention only a few whose work is well known; significantly, one of the main African literary organs in South Africa is the *Classic*, which specializes in the short story. It is essentially a protest literature, and this applies to the few novels as well (the only novelist with an important body of work is Peter Abrahams) and to the other popular form of literary expression, the autobiography. The rare poet, such as Denis Brutus, transfers to his medium the same kind of acute observation of the local scene. It is a writing which inevitably lacks the scope of the Nigerian novel, but the compact framework of the short story is often an extremely adequate and moving expression (although not without moments of humour) of the restricted world in which the South African Negro is obliged to live, both physically and emotionally.

Little use is made in South African writing of traditional material, and this applies by and large to Caribbean writing as well. The Caribbean writer has less tradition to draw on, as we have seen, but in South Africa the reason is largely the way in which tradition has been undermined by migration to the towns in search of work and the consequent breakdown of tribal life. By traditional material I do not mean the setting of the action of novels and plays in the country, although in a sense this can be seen as part of it, since it is in the country that tradition remains alive. I mean really the drawing on traditional legend and folktales as a source of thematic material by the modern writer. This kind of material is extremely difficult to use, because it needs to be made relevant to the contemporary reader and his own situation, which is basically one which makes the custom of explaining experience in terms of myth and fantasy more remote. The parallel in Europe is the use of well-known Greek myth by such writers as Eugene O'Neill, Sartre, Cocteau and so on. In modern Western culture it is an extremely fertile source of material for the expression of eternal human situations and problems. Nigerian writers have frequently drawn on the same kind of tradition in Yoruba and Ibo oral literature. John Pepper Clark's most impressive play to date, in my view, is *Ozidi*, based on an Ijaw saga, and Soyinka's most significant poem *Idanre* is drawn from Yoruba legend. But the most remarkable exponent of this form of writing in Nigeria is, of course, Amos Tutuola. It is difficult to say whether Tutuola has realized the full potential of his medium and succeeded in making it relevant to contemporary Nigeria. He has certainly demonstrated the immense fertility of Yoruba folk literature and has attempted to adapt his material to contemporary life by introducing references to the modern ways and objects brought by the white man. The use of apparently insignificant detail in this way is very effective; it reminds one, for example, of the way Jean Anouilh makes his characters in *Antigone* smoke, so as to make his rendering of the Greek myth more immediate.

It is interesting to compare Tutuola's work with that of another West African writer who has drawn mainly on folk literature: Birago Diop. The latter's *Tales of Amadou Koumba*[21] are well known and have been translated into English. But although these tales have been inspired by a very similar tradition, the final impression is very different. On the simplest level of form, where Tutuola attempts the transformation of his tales into a novel, Diop retains the form of the story. Also, Diop calls on the familiar animal tales, as well as telling stories involving people, whereas Tutuola is almost entirely concerned with human beings or creatures which have features relating them essentially to the human. These and the other differences between Tutuola and Diop probably have much to do with the different folk traditions which inspire them. Perhaps the most significant difference between them is the fact that the element of fantasy and imagination is much richer in Tutuola than it is in Diop. Tutuola's world reminds one, from the imaginative point of view, of Lewis Carroll's *Alice in Wonderland*, whereas Diop has the more restrained imagination which we associate with the conventional folktale. Whether it is in fact so or not, Tutuola gives the reader the impression that his work is the product of a truly creative imagination, whereas Diop is on the whole merely re-telling in his own way tales as they are known. I do not want to underestimate Diop's achievement, which is considerable. He is a born story-teller, and his tales reveal an admirable economy of expression and sense of structure, as well as a real eye for the dramatic. Yet his tales are clearly influenced in the telling by his French education. Diop is one of the leading exponents of negritude of Senghor's generation; he is well known for his poem *Souffles* (*Breaths*). Reading his published poems, *Leurres et Lueurs*,[22] one cannot help noticing how many of them remain faithful to traditional French verse conventions, in an age when even in France they have been largely abandoned. They certainly were not used by Senghor, who sensed immediately that a poet must refer to the conventions of his time. My point about Diop is that his loyalty to the French tradition in his poetry indicates the extent of his dependence on the French tradition which in turn is also reflected in his short stories. In every other respect, however, Diop's concept of negritude, unlike Senghor's, tends to exclude the white man altogether. Diop is a writer for whom the white man does not exist, and it is an absence which the reader cannot help being very much aware of. The white man is physically absent from Tutuola's world, but present by implication in the things he has brought to Nigeria and which have impressed themselves on the Nigerian's imagination. The 'television-handed ghostess' and many other such references to the white man's culture along these lines point to an imagination endowed with a strong sense of wonder. It reminds one of the vivid circumlocutory ways that the white man's more strange inventions have been rendered into the African languages. The white man does not exist physically in Tutuola's world, but whereas Diop's deliberate exclusion has a negative effect, Tutuola's world, because it does not exclude in this way, has a fullness and an expansiveness which makes the reader feel more at ease.

Tutuola's world must owe a lot to his language, which is nevertheless the most puzzling aspect of his work. To the English reader it gives his novels a kind of charm and an amusing quality, while to the Nigerian reader he is simply writing 'bad' English, and therefore creating a false impression of the African's ability to master the language. For one point must be made clear: Tutuola's use of English is, strictly speaking, 'bad' English, the English of a man who has imperfectly learned the language. It is not the English spoken by the majority of Nigerians for whom the preferred form of spoken English is pidgin. There are variations in Tutuola's style of writing, from book to book, which suggest that his form of English is a deliberate mannerism rather than the English he normally speaks. One small illustration of this which struck me recently is the fact that in *The Palm-Wine Drinkard*, his first book, the full stop occurs at the end of a full sentence, including, that is, the clauses. In his latest book, *Ajaiyi and his inherited Poverty*, a full stop occurs at the end of every clause. When Fagunwa writes, presumably he uses 'correct' Yoruba.

It is not my function in this essay to explain Tutuola's reasons for adopting this style, but I have raised the problem in order to emphasize the general problem of language in the writing, not only of Nigerians, but of the black world in general, and to inquire whether a new literary language is beginning to emerge either in Nigeria or elsewhere. It seems to me that Tutuola belongs to those writers who feel the need to create for themselves a radically new literary idiom which may bear little relation to the spoken language. Samuel Beckett is probably a good example of this in Europe. But there is a more important problem. The French poet and novelist, Raymond Queneau, believes that the spoken language ought to replace the hypertrophied written language (but it must be borne in mind here that spoken French and written French are more widely separated than are spoken and literary English).[23] Queneau therefore writes his novels and many of his poems in colloquial French, and in addition very often spells words and phrases as they are pronounced. The chief effect of this, it seems to me, is to suggest quaintness and therefore to heighten the reader's amusement, not unlike the effect Tutuola's language has on the English reader. Other French poets, such as Jacques Prévert, consistently use colloquial French, although they do not follow Queneau in spelling words as they are pronounced. It may be worth while noting here that it was a celebrated poem of Prévert's, *Tentative d'une description d'un Dîner de Têtes à Paris-France*,[24] which inspired the form and to some extent colloquial language used by Césaire in his poem, *Cahier d'un Retour au Pays Natal*. This practice of using colloquial speech in the narrative part of the work as well as in the dialogue, where it could be expected, is not followed, to my knowledge, by any Nigerian writer. Soyinka's plays, especially *The Road*, do contain quite a lot of pidgin and even some Yoruba, but this can be expected in plays, as it can also in the dialogue of novels. Several Caribbean writers using English have made experiments with the use of Caribbean English in certain of their novels, but Samuel Selvon is the only one to use it consistently, as for example in *The Lonely Londoners*.[25] Except for Césaire's use of colloquial French (as opposed to Caribbean French) in the *Cahier*, there has been no attempt, at least by an important French-speaking writer, to do the same as some of his English-speaking counterparts. The use of colloquial speech as a literary language has severe limitations and will not probably be generally adopted. Its essential literary function is to create an effect of realism, as in Selvon's novels, or of satire, as in Queneau's *Le Chiendent*. Césaire uses it to convey the violence of his emotion in the *Cahier*.

In his introduction to a selection of James Joyce's works, Harry Levin points out that many of the most important English writers of this century have been Irishmen, and he ascribes this to the revitalizing effect on English of the Irish writer's own linguistic background.[26] Okigbo and Soyinka have, I think, reached a stage of creative mastery of English which very likely owes a good deal to the stimulus of their mother language. I do not think this is yet true of Clark, nor of any other poet or dramatist in West Africa. Although this was his aim, too, it is doubtful whether Senghor actually achieved this to the same extent. At the same time, a new literary language, peculiar to Nigeria, Jamaica and so on is bound to develop, in much the same way as a specifically American linguistic quality has developed in the United States. The form it will take will depend on the hundred and one factors that will condition the evolution of English and French in the Third World. This process has already begun in a small way in Nigerian writing and has perhaps gone further there than it has done elsewhere. Signs of this can be seen mainly in the prose writing. Beneath the appearance of a conventional English prose style, Achebe is already beginning to use linguistic forms which are not only peculiar to him but to Nigerian English as well. One does not gain this impression from a reading of Caribbean or French-speaking writers. Wilson Harris has a very personal style, but like Tutuola's, it is personal rather than colloquial. On the whole, Caribbean and French-speaking writers use an English and a French which is hardly distinguishable from that of the European source. One does occasionally find that French-speaking novelists use a French reminiscent of French student speech, as for example in Bertène Juminer's *Les Bâtards*[27] and parts of Mongo Beti's writing.

What one does not find in Nigeria, however, with the possible exceptions of Soyinka's *The Interpreters* (in some ways reminiscent of Lamming's *Of Age and Innocence*) and Okara's *The Voice*, is the search for new, more authentic forms of creative expression, in terms of treatment of themes and character in the novel, or of theme and imagery in poetry. Achebe, the *doyen* of Nigerian novelists, uses the conventional narrative novel, which fits in well with his idea that the novelist is also a teacher, and therefore cannot afford to be obscure or too difficult. Negritude is a well-known example of the other kind of search, but it is limited in effect to an historical function; that is, it is the creation of a need at a given moment in time, the need for a myth and a rallying cry. As such it has tended to remain, in spite of its ambitions, an ideal of literary expression rather than an achievement. In the Caribbean, Wilson Harris is trying to evolve a notion of character in the novel

205

which could well have repercussions in Europe. He has attempted to put his ideas into effect in his tetralogy, *The Palace of the Peacock, The Far Journey of Oudin, The Whole Armour* and *The Secret Ladder*, and has explained them in a collection of essays, *Tradition, the Writer and Society*.[28] This kind of search has been introduced into Nigerian poetry by Christopher Okigbo, in his quest for a poetic language, an 'account' of which is given in his poem *Limits*.

I have tried in this essay to bring out what seem to me to be significant points of comparison and difference between Nigerian writing and the writing of other parts of the black world. It makes no claims to be exhaustive, and other readers would probably be struck by other features and regard them as more significant. This is inevitable when one is dealing with literatures so young as those under comparison. For the same reason, it is particularly hazardous to make generalizations of the kind I have been making; but even at this stage, provided one is not too categorical about them, generalizations can highlight striking trends and indicate possible directions being taken by the literatures under review. One is perhaps on safest ground when one is contrasting individual authors, but even here there is the danger of ascribing personal differences to national or regional characteristics, so one is bound to be careful. One thing is clear, I think, and that is that political divisions within the continent of Africa, which tend to make the ideal of Pan-Africanism an even more remote dream, are going to hasten the emergence of fairly distinctive national literatures as has occurred in Europe. In this respect, the Nigerian *rage de l'expression* which has led to such a proliferation of writers, and among them so many of quality, will give this country an important advantage over the others.

Notes

1 G. Lamming, *Of Age and Innocence*, Michael Joseph, 1958. John Hearne, *Stranger at the Gate*, Faber, 1956.

2 Cf. V. S. Naipaul, *A House for Mr Biswas*, André Deutsch, 1961.

3 Cf. W. Harris, *Palace of the Peacock*, Faber, 1960; *The Far Journey of Oudin*, Faber, 1961; *The Whole Armour*, Faber, 1962; *The Secret Ladder*, Faber, 1963. E. Mittelholzer, *Children of Kaywana*, Secker & Warburg, 1952.

4 E. Braithwaite, *Rights of Passage*, Oxford University Press, 1967.

5 A. Césaire, *Cahier d'un Retour au Pays Natal*, Présence Africaine, 1956.

6 See also his less well-known work, *Et les chiens se taisaient*, Gallimard, 1946, which deals with a theme similar to that of the *Cahier*, and is of great interest.

7 See L. S. Senghor, *Prose and Poetry*, translated by John Reed and Clive Wake, Oxford University Press, 1965, p. 99: '*Negritude* as we had then (i.e. in 1928-1935) begun to conceive and define it was a weapon of defence and attack and inspiration, rather than an instrument of construction.' In an earlier passage quoted in this same selection, Senghor defends negritude against the charge of racialism (Extract 30: *The Struggle for Negritude*, p. 96).

8 'New Sum of Poetry from the Negro World', Présence Africaine, No. 57, Premier Trimestre 1966.

9 A. Mazrui, *Abstract Verse and African Tradition*, Zuka, No. 1, September 1967.

10 Cf. D. Walcott, *The Castaway and other Poems*, Jonathan Cape, 1965.

11 A. Césaire, *Le Roi Christophe*, Présence Africaine, 1963; *Une Saison au Congo*, Seuil, 1967. I exclude *Et les chiens se taisaient*, because it is really a dramatic poem, although Césaire terms it a tragedy.

12 J. Rabémananjara, *Les Boutriers de l'Aurore*, Présence Africaine, 1957.

13 Camara Laye, *The Radiance of the King*, translated by James Kirkup, Collins, 1956. Originally published in French as *Le Regard du Roi*, Plon, 1954.

14 Cf. Michael Anthony, *The Games were Coming*, André Deutsch, 1963; *The Year in San Fernando*, André Deutsch, 1965; *Green Days by the River*, André Deutsch, 1967.

15 Cf. L. S. Senghor, op. cit.: *For Koras and Balafong*, p. 108:
'A Paradise where guard is kept against fevers by a child with eyes bright as two swords.
Paradise my African childhood, that kept guard over the innocence of Europe.'

16 L. S. Senghor, op. cit., p. 177.

17 Camara Laye, *The African Child*, translated by James Kirkup, Collins, 1955. Originally published in French as *L'Enfant Noir*, Plon, 1953.

18 Camara Laye, *Dramouss*, Plon, 1966. There is an English translation by James Kirkup, under the title *A Dream of Africa*, Collins, 1968.

19 Jacques Roumain: *Gouverneurs de la Rosée*, Club Français du Livre 1950 (first published in 1944). There is an English translation by Langston Hughes and Mercer Cook under the title *Masters of the Dew*, Reynal & Hitchcock, New York, 1947.

20 C. Achebe, *The Sacrificial Egg and other stories*, Etudo, Onitsha, 1962.

21 Birago Diop, *Tales of Amadou Koumba*, translated by Dorothy Blair, Oxford University Press, 1966. This is a selection of stories taken from *Les Contes d'Amadou Koumba*, Fasquelle, 1947, and *Les Nouveaux Contes d'Amadou Koumba*, Présence Africaine, 1958.

22 Birago Diop, *Leurres et Lueurs*, Présence Africaine, 1960.

23 Queneau expounds his theories in essays to be found in *Bâtons, Chiffres et Lettres*, Gallimard, 1965.

24 J. Prévert, *Paroles*, Gallimard, 1949. The poem mentioned was first published in 1931, in the review *Commerce*, and had an immediate popular success. Césaire's *Cahier* was first published in 1939, in the review *Volontés*.

25 S. Selvon, *The Lonely Londoners*, A. Wingate, 1956.

26 Harry Levin, editor, *The Essential James Joyce*, Penguin, 1963, p. 14: 'It is a striking fact about English literature in the twentieth century that its most notable practitioners have seldom been Englishmen. The fact that they have so often been Irishmen supports Synge's belief in the reinvigorating suggestiveness of Irish popular speech. That English was not Joyce's native language, in the strict sense, he was keenly aware; and it helps to explain his unparalleled virtuosity.'

27 Bertène Juminer, *Les Bâtards*, Présence Africaine, 1961.

28 W. Harris, *Tradition, the Writer and Society*, New Beacon, 1967.

Index

(Significant subjects of notes have been indexed only when not named in the text at the appropriate point)